Seven Strategies
of Assessment *for* Learning

Second Edition

Jan Chappuis

PEARSON

Boston   Columbus   Indianapolis   New York   San Francisco   Hoboken
Amsterdam   Cape Town   Dubai   London   Madrid   Milan   Munich   Paris   Montreal   Toronto
Delhi   Mexico City   São Paulo   Sydney   Hong Kong   Seoul   Singapore   Taipei   Tokyo

Vice President and Editorial Director: Jeffery W. Johnston
Vice President and Publisher: Kevin M. Davis
Editorial Assistant: Caitlin Griscom
Executive Field Marketing Manager: Krista Clark
Senior Product Marketing Manager: Christopher Barry
Project Manager: Lauren Carlson
Procurement Specialist: Michelle Klein
Art Director: Diane Ernsberger
Cover Designer: Carie Keller
Cover Art: Shutterstock
Media Project Manager: Caroline Fenton
Full-Service Project Management: S4Carlisle Publishing Services
Composition: S4Carlisle Publishing Services
Printer/Binder: Manufactured in the United States by RR Donnelley
Cover Printer: Manufactured in the United States by RR Donnelley
Text Font: ITC Century Std 11/16

Credits and acknowledgments for material borrowed from other sources and reproduced, with permission, in this textbook appear on the appropriate page within the text.

Every effort has been made to provide accurate and current Internet information in this book. However, the Internet and information posted on it are constantly changing, so it is inevitable that some of the Internet addresses listed in this textbook will change.

Library of Congress Cataloging-in-Publication Data

Chappuis, Jan.
  Seven strategies of assessment for learning/Jan Chappuis.—Second edition.
   pages cm
  Includes index.
  ISBN 978-0-13-336644-0
  ISBN 0-13-336644-8
Educational tests and measurements.   I. Title.
  LA3051.C43 2015
  371.26—dc23

                                           2014013911

10 18

ISBN 10:   0-13-336644-8
ISBN 13: 978-0-13-336644-0

Preface

When I began teaching, I remember walking around my fourth-grade classroom and thinking, "I can't believe they pay me to do this." I liked everything about it, except grading. I could not make peace with that part of the job. It felt like I was giving with the teaching hand and taking away with the grading hand. Some of what I did then, and later as a secondary school teacher, was unfair to students, partly because I didn't know how to assess accurately and partly because I didn't know how to do anything with assessment but grade.

My introduction to assessment for learning came one summer as a participant in the Puget Sound Writing Project, where I learned to revise my own writing based on thoughtful feedback from colleagues and to reflect on myself as a writer. I brought back to my classroom a writing-process approach, in which students had opportunities to draft and revise, to give and respond to feedback before submitting their work for a grade. These practices significantly improved both the quality of their writing and their attitude toward it. My interest in assessment's formative classroom potential grew from that experience.

During the early and middle years of my teaching career, I studied feedback, self-assessment, self-reflection, and metacognition. Like many teachers before me and since, I experimented with devising lessons and activities using these ideas to deepen students' understanding of the content and of themselves as learners. I drew ideas from the work of Grant Wiggins, Rick Stiggins, and Vicki Spandel, all advocates of using assessment to advance, not merely measure, achievement. As I moved from the classroom into curriculum development and then to staff development, I focused my work with teachers on assessment practices that help students learn.

In 2001, my husband Steve and I joined Rick Stiggins and Judy Arter at the Assessment Training Institute in Portland, Oregon. Collectively and in various combinations, the four of us have written a series of books aimed at improving teachers' classroom assessment practice. Our primary text, *Classroom Assessment for Student Learning: Doing It Right—Using It Well* (2004, 2012), is grounded in the concept of student-involved assessment. In it, we briefly describe the seven strategies of assessment for learning.

This book extends those ideas into practical applications. The seven strategies represent a synthesis of best thinking in the field about high-impact formative assessment practices. Shaped by more than 30 years of teaching, reading, experimenting, and learning from students and colleagues and refined through thousands of workshops given over the years to school faculties, the seven strategies provide a practical classroom framework for using assessment to "grow" learning.

Acknowledgments

In writing this book, I am indebted to many for their ideas, talents, and assistance: mentor teacher Bud Creighton, for insight into the power of noticing student success; teacher Claudia Rengstorf, for showing what students are capable of doing when we move from the front of the classroom to the side; writer Vicki Spandel, for her pioneering of assessment for learning strategies in teaching and assessing writing; colleagues Judy Arter, Steve Chappuis, and Rick Stiggins, from whom I have learned so much; Pearson Vice President and Publisher Kevin Davis for shepherding the book-making process from outline to final printing; Program Manager Carrie Mollette for her expertise with the permissions process and her willingness to go the extra mile; Project Manager Lauren Carlson for keeping this project on deadline; and copy editor Karen Bankston for her gift of clarity and commitment to quality in the details. I am grateful to the many people who collaborated to create the video segments: to production coordinator Eric Farnbauch for the quality of the video and his skill at stitching clips together; to Cassandra Erkens and Kim Zeidler-Watters for organizing and directing the classroom and interview videos; to classroom teachers Shannon Braun, Stephanie Harmon, Ken Mattingly, Jennifer McDaniel, Emily Roberts, Lisa Smith, Crystal Thayer, and Melissa Vernon for graciously allowing us into their classrooms to capture the seven strategies in action; to their students for their willingness to be interviewed about how assessment practices have changed their learning; and to administrators Jennifer Mattingly and Becky Smith and parent Judy Ponder for their reflections on the impact these practices have had on students.

Thank you also to the educators who reviewed the first edition and offered comments about its strengths and suggestions for changes and additions: Katrina Hunter-Mintz, Walden University; Alan Olson, Valley City State University; Connie Pohlgeers, Campbell County Schools; Rosalie M. Romano, Western Washington University; and Sigrid Yates, Gilmer Independent School District. Your thoughtful responses have been invaluable in guiding revisions.

My deepest gratitude goes to my daughter Claire for her persistence as a learner in the face of multitudes of contrary assessment practices throughout her kindergarten through university experiences and for her willingness to vent in depth about their effects, and to my husband Steve for his love, understanding, and cheerful willingness to both work and play without me during the writing of this book. Lastly, I am grateful to the hundreds of teachers and administrators who have shared examples of how they are using the seven strategies in their classrooms and districts. This book is richer for their work.

Jan Chappuis
Portland, Oregon
April 2014

Introduction to the Second Edition

Educators have come to understand formative assessment practices in greater depth since the first edition of *Seven Strategies of Assessment for Learning* went to press five years ago, and considerably more research on effective practices has been published. The second edition of this book remains grounded in the original research on which it was based, but you will find a number of changes that include more recent research, extended examples of the strategies, and additions to make the text easier to use for collaborative learning. These changes include the following:

Research

Addition of research information about goal orientations, their likely impact on student motivation, and their contribution to the establishment of a learning culture in the classroom

Expanded research base for goal-setting applications

More robust treatment of Strategies 5 and 6, drawn from John Hattie's research-based explanation about the importance of the "feedback loop" as well as research on the use of practice to improve learning

Deeper explanations of how to diagnose student needs, based on research on instructional traction of assessment items and tasks

Examples of the Strategies

Updated context and examples to address current misconceptions about what formative assessment is and what makes it most effective

More examples of the strategies in action at all levels

Inclusion of anecdotes from classroom teachers describing assessment strategies they use, the impact of these strategies on learning, and their students' reactions

Expanded treatment of problems related to grading issues

A DVD with video clips of elementary, middle school, and high school teachers using the strategies with students

Editable templates for use with students, also on the DVD

Collaborative Learning

End-of-chapter activities to assist with implementation of the strategies that can be completed independently or collaboratively

Editable forms on the DVD for use with end-of-chapter activities

Guidance on setting up and conducting collaborative learning with the text in the contexts of partner learning, learning teams, in-service classes, and university classes

Brief Contents

Table of Contents

Assessment in Support of Learning

> Innovations that include strengthening the practice of
> formative assessment produce significant and often
> substantial learning gains.
>
> —*Black & Wiliam, 1998b, p. 140*

T his conclusion, from Paul Black and Dylan Wiliam's extensive review of research on formative assessment practices, is in large part responsible for the widespread focus in education on the particular kind of assessment known as *formative*. Black and Wiliam's research review (1998a) examined studies that collectively encompassed kindergartners to college students; represented a range of subject areas, including reading, writing, social studies, mathematics, and science; and were conducted in the United States and other countries throughout the world. The gains reported in the studies they described are among the largest found for any educational intervention. Not surprisingly, a steady stream of commercial formative assessment programs and products has surfaced over the last decade, in response to the achievement gains and gap-closing powers reported by Black and Wiliam and other more recent researchers. The adjective *formative* now appears frequently in titles of commercially prepared tests and item banks, interim and benchmark tests, short-cycle assessments, and classroom assessments. In some instances, this term has become synonymous with activities designed to monitor student understanding, such as those introduced by Madeline Hunter (1982).

But, does calling a product or practice *formative* make it so? Is formative assessment an instrument or a process? Is it a test or a collection of activities involving white boards, cups, thumbs, and clickers? What is it about formative assessment that gives it power to increase learning? And most importantly, what should we be doing with formative assessment in the classroom? In this chapter, we'll look at what formative assessment is and isn't, current research on assessment practices that support learning, and how the framework of seven strategies can be used to implement high-impact formative assessment activities daily in the classroom.

> **Chapter 1 Learning Targets**
>
> At the end of Chapter 1, you will know how to do the following:
>
> 1. Understand the importance of using assessment practices that meet both teachers' and students' information needs
>
> 2. Know what the Seven Strategies of Assessment for Learning are and how they connect to
>
> research on high-impact formative assessment practices
>
> 3. Understand how formative assessment practices can help shift the classroom culture to a learning orientation

What Is Formative Assessment?

First let's look at what is and what isn't formative. For Black and Wiliam, and for many other experts in the field, formative assessment is not simply an instrument or an event, but a collection of practices with a common feature: *They all lead to some action that improves learning.* Educational researchers emphasize this point when they describe what is at the heart of formative assessment:

- "Formative assessment, therefore, is essentially feedback (Ramaprasad, 1983) both to the teachers and to the pupil about present understanding and skill development in order to determine the way forward" (Harlen & James, 1997, p. 369).

- "[Formative assessment] refers to assessment that is specifically intended to provide feedback on performance to improve and accelerate learning" (Sadler, 1998, p. 77).

- "Formative assessment is defined as assessment carried out during the instructional process for the purpose of improving teaching or learning. . . . What makes formative assessment formative is that it is immediately used to make adjustments so as to form new learning" (Shepard, 2008/2009, p. 281).

- Assessment is formative "to the extent that evidence about student achievement is elicited, interpreted, and used by teachers, learners, or their peers, to make decisions about the next steps in instruction that are likely to be better, or better founded, than the decisions they would have taken in the absence of the evidence that was elicited" (Black & Wiliam, 2009, p. 6).

- "Broadly conceived, formative assessment refers to the collaborative processes engaged in by educators and students for the purpose of understanding the students' learning and conceptual organization, identification of strengths, diagnosis of weaknesses, areas for improvement, and as a source of information that teachers can use in instructional planning and students can use in deepening their understandings and improving their achievement" (Cizek, 2010, pp. 6–7).

A common thread throughout formative assessment research is that an instrument itself cannot be called "formative." It is the *use* of the information gathered (by whatever means, formal or informal) *to adjust teaching and learning as needed* that merits the "formative" label. The definition in Figure 1.1 captures succinctly what formative assessment encompasses when it leads to achievement gains.

Figure 1.1

Formative Assessment

Formal and informal processes teachers and students use to gather evidence for the purpose of informing next steps in learning.

In the classroom we assess formally through assignments, tests, quizzes, performances, projects, and surveys. These instruments must be of high quality—that is, they must yield accurate information about the achievement expectations being taught— and they must produce evidence at a fine enough "grain size" to be instructionally useful. We assess informally through questioning and dialogue, observing, and anecdotal note taking. These questions and events must also be carefully constructed to yield accurate and useful information. In recent years conflicting opinions have arisen about whether formative assessment is an instrument or a process. We are perhaps better served by understanding that a well-designed instrument, question, or activity is essential

> Assessments provide evidence about learning. What we do with the evidence determines whether the event is formative or summative.

to formative assessment. Yet without an understanding of *effective use* of the assessment process and its results, nothing "formative" will happen. Given a well-designed instrument, question, or activity, we may or may not be engaged in formative assessment. The determining factor is not the type of assessment we use, but rather what we and our students are able to do with the information it yields.

Summative Assessment

A summative assessment can be thought of as any instrument or task whose results are intended to be used to make a judgment about level of competence or achievement (Figure 1.2). The results of such assessments are generally used to evaluate rather than shape learning, so a summative assessment is generally not formative. For example, at the program level, an assessment is summative when results are used to make judgments such as determining how many students are and are not meeting standards in a certain subject for purposes of accountability. The data may be reported to educators within the system, the school board, and the community in broad categories for this purpose.

Figure 1.2

Summative Assessment
Assessments that provide evidence of student achievement for the purpose of making a judgment about student competence or program effectiveness.

At the classroom level, an assessment is summative when it is given to determine how much students have learned at a particular point in time, for the purpose of communicating achievement status to others. The communication usually takes the form of a symbol, a letter grade or number, or a comparison to a standard such as "Meets the Standard" or "Proficient" that is reported to students and parents.

Formative and Summative Use of the Same Assessment

A misconception arises when we think an assessment can never serve both purposes. Sometimes an assessment intended to be used formatively can be used summatively, such as when the evidence indicates that students have attained mastery and no further instruction is needed. Sometimes an assessment intended to be used summatively can and should be used formatively, such as when a test reveals significant problems with learning that we can address through examining the results and designing appropriate next steps. Often with performance assessment, the same task is first used formatively and then summatively. For example, with a writing task, the student creates a draft, revises it, submits it to the teacher or a peer writing group for feedback, and revises again before submitting the final piece to the teacher for a grade.

Researcher Randy Bennett (2011) offered a strong case for attending to the learning support offered by carefully crafted summative assessments:

- Preparing for the test can lead to deeper learning by helping students consolidate and organize knowledge, rehearse processes and strategies, make stronger links to ways the knowledge can be used, and develop automaticity of application.

- Taking a test can contribute to long-term retention of the content.

- The results of the test can be used to identify students needing further instruction either immediately or in the next teaching cycle.

In a nutshell, think carefully about the intended uses of assessment information prior to selecting or designing the instrument. If you intend to use it both formatively and summatively, make sure the instrument is designed to support both uses.

 Formative Use of Summative Data

Don't overlook appropriate formative uses of summative information.

Requirements for Maximizing Impact of Formative Assessment

Whether the original intent of the assessment instrument or event is formative or summative, achievement gains noted in research studies will not materialize unless certain conditions are met. At least some of these conditions are often *not* met by assessments whose primary purpose is summative; sadly, they are often not met even by assessments intended to be formative. The conditions are as follows:

- Aligned to instruction. The assessment instrument or event is designed so that it aligns directly with the content standards to be learned. All items or tasks match what has been or will be taught.

- Diagnostic for teachers. The instrument or event provides accurate information of sufficient detail to pinpoint specific problems, such as misunderstandings, so that teachers can make good decisions about what actions to take and with whom.

- Diagnostic for students. If the instrument or event is intended for student decision making, the information provided gives specific guidance on what parts of the learning targets have been mastered and what parts are in need of further action.

- Timing of results. The results are available in time to take action with the students who generated them.

- Time for action. Teachers and students have time to and do indeed take action based on the results.

If one or more of these conditions is not fulfilled, we have lost an opportunity to improve achievement. For example, the first four conditions may be in place, but if a pacing guide's schedule precludes further learning opportunities even when formative assessment results clearly indicate more learning is needed, there might just as well have been no formative assessment at all. Another wasted opportunity occurs if the first four conditions are in place but the assessment is simply graded, as is sometimes the case with common formative assessments. Assessment does not accomplish a formative purpose when "the information is simply recorded, passed on to a third party who lacks either the knowledge or the power to change the outcome, or is too deeply coded (for example, as a summary grade given by the teacher) to lead to appropriate action" (Sadler, 1989, p. 121). No action—no gains.

It is a good idea to review the assessments considered formative in your context against the requirements for effective formative use. You may also want to refer to the table in Figure 1.3, which lists types of assessments present in many current school systems, identifies their primary purposes, and classifies their intended uses.

High-Impact Formative Assessment Practices

The collection of studies Black & Wiliam (1998a, 1998b) examined represents a diverse array of interventions, all of which featured some formative use

Figure 1.3

Formative or Summative?

Type of Assessment	What Is the Purpose?	Who Will Use the Information?	How Will It Be Used?	Is the Use Formative or Summative?
State/ provincial test	Measure level of achievement on state/ provincial content standards	State or Province	Determine achievement level of each student	Summative
		District, Teacher Teams	Determine program* effectiveness	Summative
	Identify percentage of students meeting performance standards on state/provincial content standards	State or Province	Comparison of schools/ districts	Summative
		District, Teacher Teams	Develop programs/ interventions for groups or individuals	Formative
District benchmark, interim, or common assessment	Measure level of achievement toward state/provincial content standards	District, Teacher Teams	Determine program* effectiveness	Summative
		District, Teacher Teams	Identify program* needs	Formative
	Identify students/ portions of the curriculum needing additional instruction	District, Teacher Teams, Teachers	Plan interventions for groups or individuals	Formative
Classroom assessment	Measure level of achievement on learning targets taught	Teachers	Determine grade for reporting purposes	Summative
	Diagnose student strengths and areas needing further work	Teacher Teams, Teachers	Revise teaching plans for next year/semester	Formative
			Plan further instruction/ differentiate instruction for these students	Formative
		Teachers, Students	Provide feedback to students	Formative
	Understand strengths and areas needing further work	Students	Self-assess, set goals for further study/work	Formative

* Program = curriculum, texts/resources, and pedagogy

Identifying program needs:

- Are we teaching to the right content standards/learning targets?
- Do we have sufficient texts and other resources?
- Are our teaching strategies effective?

of assessment data or processes. Practices yielding large achievement gains involved the following actions:

- Use of classroom discussions, classroom tasks, and homework to determine the current state of student learning and understanding, with action taken to improve learning and correct misunderstandings

- Provision of descriptive feedback, with guidance on how to improve, during the learning

- Development of student self- and peer-assessment skills

Notice where these recommended practices fall on the chart in Figure 1.3—all in the Classroom Assessment category. Classroom assessment, designed to reflect gains in learning related to what teachers and students are doing daily, is most capable of providing the basis for understandable and accurate feedback about the learning while there is still time to act on it. This level of assessment also has the greatest capacity to develop students' ability to monitor and adjust their own learning. Formative assessment is a powerful tool in the hands of both teachers and students, and the closer it comes to everyday instruction, the stronger it is.

Formative Assessment in Teachers' Hands

In Black and Wiliam's (1998b) first category of formative assessment practices—"Use of classroom discussions, classroom tasks, and homework to determine the current state of student learning/understanding, with action taken to improve learning/correct misunderstandings"—the teacher is the one who is gathering the information, interpreting it, and acting on it. Many strong programs and practices help teachers obtain, interpret, and act on student achievement information. Data-driven decision making, developing interim assessments, Response to Intervention, differentiated instruction, minute-by-minute assessment, and questioning strategies are among the more well-known of those focusing on one or more aspects of teacher decision making. If you are already familiar with the term *formative assessment*, you probably have encountered its use in these contexts. They are generally designed to help teachers answer questions critical to good instruction:

- Who is and is not understanding the lesson?

- What adjustments should I make to instruction?

- What are each student's strengths and needs?

- What misconceptions do I need to address?

- How should I group students?

- What differentiation do I need to prepare?

- Are students ready for feedback? If so, what feedback should I give?

"Formative" Isn't Always Fast

Formative assessment is more than a menu of quick-check activities.

Formative Assessment in Students' Hands

There is no doubt that, acting on good information gathered during the course of instruction, teachers can increase what and how well students learn. Significant achievement gains attributable to formative assessment are due to enhanced questioning and dialogue techniques (Black, 2013, p. 168). It would be hard to dispute the value of noticing problems in learning and taking time to address them. However, if teacher use of assessment information is our total picture of formative assessment, one very important player is sitting on the sidelines, and it's not the principal or the superintendent. We have benched the student. Happily, more recent definitions of formative assessment demonstrate awareness of the importance of the student as a central decision maker.

> "Whatever the procedures by which the assessment message is generated, it would be a mistake to regard the student as the passive recipient of a call to action."
>
> —*Black & Wiliam, 1998a, p. 21*

In Black and Wiliam's (1998b) second category of high-impact practices— "Provision of descriptive feedback, with guidance on how to improve, during the learning"—the teacher is gathering the information and interpreting it, but the student must also interpret either the information or the teacher's reframing of it, and then the student must act on it. It is not the provision of feedback that increases learning, but rather the student's actions in response to feedback. Again here, no action, no gains.

In the third category of high-impact formative assessment practices— "Development of student self- and peer-assessment skills"—it is the student who is doing the work of gathering the information, interpreting it, and acting on it. In an often-cited article describing how formative assessment improves achievement, Australian researcher Royce Sadler (1989) concluded that the greatest potential for formative assessment derives from developing

Figure 1.4

Sadler's Indispensable Conditions for Improvement

1. The student develops a vision of quality in accordance with that of the teacher.
2. The student is able to monitor, i.e., self-assess, his or her progress during the learning.
3. The student is able to draw from a repertoire of strategies to improve whenever needed.

students' capacity to monitor the quality of their own work during production (Figure 1.4):

> The indispensable conditions for improvement are that the *student* comes to hold a concept of quality roughly similar to that held by the teacher, is able to monitor continuously the quality of what is being produced *during the act of production itself*, and has a repertoire of alternative moves or strategies from which to draw at any given point (p. 121, emphasis in original).

The ultimate goal of formative assessment then is that both the teacher and the student know what actions to take to keep learning on a successful track.

Seven Strategies of Assessment for Learning

Sadler's conditions are at the heart of what is known as "assessment *for* learning"—formative assessment practices designed to meet teachers' *and students'* information needs to maximize both motivation and achievement, by involving students from the start in their own learning (Stiggins, Arter, Chappuis, & Chappuis, 2004). These practices are fleshed out in a framework of seven strategies that apply high-impact formative assessment actions across disciplines and content standards. The Seven Strategies of Assessment for Learning offer direction as to how to meet Sadler's three conditions, phrased as questions from the student's point of view (Figure 1.5):

- Where am I going?

- Where am I now?

- How can I close the gap?

As you read through the description of each strategy, you will notice that many are familiar. They reflect practices that have always been a part of good

Figure 1.5

Seven Strategies of Assessment for Learning

Where Am I Going?
Strategy 1: Provide students with a clear and understandable vision of the learning target.
Strategy 2: Use examples and models of strong and weak work.
Where Am I Now?
Strategy 3: Offer regular descriptive feedback during the learning.
Strategy 4: Teach students to self-assess and set goals for next steps.
How Can I Close the Gap?
Strategy 5: Use evidence of student learning needs to determine next steps in teaching.
Strategy 6: Design focused instruction, followed by practice with feedback.
Strategy 7: Provide students opportunites to track, reflect on, and share their learning progress.

teaching. What may be new is their strategic use, focusing on ways both we and our students can use assessment intentionally in support of learning.

Where Am I Going?

Strategy 1: Provide a Clear and Understandable Vision of the Learning Target

Begin by giving students a vision of the learning destination. Share with your students the learning targets, objectives, or goals either at the outset of instruction or before they begin an independent practice activity. There are three ways to do this: (1) state the learning target as is, (2) convert the learning target into student-friendly language, or (3) for learning targets assessed with a rubric, convert the rubric to student-friendly language. Introduce the language of quality to students. Check to make sure students understand what learning target is at the heart of the lesson by asking, "Why are we doing this activity? What are we learning?"

Strategy 2: Use Examples and Models of Strong and Weak Work

Help students sort through what is and isn't quality work by using strong and weak models from anonymous student work, examples from life beyond school, and your own work. Begin with examples that demonstrate strengths and weaknesses related to problems students commonly experience, especially the problems that most concern you. Ask students to analyze these samples for quality and then to justify their judgments. Use only anonymous work. When you engage students in analyzing examples or models, they develop a vision of what the knowledge, understanding, skill, product, or performance looks like when it's executed well.

Model creating a product or performance yourself. Show students the true beginnings, the problems you encounter, and how you think through decisions along the way. Don't hide the development and revision part, or students will think they are doing it wrong when it is messy at the beginning, and they won't know how to work through the rough patches.

Where Am I Now?

Strategy 3: Offer Regular Descriptive Feedback During the Learning

Effective feedback can be defined as information provided to students that results in an improvement in learning. In our current system, most of the work students do is graded, and marks or grades may be the only formal feedback they receive. Unfortunately, marks and grades deliver a coded summary evaluation without specific information about what students did well or what their next steps in learning might be.

Effective feedback identifies student strengths and weaknesses with respect to the specific learning target(s) they are trying to achieve in a given assignment. It helps students answer the question, "Where am I now?" with respect to "Where do I need to be?" And it points the way to "How can I close the gap?" With those answers in mind, offer feedback instead of grades on work that is for practice and offer students opportunities to act on it before holding them accountable for mastery. Giving students time to act allows them to grow with guidance. Also, providing this kind of feedback models the kind of thinking you want students to engage in when they self-assess and identify next steps.

Involve students as peer feedback-givers. Research literature includes promising learning gains attributable to peer feedback (c.f., White & Frederiksen, 1998). To offer each other useful feedback, students must understand the intended learning targets, objectives, or goals (Strategy 1); be clear about how to distinguish levels of quality (Strategy 2); and have practiced with protocols for offering feedback in a controlled situation (Strategy 3).

Strategy 4: Teach Students to Self-Assess and Set Goals for Next Steps

With this strategy, we transfer the ownership of learning to the student. In essence, when we teach students to self-assess and set goals, we teach them to provide their own feedback. To be accurate self-assessors, students need a clear vision of the intended learning (Strategy 1), practice with identifying strengths and weaknesses in a variety of examples (Strategy 2), and exposure to feedback that models "self-assessment" thinking: "What have I done well? Where do I need to continue working?" (Strategy 3).

This strategy is a proven contributor to increased learning and a necessary part of becoming a self-regulated learner. It is *not* what we do if we have the time or if we have the "right" students—those who can already do it. Monitoring and regulating their own learning can be taught to all kinds of students, including those with mild to moderate learning disabilities (Andrade, 2010). Struggling students *especially* are the right students, and they have the most to gain from learning how to do this kind of thinking.

How Can I Close the Gap?

Strategy 5: Use Evidence of Student Learning Needs to Determine Next Steps in Teaching

With this strategy, we build a feedback loop into the teaching cycle, checking for understanding and continuing instruction guided by information about what students have and have not yet mastered. After having delivered a lesson and after students have done something in response, we use what they have done to determine further learning needs. Do their responses reveal incomplete understanding, flawed reasoning, or misconceptions? Are they ready to receive feedback? Strategy 5 includes a repertoire of approaches to diagnose the type of student learning needs in preparation for addressing them.

Strategy 6: Design Focused Instruction, Followed by Practice with Feedback

This strategy scaffolds learning by narrowing the focus of a lesson to address specific misconceptions or problems identified in Strategy 5. If you are working on a learning target having more than one aspect of quality, build competence one block at a time by addressing one component at a time. For example, mathematics problem solving requires choosing the right strategy as one component. A science experiment lab report requires a statement of the hypothesis as one component. Writing requires an introduction as one component. Identify the components of quality and then teach them one part at a time, making sure students understand that all of the parts ultimately will come together.

After delivering instruction targeted to an area of need, let students practice and get better before reassessing and grading. Give them opportunities to revise their work, product, or performance, based on feedback focused just on that area of need prior to the graded event. This narrows the volume of feedback students, especially struggling learners, need to attend to at a given time and raises their chances of success in doing so. It is a time saver for you and more instructionally powerful for students.

Strategy 7: Provide Opportunities for Students to Track, Reflect on, and Share Their Learning Progress

Any activity that requires students to reflect on what they are learning and to share their progress reinforces the learning and helps them develop insights into themselves as learners. These kinds of activities give students the opportunity to notice their own strengths, to see how far they have come, and to feel in control of the conditions of their success. By reflecting on their learning, they deepen their understanding and will remember it longer. By sharing their progress, students develop a deeper commitment to making progress.

These Strategies as a Progression

The seven strategies are not a recipe to be followed step by step, although they do build on one another. Strategy 4 and Strategy 7 are "destinations," Strategies 1 through 3 are "enablers," and Strategies 5 and 6 are "floaters." The destination strategies are where we want students to arrive as a result of being learners in our classrooms. These essential college and career readiness skills can be developed as early as prekindergarten. The enabler strategies, especially Strategies 1 and 2, are generally undervalued, and yet without them—without a clear picture of where we are going—it is hard to determine where we are now and even harder to identify actions to close the gap. Imagine attempting to get from Point A to Point B using a GPS system that only gives your current location, which is akin to what grades do. Strategies 1 and 2 equip the GPS system with information it needs to communicate next steps. The floater strategies 5 and 6 can happen any time and often employ the use of the preceding strategies as part of the lessons. Taken together, these formative assessment strategies represent actions that will strengthen students' sense of self-efficacy (their belief that effort will lead to improvement), their motivation to try, and ultimately, their achievement.

Video 1.1: Impact of the Seven Strategies in Elementary Classrooms

Video 1.2: Impact of the Seven Strategies in Secondary Classrooms

Watch Videos 1.1 and 1.2 to hear teachers and students discuss how the Seven Strategies of Assessment for Learning have changed their teaching and learning.

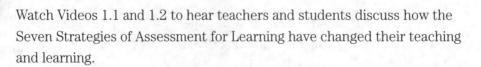

Goal Orientations, Effects on Student Motivation, and Connections to the Seven Strategies

It would be so much easier to teach if all students decided to put forth the effort needed to succeed. Many studies (Ames, 1992; Black & Wiliam, 1998a; Butler, 1988; Halvorson, 2012a; Hattie & Timperley, 2007; Schunk, 1996) have found that students' willingness to persist at a task is influenced by their *goal orientation*. This is a term researchers use to define different ideas students have about why they are doing their work in school. A goal orientation can be thought of as how a student answers the question, "What is the aim of my work?" or "Why am I doing this assignment?"

To illustrate the concept of goal orientation, let's say you ask a student what she learned today in school. It's possible she'll draw a blank. She may tell you what she did—"We worked on a math problem about camping," or "We watched our teacher cook stuff in Science and then we got to eat it"—but she may not be able to tell you why. This student's attention is focused not on what she is supposed to be *learning* from the activity but on what she is supposed to be *doing*. She may not even know the goal in math class is to learn to use the problem-solving strategy "draw a picture" to solve a problem or that the intended learning behind the teacher's cooking was for students to draw inferences about the differences between a physical change and a chemical change.

Goal orientations typically fall into one of three categories (Figure 1.6) (Ames, 1992; Black & Wiliam, 1998a; Halvorson, 2012a):

1. A learning orientation, where the student's goal is to get better

2. A performance or ego orientation, where the student's goal is to prove ability or hide a perceived lack of ability

3. A task-completion orientation, where the student's goal is to get it done and get a grade

Figure 1.6

Three Common Goal Focuses

What is the aim of my work?
1. Learning Orientation: "To get better"
2. Performance/Ego Orientation: "To prove ability" or "To hide perceived lack of ability"
3. Task Completion Orientation: "To get it done and get a grade"

Learning Orientation

Students with a *learning goal* approach focus their effort on improving their work and getting better. Their goal is to find out what they don't know and master it. Students with this orientation believe that success means improving their level of competence and that their job in school is to develop new skills and master the intended learning. Their goals focus on continuous improvement; they are motivated by a desire to become competent and by evidence of increasing mastery. They tend to seek help more frequently in developing competence and explain help avoidance in terms of attempting independent mastery.

A learning goal orientation results in the following beliefs and behaviors (Ames, 1992, p. 262; Halvorson, 2012a, pp. 43–52):

- Belief about effort: Effort will lead to success ("I can do this if I keep trying")

- Direction of effort: Developing new skills, trying to understand their own work, improving their level of competence, and achieving a sense of mastery relative to their own past level

- Response when faced with difficulty: Increased level of involvement and commitment to effort-based strategies

- Motivation to learn and a willingness to engage in the process of learning

- "Failure tolerance": Belief that failure can be overcome by a change in strategy

- Development of an intrinsic valuing of learning

"What does 'done well' look like?" is the guiding question of students with a learning orientation.

Performance and Ego-Involved Orientations

Students with a *performance goal* or an *ego-involved goal* approach to school focus their effort on protecting their sense of self-worth. Their goal is to attain public recognition of having done better than others or having performed at a superior level. Students with this orientation often believe successful achievement is a function of ability, not a result of effort. Their sense of self-worth is tied to their capacity to demonstrate high ability by doing better than others or achieving success with little effort. Their goals focus on being judged as smart or being seen as competent in relation to others. They are motivated by judgments indicating superior performance. Students with *ego-involving goals* are working with a focus primarily on maintaining positive self-esteem by demonstrating that they have high ability or masking their perceived low ability. They tend to avoid seeking help and in research studies have explained this behavior in terms of hiding their lack of ability.

A performance goal or ego-involved goal orientation results in the following beliefs and behaviors (Ames, 1992, pp. 262–263; Halvorson, 2012a, pp. 43–52):

- Belief about effort: Trying hard when it doesn't lead to success proves lack of ability

- Direction of effort: To exceed the performance of others or hide perceived lack of ability

- Response when faced with difficulty: Anxiety and poor performance ("I don't know what I'm doing, so I lack ability"); quits, cheats, or chooses easier work

- Highest value is achieving success with little effort, which leads to unwillingness to try effort-based strategies

- Help avoidance to hide perceived lack of ability

"How do I get an A?" or "How do I avoid being seen as stupid?" are the guiding questions of students with a performance or ego-involved orientation.

Task-Completion Orientation

Students with a *task-completion* approach to school focus their effort on assignment completion. They believe it is their job to finish the task—to get it done—and to get the points. Students with this orientation believe that points and grades, rather than learning and mastery, are the aim of their work.

A task-completion orientation results in the following beliefs and behaviors (Schunk, 1996; Black & Wiliam, 1998a):

- Belief about effort: Will expend as much as needed to get work turned in or earn points

- Direction of effort: Activity completion rather than producing quality

- Response when faced with difficulty: Works for points rather than understanding; looks for ways to get points

- Attitude that it matters less who does the work as long as it's turned in

"When is it due?" or "How much is this worth?" are the guiding questions of students with a task-completion orientation.

How the Seven Strategies of Assessment for Learning Contribute to a Learning Culture in the Classroom

Goal orientations are a response to a set of conditions: students can hold one set in one classroom and another in a different one. Our assessment practices do a great deal to shape students' goal orientations. The following quotes are from a group of eighth-graders in a science class where the teacher uses the Seven Strategies of Assessment for Learning as a regular part of instruction (Westerville City School District).

- Jordan: "I like Mr. Holman's class because he's more based on that you get the concept of his class instead of just trying, like, to give you a grade. He wants to make sure you understand the material he's teaching you."

- Emmanuel: "I like it. You feel good when you get the quiz because you know, no pressure, you're just going to find out what you need help in. I actually look forward to taking quizzes in his class because I myself don't normally ask that much questions, so when I take the quiz . . . it points out what you're doing wrong. So I love taking quizzes in his class. That's a first."

- Patricia: "He teaches us that it's fine not to get it right the first time as long as when we do it again it's better than last time."

- Bintu: "Instead of my trying to get done just because of the points, I truly take my time on it and complete it and make sure I learn something. The other classes, the work that's worth points, I just rush through, just to get my points in, but in his class I take my time, do the work, and learn from it."

Contrast these students' beliefs with ninth-grader Claire, who came home from the first week of school and stated: "I'm doomed in English this year. All of my mistakes count against me." Although Mr. Holman did not teach his students about goal orientations, their comments clearly demonstrate a learning orientation to the work they do in response to how he has structured the learning environment and how that has affected their sense of competence as learners.

Watch Video 1.3 to hear a teacher and students discussing a classroom learning environment that focuses on learning.

Video 1.3: Developing a Learning Culture in the Classroom

Formative Assessment Practices and Grading Issues

Based on my own teaching experiences, reading research, and working with teachers and students in classrooms over the past 30 years, I believe the key to creating a level playing field for all students is in establishing a different relationship between assessment and learning. The research on the impact of goal orientations on student motivation shows us that students are prevented from learning by assessment practices embedded in our traditional grading practices.

To consider this issue from another perspective, think of basketball. Basketball generally is a "cut" sport: Players try out and not everybody makes the team. We don't usually think of our classrooms as places where learning is a cut sport. No teacher wakes up in the morning and says, "Today I need to exclude a few students." Yet some of our traditional assessment practices structure the rules of success so that education becomes a "sport" many students feel "cut" from and choose to drop.

How does assessment do this? Three typical classroom causes are (1) not allowing students sufficient time to practice, (2) grading for compliance rather than learning, and (3) using assessment practices that distort achievement.

Not Allowing Sufficient Time for Practice

Let's assume that the reason teachers have jobs is because students don't already know what we are teaching. It follows that we can expect a need for instruction accompanied by practice, which will not be perfect at the start. We can expect that we'll need to monitor the practice to intervene with correctives so students don't spend time learning it wrong. If practice time is cut short by a pacing guide or other directive about what to "cover," only those students who need a minimum of practice to improve will succeed. The others will tend to conclude they aren't very good at the task or subject. But that is our premise: They *aren't* good at it. Our job is to give them sufficient opportunity to improve through instruction, practice, and feedback. If we cut learning short by assessing for the grade too soon, we have, in effect, decided to exclude those students.

Grading for Compliance Rather Than Learning

Awarding points for work completion tends to cause students to believe the aim of their effort in school is to get work done and to get points. When completion rather than learning is the trigger for earning points, it matters less who does the work or whether learning has occurred. The intent is to get students to do the practice, but the effect is to send the wrong message about the purpose of practice—to improve learning. When *done* is the goal rather than *improved learning*, growth is often marginal. In addition, when we don't look at the work, we can't use it as evidence to guide further instruction. We close our eyes to information about learning needs and shut more students out of the game.

Distorting Achievement

Including scores on practice work in the final grade is a common grading procedure that distorts achievement. When students need practice to learn, their beginning efforts are not generally as strong as their later performance. Averaging earlier attempts with later evidence showing increased mastery doesn't accurately represent students' true level of learning, and some give up trying altogether when they realize that they can't overcome the blow to their grade inflicted by early imperfect trials. This also reinforces the damaging inferences that being good means not having to try and that if you have to try, you aren't good at the subject. If one of our goals is to get students to try, then trying shouldn't result in the punishment of a low grade assigned too soon.

A less common but equally damaging procedure used when students don't do well as a group on a test is to "curve" the grades by reapplying the grade point cutoffs at lower levels, so for example, what was a "C" becomes an "A." This distortion of achievement masks the cause of low performance. Were the results inaccurate because of flaws in certain items? Were items too difficult for the level of instruction preceding the test? Were there items on the test representing learning that wasn't part of instruction? Each of these problems has a different solution, and each of them leads to misjudgments about students' levels of achievement. Perhaps the most harmful are those judgments students make about themselves as learners. Or did the results accurately represent learning not yet mastered? When we engage in practices that misrepresent achievement, we cut more than a few students out of learning.

Changes to Consider

All of these customs can be justified, but if learning suffers, we have created a more serious problem than the one we intended to solve. These practices lead us to ignore students' learning needs, and they discourage students from seeing themselves as learners. What is the antidote? Here are some key places to start:

- Emphasize that learning is the goal of education, and focus instruction and activities on clear learning targets.

- Ensure that your classroom assessment practices treat learning as a progression and mistakes as a way to learn.

- Offer penalty-free feedback during the learning that helps students improve.

- Use assessment as a means to know your students and to guide your own actions.

- Use assessment practices that help students see and know themselves as learners.

Adopting formative assessment practices does not mean grades aren't important. Grades are important. Grades do matter. They simply don't work well to guide learning. Grades are an accountability device that should be applied after (hopefully) sufficient opportunity to get better. The question in a learning culture is not "How can I improve my grade?" but "What do I need to do to master this?" In such a classroom culture, learning happens first and grades follow.

We can create a learning culture in our classrooms by emphasizing that learning is the aim of our work together. Formative assessment is essentially assessment focused not on judging but on helping students to learn. When we share the learning targets up front with students and use some of our precious instructional time helping them understand where they are headed (Strategies 1 and 2), we take the first steps toward establishing a focus on learning. When we offer feedback focused on the learning targets on work that is for practice, rather than giving grades or points (Strategy 3), we allow students a penalty-free opportunity to improve their learning. When we use assignments and quizzes as opportunities for students to find out what they haven't yet mastered coupled with reteaching opportunities (Strategies 4 and 6), we emphasize that learning is the goal. When we take a closer look at the work they are doing to understand what their learning needs are (Strategy 5), we communicate that their learning matters to us. When we teach students how to revise their work and deepen their learning (Strategy 6), we give them opportunities to improve as learners before the graded event. When we give students opportunities to track their progress, to notice how far they have come, and to share their achievement in those terms, we help them connect success to effort (Strategy 7).

Video 1.4: Formative Assessment Practices and Grading Issues

The relationship between motivation to learn and assessment does not run through accountability. It runs through formative practices that show students *who they are as learners*—practices that offer students a hopeful, forward-looking stance to the road ahead. If learning is truly the intended goal of the education game, all students can play successfully.

Watch Video 1.4 to hear teachers and students talk about how changes in grading practices have influenced learning.

Conclusion

Video 1.5: Implementation Advice: Elementary Teachers

The Seven Strategies of Assessment for Learning represent a progression of teaching activities that link *assessment* and *learning*. They call for a use of assessment information that differs from the traditional practice of associating *assessment* with *test* and *test* with *grade*. These assessment practices will not result in more grades in the gradebook. Rather, they ask us to think more broadly about what assessment is and what it is capable of accomplishing.

Video 1.6: Implementation Advice: Secondary Teachers

These activities won't eliminate all learning problems in your classroom. Too many factors are at work to be completely overcome by one set of strategies. However, they will take you farther in a more positive direction by helping you reclaim assessment as an integral part of teaching and learning. The seven strategies offer a sequence of effective research-based practices that develop in students the patterns of thought they need to substantially improve their own achievement. In doing so, they will introduce your students to the motivational power of being in control of the conditions of their success. Assessment can be your friend. It can be your students' friend, too—and it can even be fun.

Watch Videos 1.5, 1.6, and 1.7 for suggestions from teachers and administrators about getting started with formative assessment practices.

The Chapters Ahead

Video 1.7: Implementation Advice: Administrators

The following chapters will explain the strategies in detail, provide a research-based rationale for their use, describe how they work, and offer hands-on classroom activities that you can use tomorrow. Each chapter includes instructions for carrying out core procedures and suggestions for adaptations, all selected to make the intent and the execution of the strategy as clear as possible. Examples come from prekindergarten to college levels in a range of content areas. The majority can be adapted to work well in most contexts. Even if an example is not from your grade level or subject, you may find it useful. Information about key research recommendations will help you modify the ideas to fit your context without diluting their potential for positive impact.

Further Reading

The following resources elaborate on topics presented in this chapter.

Ames, C. (1992). Classrooms: Goals, structures, and student motivation. *Journal of Educational Psychology, 84*(3), 261–271.

> This article examines the impact of different goal orientations on student achievement and makes recommendations about which classroom structures best support development of a mastery (learning) orientation.

Chappuis, J., Stiggins, R., Chappuis, S., & Arter, J. (2012). *Classroom assessment for student learning: Doing it right—using it well* (2nd ed.). Upper Saddle River, NJ: Pearson Education.

> This textbook teaches what classroom teachers need to know and be able to do with all aspects of classroom assessment. Chapter 1 defines assessment literacy and gives an overview of the knowledge and skills educators need to ensure they are using high-quality classroom assessment practices in their classrooms. Chapter 2 explains formative and summative uses of assessment information. The rest of the chapters go into depth on assessment design and use, including grading issues.

Halvorson, H. G. (2012). *Succeed: How we can reach our goals*. New York, NY: Penguin.

> This book combines research in psychology with anecdotes and practical examples to explain the types of thinking that lead to commitment to effort-based strategies and success at achieving difficult goals.

Hattie, J. (2009). *Visible learning: A synthesis of over 800 meta-analyses relating to achievement*. New York, NY: Routledge.

> In this book, Hattie pulls together results from meta-analyses of studies relating to all facets of student achievement and identifies those with the most power to influence learning.

Hattie, J. (2012). *Visible learning for teachers: Maximizing impact on learning*. New York, NY: Routledge.

> In this follow-up to his 2009 book *Visible Learning*, John Hattie summarizes the most successful practices that impact achievement and offers recommendations for implementation in the classroom.

Shepard, L. A. (2008/2009). The role of assessment in a learning culture. *Journal of Education, 189*(1/2), 95–106.

This article addresses the issue of how assessment came to be viewed as separate from teaching and why it is so important to consider assessment practices as a part of effective pedagogy in every classroom.

Understanding and Applying the Content of Chapter 1

End-of-chapter activities are intended to help you master the chapter's learning targets and apply concepts to your classroom. They are designed to deepen your understanding of the chapter content, provide discussion topics for collaborative learning, and guide implementation of the content and practices taught in the chapter. Forms and materials for completing each activity appear in editable Microsoft Word format in the Chapter 1 DVD file. Each form needed for an activity is listed after the activity directions and marked with this symbol:

Chapter 1 Learning Targets

1. Understand the importance of using assessment practices that meet both teachers' and students' information needs
2. Know what the Seven Strategies of Assessment for Learning are and how they connect to research on high-impact formative assessment practices
3. Understand how formative assessment practices can help shift the classroom culture to a learning orientation

Chapter 1 Activities

Discussion Questions (All learning targets)

Activity 1.1   Keeping a Reflective Journal (All learning targets)

Activity 1.2   Defining Formative Assessment (Learning target 1)

Activity 1.3   Balancing Formative and Summative Uses (Learning target 1)

Activity 1.4   Maximizing Impact of Formative Assessment (Learning targets 1 and 2)

Activity 1.5   Meeting Teachers' and Students' Information Needs (Learning targets 1 and 2)

Activity 1.6   Inventorying Formative Practices (Learning targets 1 and 2)

Activity 1.7   Thinking More About Student Goal Orientations (Learning target 3)

Activity 1.8   Surveying Students (Learning targets 1 and 3)

Activity 1.9   Collecting Samples of Student Work (Learning target 1)

Activity 1.10 Reflecting on Your Own Learning (All learning targets)

Activity 1.11 Setting Up a Growth Portfolio (All learning targets)

Chapter 1 Discussion Questions

Discussion questions are also explored in depth in the activities listed in parentheses.

Questions to Discuss Before Reading Chapter 1

1. What is *formative assessment*? (Activity 1.2)
2. What do you currently do with assessment information? (Activity 1.4)
3. What do your students do with assessment information? (Activity 1.4)

Questions to Discuss After Reading Chapter 1

4. Which of the seven strategies are you most interested in doing more with? (Activity 1.6)
5. How does your use of assessment practices influence your students' goal orientations? (Activity 1.7)
6. Which ideas from this chapter were most significant to you? (Activity 1.10)
7. What one action might you take based on your reading and discussion of Chapter 1? (Activity 1.10)

Activity 1.1

Keeping a Reflective Journal

This is intended as an independent activity. If you choose to do it, you may want to discuss the thoughts you record with your learning team.

1. Keep a record of your thoughts, questions, and any implementation activities you tried while reading Chapter 1.

Activity 1.1 Chapter 1 Reflective Journal Form

Activity 1.2

Defining Formative Assessment

This is intended as an independent activity. If you choose to do it, you may want to discuss the results with your learning team.

1. Before reading Chapter 1, write your own definition of the term *formative assessment*. When you finish the chapter, revisit your definition. Make changes if needed, based on the chapter information. Identify what changes you made and why you made them.

Activity 1.2 Defining Formative Assessment

Activity 1.3

Balancing Formative and Summative Uses

This is intended as a team activity.

1. After reading the section titled "What Is Formative Assessment?" review Figure 1.3 with your learning team. Identify which assessment uses are present in your school and district.

2. Discuss: Are formative and summative uses in balance? If not, what modifications might you recommend? With whom might you share your recommendations? What rationale might you give for your recommendations?

 Activity 1.3 Balancing Formative and Summative Uses

Activity 1.4

Maximizing Impact of Formative Assessment

This activity can either be completed independently or with a team.

1. After reading through the section "Requirements for Maximizing Impact of Formative Assessment," make a list of formative assessment instruments and practices you have used over the past grading period.

2. Evaluate each entry against the five conditions for maximizing impact.

3. Note any revisions you would make to ensure effective formative use.

 Activity 1.4 Maximizing Impact of Formative Assessment

Activity 1.5

Meeting Teachers' and Students' Information Needs

This is intended as an independent activity, followed by a team discussion.

1. After reading the section titled "High-Impact Formative Assessment Practices," make a list of formative assessment instruments and practices you have used over the past grading period.

2. For each practice, determine who is gathering the information, who is interpreting the information, and who is acting on it.

3. Discuss your list with your learning team. Do your current practices meet both teacher and student information needs?

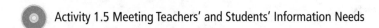

Activity 1.5 Meeting Teachers' and Students' Information Needs

Activity 1.6

Inventorying Formative Practices

This is intended as an independent activity, followed by a team discussion.

1. After reading the section titled "Seven Strategies of Assessment *for* Learning," make a list of formative assessment instruments and practices you have used over the past grading period.

2. Categorize your list according to the seven strategies.

3. Discuss with your team where your current practices fall: Are some strategies more populated than others? Which of the seven strategies are you most interested in doing more with?

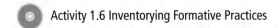

Activity 1.6 Inventorying Formative Practices

Activity 1.7

Thinking More About Student Goal Orientations

This is intended as a learning team discussion activity.

After reading the section "Goal Orientations, Effects on Student Motivation, and Connections to the Seven Strategies," discuss one or more of the following questions with your learning team:

1. What else might students be focused on as the goal of school work, *other than learning*?

2. How might that other focus *inhibit success* in learning?

3. What are key factors in *developing* a learning focus in students?

4. How can *assessment practices* contribute to a learning culture and to creating college- and career-ready students?

Activity 1.8

Surveying Students

This is an independent activity. If you choose to do it, you may want to discuss the results with your learning team.

On the DVD in the Chapter 1 file you will find two sets of surveys—an elementary version and a secondary version—designed to elicit students' responses to important aspects of assessment. Each set has a presurvey and a postsurvey. The only difference between the surveys is the instructions. The surveys are anonymous; the information is intended to be examined and compared as a classroom set of data.

1. Select either the elementary or the secondary survey and print out the presurvey form. Administer it to students at the start of your study of the Seven Strategies of Assessment for Learning.

2. Print out the postsurvey. Administer it to the same students at the end of the grading period, semester, or school year.

3. Compare the results of the pre- and postsurveys. Use this information as one indicator of the impact of the practices you are using on students' attitudes about assessment and understanding of themselves as learners.

⊙ Activity 1.8a Elementary Student Pre-Survey   ⊙ Activity 1.8c Elementary Student Post-Survey

⊙ Activity 1.8b Secondary Student Pre-Survey   ⊙ Activity 1.8d Secondary Student Post-Survey

Activity 1.9

Collecting Samples of Student Work

1. To document students' changes in achievement throughout the course of your study, collect samples of their work from the beginning. If you teach a large number of students or a number of subjects, you may want to focus on a handful of students—a few typically strong learners, a few midrange learners, and a few struggling learners.

2. Collect samples of their work periodically throughout the year.

3. Look for changes that are different from what you would normally expect to see.

4. Save these samples and include them in your own personal growth portfolio (Activity 1.11). These artifacts can be a powerful testament to your learning, as increased student growth is an important goal of your work.

Activity 1.10

Reflecting on Your Own Learning

This is an independent activity. If you choose to do it, you may want to discuss the results with your learning team.

Review the Chapter 1 learning targets and select one or more that represented new learning for you or struck you as most significant from this chapter. Write a short reflection that captures your current understanding. If you are working with a partner or a team, use this as a discussion prompt.

 Activity 1.10 Reflecting on Chapter 1 Learning

Activity 1.11

Setting Up a Growth Portfolio

This is an independent activity. If you choose to do it, you may want to share the artifacts you select with your learning team.

Part A: Growth Portfolio Option

In this activity, you will collect evidence of your progress throughout the course of your study and assemble the evidence in your own growth portfolio—a collection of artifacts selected to show growth over time—focused on formative assessment practices.

You may not want to include evidence of everything you have learned. You may choose to narrow your focus. Each chapter begins with a list of learning targets. If one or more of those learning targets is an area of improvement for you, you may wish to complete the corresponding chapter activity or activities and use them as portfolio entries, along with any other related artifacts you develop.

Many people find it helpful to keep a record of their thoughts and questions as they read each chapter and try out activities, both for their own learning and to prepare for learning team discussions. Therefore, the first activity in each chapter is to create a reflective journal entry that documents your thoughts, questions, and activities. This can also become part of your growth portfolio.

Part B: Portfolio Artifacts from Chapter 1

Any of the activities from this chapter can be used as portfolio entries for your own growth portfolio. Select activities you have completed or artifacts you have created that will illustrate your competence at the Chapter 1 learning targets. If you are keeping a reflective journal, you may want to include Chapter 1's entry in your portfolio. The portfolio entry cover sheet provided on the DVD will prompt you to think about how each item you select reflects your learning with respect to one or more of these learning targets.

Activity 1.11 Chapter 1 Portfolio Entry Cover Sheet

Where Am I Going?
Clear Learning Targets

Strategy 1
Provide a clear and understandable vision of the learning target.

Strategy 2
Use examples and models of strong and weak work.

> "Involving pupils in their own assessment means that they must know what are the aims of their learning. Communicating these aims is not easy, but the rewards of successfully attempting it are quite considerable, not only for help in assessment, but also in the obvious potential for self-direction in learning."
>
> —*Harlen & James, 1997, p. 372*

*T*aken together, Strategies 1 and 2 make the intended learning clear. They help students understand that the assignment is the *means* and the learning is the *end*. As we saw in Chapter 1, too often they may believe that getting work turned in or getting a good grade is the purpose of their effort—a limiting view of what they are in school to accomplish. We help them understand that learning is their goal by setting up a classroom culture that showcases *learning*. Being clear up front about what that learning looks like is the first step.

Teachers are often asked to post learning targets on the wall. Posting targets without using them actively throughout the lesson will not lead to increased achievement. Targets on the wall are not targets in the head. In this chapter we will focus on Strategies 1 and 2, examining ways to insert understanding of the intended learning into instruction. These activities lay the groundwork for a learning-goal approach to school, a valuing of improvement toward mastery, and a commitment to the effort-based strategies required to attain it—outcomes that will contribute to increased achievement.

In addition, Strategies 1 and 2 act as *enabling strategies* for Strategies 3 and 4: They prepare students to respond effectively to feedback and to engage in accurate self-assessment and productive goal setting. In Strategy 3, the role of feedback is to show students where they are now with respect to where they are headed. If students don't have a clear vision of their destination, feedback does not hold much meaning for them. In the case of Strategy 4, good self-assessment mirrors good feedback; the student is self-diagnosing and self-prescribing. Self-assessment, Black and Wiliam (1998a) note, is an indispensable condition for effective learning (p. 25), which cannot be done well without accurate understanding of the intended learning outcome. While it may be tempting to regard Strategies 1 and 2 as less important than later strategies, they are the foundation on which students develop self-reliant learning capabilities.

Chapter 2 Learning Targets

At the end of Chapter 2, you will know how to do the following:

1. Share different types of learning targets with students so they have a clear vision of the intended learning
   - Convert learning targets into student-friendly language
   - Identify rubrics suited for formative use
   - Convert rubrics to student-friendly language

- Introduce the concepts of quality represented in a rubric to students

2. Monitor student awareness of the intended learning

3. Use strong and weak examples effectively to deepen conceptual understanding and to make standards of quality clear

---

Prerequisite: Clear Learning Targets

The term *learning targets* refers to any statement of what students are to know and be able to do as a result of instruction. These statements of intended learning take many forms, such as *content standards*, *Common Core State Standards*, *benchmarks*, or *objectives*. Learning targets range from simple to complex, a feature sometimes called *grain size*. They can be written at the pebble-sized lesson level ("Represent addition on a number line," CCSS Mathematics, 2010b, p. 48), at the rock-sized outcome of a unit of study ("Use measures of center and measures of variability for numerical data from random samples to draw informal comparative inferences about two populations," CCSS Mathematics, p. 50), or at the boulder-sized culmination of a year's study ("Reason abstractly and quantitatively," CCSS Mathematics, p. 47).

Types of Learning Targets

Learning targets fall into one of four categories: knowledge, reasoning, skill, and product (Chappuis, Stiggins, Chappuis, & Arter, 2012, pp. 44–58).

- Knowledge-level learning targets represent factual knowledge (knowing from memory), procedural knowledge (knowing how to execute a series of steps), and conceptual understanding (being able to explain a concept). Because *knowledge* as defined here includes procedural knowledge and conceptual understanding, we do not consider all knowledge targets to be "low-level."

- Reasoning-level learning targets define thought processes students are to learn to execute, such as *predict*, *infer*, *compare*, *hypothesize*, *critique*, *draw conclusions*, *justify*, and *evaluate*.

- Skill-level targets require a real-time demonstration or physical performance. The *skills* category can be confusing, as we commonly talk about problem-solving skills (a reasoning target), reading skills (also reasoning targets), thinking skills (reasoning targets, again), and so on. This category is not set up to change how you use the word *skills*, but it is the term we use to identify a small set of content standards that have a performance of some type at the heart of the learning. Some subjects have no skill targets as part of their curriculum, and others have quite a few, such as world languages, physical education, and fine and performing arts.

- Product-level targets are just what they sound like: The content standard as written calls for the creation of a product, and the evaluation of learning will be of the qualities of the product. We often have students create products to demonstrate other types of learning targets, in which case what should be evaluated is the intended learning, not the qualities of the product.

Figure 2.1 shows examples of targets classified by type. For a more detailed explanation of target types, see Chapter 3 in *Classroom Assessment for Student Learning* (Chappuis et al., 2012).

Figure 2.1

Examples of Learning Target Types

These examples are drawn from district-level curriculum guides throughout the United States.

Knowledge-level targets	Know that plants and animals need certain resources for energy and growth Comprehend vocabulary Explain the important characteristics of U.S. citizenship
Reasoning-level targets	Use statistical methods to describe, analyze, evaluate, and make decisions Analyze fitness assessments to set personal fitness goals Compare and contrast points of view from an historical event
Skill-level targets	Use simple equipment and tools to gather data Read aloud with fluency and expression Use kinesthetic awareness, concentration, and focus in performing movement skills
Product-level targets	Construct physical models of familiar objects Create a scripted scene based on improvised work Write arguments to support claims

Clear learning targets guide instruction, assignments, formative assessments, and summative assessments. Learning targets determine how we track achievement and, ultimately, how we figure grades. Classifying them prior to instruction offers several benefits. First, it helps us know how to structure the lesson. Second, it clarifies which activities and assignments will best lead to mastery of the target. Third, the type of target determines which assessment method or methods will yield the most accurate achievement data.

For example, let's say you are planning to teach the learning target "Knows how to measure cardiorespiratory fitness." Does this mean "Knows the steps in measuring cardiorespiratory fitness" (a knowledge target) or "Measures own cardiorespiratory fitness accurately" (a skill target)? If you classify it as a knowledge target, you will likely teach the steps and assess whether students know them, which could take the form of a written response test item. If you classify it as a skill target, you will likely teach the steps and provide opportunities for students to practice executing them. Your assessment will be a performance assessment, rather than a written response, as each student demonstrates his or her ability to carry out the steps accurately.

More About Assessment Methods and the Match to Learning Targets

Because the formative assessment practices embedded in the seven strategies vary depending on the assessment method to be used, we will briefly review the four assessment methods at our disposal—selected response, written response, performance assessment, and personal communication—and when to use each one (Chappuis et al., 2012, pp. 88–102).

> "Assessment methods are not interchangeable. To ensure accurate assessment results, the overriding criterion for selection of method is consideration of the type of learning targets to be assessed."
>
> *Chappuis, et al., 2012*

Selected Response Assessment

This method includes multiple-choice items, matching exercises, true/false questions, and fill-in-the-blank questions. In general, these kinds of items have one right or best answer (or a small number of acceptable answers) and one or more wrong answers. Students select the correct or best response (or provide it), and scores are usually recorded in terms of points representing number of correct answers.

Whether an assessment method is a good choice for a target type is determined by whether it will produce accurate results for the target to be assessed. We usually think of selected response items as a good choice for knowledge-level targets, but they are also a good choice for a number of patterns of reasoning. Students' aptitude at taking selected response tests is not a consideration in determining the method to be used. When they can read sufficiently, we need to help them learn to demonstrate their achievement in formats similar to those they will see on high-stakes tests. If they can't read well enough to understand the item, we can substitute personal communication—in other words, conduct the assessment orally—provided it is not a test of reading. With younger primary students, selected response methodology may be of limited use in getting at reasoning, but may be appropriate to determine if they know such things as beginning letter sounds. Selected response is not a good match for skill targets, except in limited cases of measurement skills such as "Uses a protractor to measure angles accurately." It is not a good match for product targets.

Written Response

Often referred to as "constructed response," this method calls for a response to a question or short prompt. There are two types of written response: short answer and extended written response. Short answer items can be answered briefly, often with a limited range of correct responses, and are usually evaluated with a simple scoring guide in the form of a list of possible correct answers or desired features. Extended written response items require an answer that is at least several sentences in length. These items have a wider range of possible correct or acceptable answers and are scored either with a more extensive scoring guide in list form or a rubric describing features of quality at different levels.

Written response items are a good match for knowledge targets and for reasoning targets, if students can read and write sufficiently well enough to demonstrate their achievement through writing. If not, they can also be administered as personal communication. These items are not a good match for skill or product targets.

Performance Assessment

Performance assessment is assessment based on observation and judgment. It has two parts: the task and the rubric. For skill targets, the task requires students to give a real-time demonstration of the learning target to be mastered. For product targets, the task requires students to create the product at the heart of the learning target. Both types of tasks are evaluated with a rubric describing features of quality at different levels.

Performance assessment (demonstration or product creation + rubric) can be used to evaluate some reasoning and knowledge targets, with caution. Generally a performance assessment requires students to go beyond the confines of the knowledge or reasoning target and therefore may interfere with our ability to get a good read on their mastery of the knowledge or reasoning. Performance assessment relies on knowledge and reasoning, but we can't always tell if the lack of underpinning knowledge or reasoning is the cause of a poor performance. When students don't do well on the task, we may not be able to use that as evidence of their level of mastery of the knowledge or reasoning to be assessed. In short, use performance assessment with caution for knowledge and reasoning targets.

Personal Communication

With this assessment method, we find out what students have learned through talking with them. We can use it informally for formative purposes or formally for summative purposes. Personal communication includes activities such as asking questions, conducting interviews, listening to students as they participate, giving examinations orally, and having students keep journals or logs to be used as dialogue with us.

Personal communication can yield accurate information about achievement of knowledge and reasoning targets. With skill targets, when the skill is a communication skill, such as "Converses with a host family in the target language," personal communication is the medium of the performance assessment, so it could be said that personal communication is the method of choice. However with a skill target such as "Performs CPR correctly," talking about it will not yield accurate achievement information. Personal communication is not a good match for product targets.

Deconstructing Complex Content Standards

If you are using complex content standards such as the Common Core State Standards as the basis for your curriculum, you may need to deconstruct the standards to identify the lesson-level learning targets that form the scaffolding for the overall attainment of the content standard. There are several ways to accomplish this deconstruction, but the first step always is to classify the content standard according to target type. Figure 2.2 shows an example with a content standard beginning with the word "Understands." In this case, it is the word "understands" that needs to be clarified and then classified. Figure 2.3 shows a high school biology teacher's deconstruction of content

> "Deconstructing standards is the process of breaking a broad standard, goal, or benchmark into smaller, more explicit learning targets that can be used to guide daily classroom instruction."
>
> *Chappuis, et al., 2012*

Figure 2.2

FAQ: What Kind of a Target Is "Understands"?

When learning targets begin with the word "Understands," such as "Understands the concept of diversity," you and your colleagues must decide how you will define *understands* in your context and at your grade level. Will you ask students to explain the concept of diversity, a knowledge-level target? Or will you ask students to go beyond the knowledge level to do something with the concept? If you choose "go beyond," you will want to specify the pattern(s) of reasoning (compare and contrast? analyze and draw conclusions? evaluate?) you will teach to move conceptual understanding into some form of application.

standards into lesson-level learning targets that guide his instruction. For more information on deconstructing complex content standards, see Chappuis et al. (2012, pp. 60–68).

Figure 2.3

Deconstructing Biology Standards	FOR EXAMPLE

1. *Describe the structures of viruses and bacteria*

   The word "describe" in this standard is tricky. Do they really want students to *describe* a capsid or flagellum? Or do they want them to identify structures on a diagram (a vastly more probable assessment)? I expect the students to be able to identify basic bacterial and viral structures on a simple diagram. To ensure that the benchmark is covered as completely as possible, they also need to describe the function of several structures as well. As written, this is knowledge/understanding. They should also use this information to compare and contrast the two. (Most students think they are the same thing.)

2. *Recognize that while viruses lack cellular structure, they have genetic material to invade living cells*

   The reading of the content standard is the teaching of it. This standard is, in a peripheral way, addressing the notion of whether or not viruses are alive. While they do not possess every characteristic of life (a requirement to be considered alive by the standard definition), they do have characteristics that are distinctly lifelike (specifically genetic material). Modern science does not have a consensus on this issue, so it lends itself well to having students evaluate the problem and propose a solution. This content standard is knowledge/understanding, but the analysis of the life status of viruses is reasoning.

3. *Relate cell parts/organelles to their function (limited by clarification document to cell membrane, cell wall, chloroplast, Golgi apparatus, mitochondria, nucleus, ribosome, and vacuole)*

   This content standard is knowledge/understanding. It asks students to effectively define a variety of cell structures. Later in the class, students are expected to be able to connect the functions of the organelles to each other and to the processes we learn later on. For now, simple definitions are sufficient.

4. *Compare and contrast plant and animal cells*

   This is the first standard in this unit that explicitly requires reasoning. Primarily, students are expected to list the organelles specific to plants and animals. In some cases, they may be expected to explain why the cells differ (for example: why don't animals have cell walls or why do plants have larger vacuoles?).

Source: Used with permission from Andy Hamilton, West Ottawa Public Schools: Holland, MI. Unpublished classroom materials.

*Strategy 1: Provide a Clear and Understandable Vision
of the Learning Target.*

Once you have identified lesson-level learning targets, there are three basic ways to communicate them to students. The first is to simply share the intended learning for the lesson: "Today we're going to learn how to read decimals to the tenths place and put them in order." The second is to convert the learning target into student-friendly language and then share it: "Today we are working on summarizing, so we'll be learning how to make a brief statement of the main ideas of what we have read." The third is to convert a rubric into student-friendly language and then introduce the concepts of quality represented. Which path you choose depends in large part on the type of learning target you are teaching to (Figure 2.4). For *knowledge* and some *reasoning* targets—those you can assess using selected response or short answer formats—you can create a student-friendly definition. For other *reasoning* targets, as well as *skill* and *product* targets—those you will assess with a performance assessment—you will need to find or create a student-friendly rubric.

Figure 2.4

Making Targets Clear to Students: Three Options

Provide a clear and understandable vision of the learning target.

- Share the learning target "as is"
- Convert the target into language students understand, then share it
- Convert the rubric into student-friendly language, then introduce the concepts represented

Sharing Straightforward Targets "As Is"

When I taught fourth grade, I might have begun a math lesson with this introduction:

> "Okay students, it's time for math. Take out your math books (rustle, rustle), your *math* books. Remember, we've been studying decimals. Turn to page 142 and read the first half of the page. When you have finished, send your table leader up to get your materials because we are going on a decimal hunt."

What did I tell my students? The subject (math), the topic (decimals), the resource (p. 142), and the activity (going on a decimal hunt). What did I not tell them? The *learning target*: "We are learning to read decimals and put them in order." I am sure most of my students didn't spend time inferring the intended learning from the information I provided, so if they had an activity-completion orientation to their work, I caused it or at least enabled it. How hard would it have been for me to share the target as well? And because targets from my lips also are not targets in their heads, I could have had students write the learning target at the top of their papers along with the other heading information we are so careful to insist on. Then as we were engaged in the activity, I could have moved around the room asking individuals, "Why are we going on a decimal hunt?" When they offered answers such as "Because you told us to" or "Because it's for a grade," I could ask them, "What is the intended learning?" By repeating this exercise often, students learn that the answer to why we are doing something has to do with what they are supposed to be mastering.

Sharing targets "as is" as a stand-alone strategy works well for many knowledge targets and for straightforward procedural skill targets, such as "Today we're learning how to prepare microscope slides" or "Today we're learning how to make slip correctly."

Converting Targets to Student-Friendly Language

Converting targets to student-friendly language is especially well suited to reasoning targets. Consider the reading learning target, "Summarizes what is read." Does every student who reads that phrase know what it means to summarize? If the summaries your students write are almost as long as the passage itself, you can be sure they have missed the essence of *summarize*: *brief*. They need to know that *summarize* has two working parts: *brief* and *main*. Actually most students don't miss *brief*, they usually miss *main*. A student-friendly definition might look like this:

> "I can summarize text. This means that I can make a brief statement of the main ideas or important events in what I read."

⚠️ **Consult Your Curriculum**
Consult your own curriculum documents when creating student-friendly definitions to ensure that your interpretations represent the intent of the content standards you are translating.

Here is a process you can use to turn learning targets into statements your students will understand. This process takes a little time, so it's best to remember that not all content standards need

42

to be translated. For example, "We are learning to use a balance beam to weigh things accurately" will most likely work fine as is.

1. Identify the word(s) and/or phrase(s) needing clarification. Which terms will students struggle with? Imagine stating the target in its original form to your class. Then envision the degree of understanding reflected on faces throughout the room. At which word did they lose meaning?

2. Define the term(s) you have identified. Use a dictionary, your textbook, your state content standards document, or other reference materials specific to your subject. If you are working with a colleague, come to agreement on definitions.

3. Convert the definition(s) into language your students are likely to understand.

4. Turn the student-friendly definition into an "I" or a "We" statement: "I am learning to _____," or "We are learning to _____." Run it by a colleague for feedback.

5. Try the definition out with students. Note their response. Refine as needed.

6. Let students have a go at this occasionally, using learning targets you think they could successfully define and paraphrase. Make sure the definition they settle on is congruent with your vision of the target.

Figure 2.5 shows an example of this process applied to the second-grade learning target, "Makes inferences from informational/expository and literary/narrative text."

A second example, in Figure 2.6, defines a middle school reasoning learning target: "Generalizes information beyond the text." Although the context here is language arts, this reasoning proficiency plays an important role in other subjects such as mathematics, social studies, and science. It is a good idea to work with your colleagues in other content areas when you are translating reasoning learning targets to student-friendly language. Most patterns of reasoning are used across disciplines, and having a common definition for each gives students opportunities to learn, build proficiency, and apply what they have learned in multiple contexts.

Teachers of younger students may want to use a combination of words and pictures to make the meaning of the targets clear to them. Figure 2.7 shows an example of kindergarten music targets written this way.

Figure 2.5

Student-Friendly Language: *Inference*	**FOR EXAMPLE**

1. Learning target: "Makes inferences from informational/expository and literary/narrative text" (Grade 2)

2. Word to be defined: inference

3. Definition: conclusion drawn based on evidence and logic

4. Student-friendly definition: a guess based on clues

5. Student-friendly target: I can make inferences from what I read. This means that I can make guesses based on clues given in the text.

Notice that for second graders, you may not want to define informational/expository and literary/narrative text in the statement. If you want to define those terms, you may want to create separate statements, e.g., "I can read informational text. This means I can read books and articles that tell me facts." And, "I can read literary text. This means that I can read stories."

Figure 2.6

Student-Friendly Language: *Generalize*	**FOR EXAMPLE**

1. Learning target: "Generalizes information beyond the text" (Grades 6–8)

2. Word to be defined: generalize

3. Definition: to make a broad statement based on observations of specific cases

4. Student-friendly definition: identify similarities in specific examples and make one statement that applies to all of them and to others like them

5. Student-friendly target: I can generalize information beyond the text. This means that I can find how several examples are alike and make a statement that is true for them and is also true for other cases like them.

When Not to Convert the Language

For some content standards, defining all of the terms will derail the learning. Sometimes when students do not understand the vocabulary at the outset learning it will be a central part of the lesson. Take, for example, the learning target, "Understand literary devices." You can list the literary devices students will be learning—similes, metaphors, alliteration, onomatopoeia, and so forth—but the point of the learning is that they be able to define them

Figure 2.7

	FOR EXAMPLE
Student-Friendly Learning Targets for Kindergarten Music	

Kindergarten Music Targets

K1	**Language of Music**	I can tell when music is fast or slow. This means I know when music is fast like a [rabbit] or slow like a [tortoise].
K2		I can tell when music is loud or soft. This means I know when music is loud *(f)* like a [lion] or soft *(p)* like a [mouse].
K3		I can recognize high and low sounds: When music is high it sounds like a baby bear. [baby bear] When music is low it sounds like a papa bear. [papa bear]
K4		I can hear the different ways voices are used. This means I know when someone is using their voice to: Whisper [face] Sing [face with notes] Speak [face] Shout [face]

Source: Used with permission from Jill Meciej, Community Consolidated School District 93, Bloomingdale: IL.

> ⚠️ **Use Professional Judgment**
>
> Not every learning target needs to be translated into student-friendly language. And learning targets don't always have to be shared at the outset of the lesson, as when beginning instruction with a discovery learning experience.

and identify them. The student-friendly version might be, "We are learning to identify similes and metaphors in what we read." Another example is the learning target, "Understand the binomial theorem." You may want to define what "understand" will look like: Identify it? Define it? Explain it? Know when to use it? However, you would leave the phrase "binomial theorem" alone, because learning it is at the heart of the lesson.

Video 2.1: Making Targets Clear to Students: Kindergarten

"I Can . . ." or "I Am Learning to . . ."

Instead of "I can . . ." statements, some teachers like to phrase the targets students are working on as "We are learning to . . ." (or "I am learning to . . .") statements. When students have demonstrated evidence of mastery for the target, they convert it into an "I can . . ." statement, staple it to the evidence, and place it in a folder they can use when sharing what they have learned. This idea is explained more fully in Strategy 7 in Chapter 7.

Watch Videos 2.1 and 2.2 for examples of how elementary teachers help students understand a learning target.

Video 2.2: Making Targets Clear to Students: Grade 4

Ways to Share Learning Targets with Students

Third-grade teacher Amy Meyer puts the learning targets on the assignment page itself and then makes sure to include the student-friendly definition in the writing prompt (Figure 2.8).

You can also let students discuss the meaning of a learning target and write it in terms that are clear to them. This can work as a quick "anticipatory set" activity, or it can be the focus of an in-depth exploration. For example, middle school language arts teacher Jessica Hendershot has her students record the "adult" version of the indicator (learning target) they will be working on in their writing journals. They discuss in small groups what they think the indicator means, and she then facilitates a whole-class discussion to create one common definition. High school science teacher Stephanie Harmon begins each unit by "dissecting" the targets with students (the science equivalent of deconstructing), which students then record in their academic notebooks and refer to throughout the unit (Figure 2.9).

Figure 2.8

Targets Printed on the Assignment	FOR EXAMPLE

Name _____ Date _____

I can comprehend what I read by reflecting on important information.

I can summarize main ideas in a text.

Title _____

What do you think is the most important thing you learned from reading this book?

_____

_____

_____

Tell why you think it is important.

_____

_____

_____

Summarize what this book was about. (Squish up the main ideas or most important points about the topic.)

_____

_____

_____

Source: Used with permission from Amy Meyer, third-grade teacher, Worthington City Schools: Worthington OH. Unpublished classroom materials.

Watch Video 2.3 for an explanation of how Ms. Harmon dissects learning targets with her students.

If you are working with standards that you have deconstructed, the list of learning targets you created can form the basis for student-friendly targets you give students. High school biology teacher Andy Hamilton has his students record the daily learning targets in a weekly log, which typically look like "I can" statements, but without the "I can" (for brevity). Figure 2.10 shows how he has deconstructed two content standards into lesson-level learning targets and then turned them into student-friendly statements.

Video 2.3: Dissecting Learning Targets With Students

AP calculus teacher Jennifer McDaniel hands out a "target table" at the beginning of each unit of study. The target table has five columns: Learning Targets,

Figure 2.9

From the Classroom

Strategy #1: Dissecting the Learning Target

What We Do

At the beginning of each unit, I give the students a copy of the unit's learning targets. We take a bit of time to dissect the targets – circle the critical vocabulary and underline the verb(s). We talk about what each learning target will require and what we may do to help us show mastery of the target. As we continue through the unit, we begin each day's learning experience by identifying the learning target being addressed in the lesson.

This dissection becomes a part of their academic notebooks. It is particularly helpful in putting critical vocabulary into the context of the learning and helps students shape their questions as we move through the unit. In addition, everything we do is connected to the learning target that it addresses. Every formative assessment and summative assessment is organized around the learning targets. Students quickly learn that the learning targets are central to our class.

Impact on Learning

Students take ownership of their learning. They know what is expected and how each day's experience is connected to the learning targets. They can talk about what they need to know and do in order to achieve mastery. The dissection helps student focus on content-specific vocabulary and what they must do (from the identified verbs) in order to show mastery.

What My Students Say

"I used to focus on my grades. All that mattered was an A. Now I realize that if I focus on the learning, the grade takes care of itself." Rebekah P., 11th grade student

Source: Used with permission from Stephanie Harmon, science teacher, Rockcastle County High School: Mt. Vernon, KY. Unpublished classroom materials.

Video 2.4: Making Targets Clear to Students: AP Calculus

Working Log, Strengths, Challenges, and Green/Yellow/Red (Figure 2.11). In the Working Log column, students note the activities and resources they are using to master the target. In the Strengths column, students identify what aspects of the target they have mastered. In the Challenges column, they note the difficulties they encounter, and in the Green/Yellow/Red column, they assess their learning progress. Ms. McDaniel and her students use the target tables to guide their study and review throughout the unit.

Watch Video 2.4 to hear Ms. McDaniel and her students share their thoughts about the value of clear targets.

Figure 2.10

Content Standards→Learning Targets→ Student-Friendly Targets	**FOR EXAMPLE**

Content Standard: Explain that some structures in the modern eukaryotic cell developed from early prokaryotes, such as mitochondria, and in plants, chloroplasts

Learning Targets: The wording of this standard implies knowledge/understanding. In fact, reading the standard effectively teaches it to you. I expect my students to explain a little more about how those structures developed. This standard requires an understanding of the vocabulary terms *prokaryote* and *eukaryote* primarily, with *mitochondria* and *chloroplasts* being secondary vocabulary terms (you don't actually need to know what a chloroplast or mitochondrion is to learn the standard). Students should be able to describe the pieces of evidence that lead scientists to the conclusion that the standard is true.

Student-Friendly Targets:

- I can define *prokaryote* and *eukaryote* and give examples of each.
- I can describe where mitochondria and chloroplasts come from.
- I can describe the evidence that explains where mitochondria and chloroplasts come from.

Content Standard: Explain the role of cell membranes as a highly selective barrier (diffusion, osmosis, and active transport)

Learning Targets: If you were to limit the scope of this standard to only what is written, students would simply have to describe that cell membranes are selective—that is, they let some things in and out but not others. I expect my students to do a lot more with this standard. They should be able to distinguish between types of membrane transport and describe what would happen in a variety of scenarios. As written, the content standard is knowledge/understanding, but it lends itself well to reasoning learning targets.

Student-Friendly Targets:

- I can define *osmosis*, *diffusion*, and *active transport*.
- I can predict what will happen when cells are placed in a variety of solutions.
- I can determine if a process is *osmosis*, *diffusion*, or *active transport* based on how materials are moving into or out of a cell.

Source: Used with permission from Andy Hamilton, West Ottawa Public Schools: Holland, MI. Unpublished classroom materials.

Figure 2.11

	Target Table: Introduction to Limits			**FOR EXAMPLE**
Learning Targets	Working Log	Strengths	Challenges	Green/Yellow/Red
I can estimate a limit using a numerical table.	• Aug 10, # 1-8 • Aug 14, # 1-3 • Aug 16, # 1-3	• Easy to determine limit	• I find there is nothing challenging about using a numerical table.	Green
I can justify a limit algebraically: factoring, rationalizing, LCD.	Factoring • Aug 10, # 1, 2 • Aug 14, # 1 • Aug 15, # 1, 2 • Aug 16, # 1 Rationalizing • Aug 10, # 3, 4 • Aug 14, # 2 • Aug 15, # 3 • Aug 16, # 2 LCD • Aug 10, # 5, 6 • Aug 14, # 3 • Aug 15, # 4 • Aug 16, # 3	• I think LCD problems are the easiest. • I'm good at rationalizing. • After factoring the problem is a piece of cake.	• Some problems or factoring can be hard to factor (Aug 16 # 1). • Easy to target negative signs on LCD problems.	Red Yellow Green I am here · · ·
I can determine a limit from a graph.	• Aug 14, # 1-12 • Aug 16, # 4-11	• It is a very quick way to find a limit. • Easy to do in general.	• Graphs with symptopes can be a bit confusing at times.	Green

Source: Used with permission from Jennifer McDaniel, Clay County Schools: Manchester, KY. Unpublished classroom materials.

Using Rubrics to Communicate Learning Targets

In general, more complex reasoning targets are most accurately measured with written response assessment; skill and product targets are most accurately measured with performance assessment. With both methods, we use a rubric to evaluate the response, performance, or work. Examples of learning targets requiring assessment with a rubric include the following:

- Plan and conduct a simple scientific investigation.

- Make sense of problems and persevere in solving them (CCSS Standards for Mathematical Practice, 2010b, p. 6).

- Represent sample spaces for compound events using methods such as organized lists, tables, and tree diagrams (CCSS for Mathematics, Grade 7, Statistics and Probability, 8b, p. 51).

- Present claims and findings, sequencing ideas logically and using pertinent descriptions, facts and details to accentuate main ideas or themes; use appropriate eye contact, adequate volume, and clear pronunciation (CCSS for English Language Arts, Speaking and Listening Standard 4, Grade 6, p. 49).

- Read aloud with fluency.

- Create a personal health-related fitness plan.

- Participate in civic discussions.

It is not crucial that these types of targets be translated into student-friendly terms. What is important is that the rubric you will use accurately describes features of quality with respect to the learning target and that it is written so that students can understand the language.

In an assessment for learning environment, we introduce the concepts in the rubric at the outset of instruction. This follows the research: Many studies focus on the positive effects of sharing the scoring rubric with students in advance of completing the assessment task, especially for lower-achieving students. See Chapter 4 for an explanation of White and Frederiksen's (1998) findings on the achievement effects of peer feedback and self-assessment with a rubric.

> "Introducing students to the criteria by which their work will be evaluated enables students to better understand the characteristics of good performance."
>
> *White & Frederiksen, 1998, p. 28*

Prerequisite: A Suitable Rubric

It makes sense that if students are to be able to self-assess, they must first understand the concepts that define quality. A good rubric answers the question "Where am I going?" by describing in specific terms the features that constitute quality for a given learning target. Its content derives from the learning target and from expertise in the field about what constitutes quality in mastering the learning target. Figure 2.12 illustrates the alignment needed.

> Scoring criteria must include qualitative descriptors if they are to function formatively to diagnose needs, provide feedback to students, and engage students in self-assessment.

Formative uses of a well-designed rubric include the following:

- To diagnose strengths and areas for improvement

- To provide feedback that guides students in revision of their work

- To help students develop their understanding of quality, self-assess, and set goals for improvement

Figure 2.12

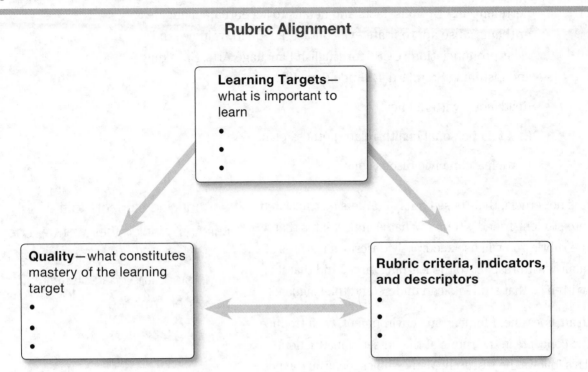

Rubric Alignment

As you may have experienced, not all rubrics are suited to formative use. Three essential characteristics that make them work formatively are: (1) descriptive of quality, (2) generalizable across tasks, and (3) analytic in structure rather than holistic, if describing a complex learning target.

1. Descriptive of Quality

To be used as a formative assessment tool, a rubric must be diagnostic. It must describe strengths and weaknesses. Rubrics that use descriptive, rather than evaluative or quantitative, language generally do a far better job of yielding diagnostic information. To illustrate this, we will look at three versions of a rubric for *Display of Information*, one criterion in a rubric for science investigation.

Example 1: Descriptive Language

4: Display of information is accurate, complete, and organized so that it is easy to interpret.

3: Display of information is accurate, mostly complete, and is mostly organized so that it is easy to interpret. It may have one or two small omissions.

2: Display of information is partially accurate, partially complete, and may have some organization problems.

    1:   Display of information is inaccurate, incomplete, and not well organized.

Example 2: Evaluative Language

    4:   Excellent display of information

    3:   Good display of information

    2:   Fair display of information

    1:   Poor display of information

Example 3: Quantitative Language

    4:   Displays four pieces of information

    3:   Displays three pieces of information

    2:   Displays two pieces of information

    1:   Displays one piece of information

Which of these three versions of the rubric work best diagnostically, as feedback, and to guide students toward mastery of the target? The descriptive version identifies in specific terms what students are doing well as well as what needs work. The evaluative version simply repeats the judgment of the number at each level; it offers no insight into features of quality present or absent. The quantitative version substitutes number counts for explanations of levels of quality; unless it is truly the number of instances that determines level of quality, the rubric inaccurately represents the learning target.

2. Generalizable Across Tasks

Rubrics that work best as formative tools are general, rather than task-specific. For example, one of the hallmarks of good writing is the quality of the introduction. A *general* rubric for writing describes the characteristics of a good introduction in a way that applies to any introduction:

    4:   The introduction captures the reader's attention and introduces the topic so the reader can move smoothly into the ideas.

    3:   The introduction connects the reader to the topic, but it doesn't yet hook the reader's attention as well as it might.

    2:   The introduction bears some connection to the topic. There is no hook to the reader's attention yet.

    1:   The introduction is missing or does not connect to the topic.

Different writing rubrics may define those characteristics in a slightly different way for different modes (e.g., narrative, expository, persuasive), but you should be able to use the mode-specific rubric to judge quality of the introduction for all writing in that mode. On the other hand, a *task-specific* rubric specifies what a good introduction looks like for one particular writing assignment only. It includes references to one specific assignment and so cannot be used to evaluate the quality of an introduction for any other assignment. A good reason for using general over task-specific rubrics is that you want students to internalize the characteristics of quality that apply to all instances of their work on that particular learning target. Another is that task-specific rubrics give away "the answer": they do all of the thinking for the student, so if handed out in advance, they reduce the learning demonstrated to the level of rote direction-following. See Figure 2.13 for a general and a task-specific rubric for the learning target "Interpret a graph." Notice that the concepts of a quality interpretation in the general rubric are embedded in the task-specific rubric, but the task-specific rubric also tells exactly what the student is to do.

> ⚠️ **Structure of the Rubric**
>
> The structure of your rubric will determine its usefulness as a teaching tool with students. Not every rubric is suited to formative use.

A strength of task-specific rubrics is that they make it relatively easy to score large numbers of responses quickly, so they are often used in large-scale assessment contexts. A weakness, again, is that they cannot be given to students in advance to help them understand what quality work looks like.

3. Analytic in Structure

A third feature essential to formative usefulness is an analytic, rather than a holistic, structure when the rubric is intended to assess complex or multidimensional learning targets. The terms *analytic* and *holistic* refer to how many scoring scales the rubric has—one or more than one. A holistic rubric has only one scale; all features of quality are combined into one score. An analytic rubric has two or more scales; the features of quality have been broken into categories and scored separately. These separate categories are often referred to as *criteria* or *traits*.

Holistic Example

If the learning target is relatively straightforward, such as "Summarize text," a holistic rubric is a better choice. A simple holistic rubric for a summary could look like this:

3: A concise explanation that includes all of the main ideas or important events in the passage

Figure 2.13

General and Task-Specific Rubric Examples

FOR EXAMPLE

General Rubric for Interpreting a Graph

5: Interprets information from graph to provide correct answers. Provides accurate and complete explanation of how conclusions were drawn.

4: Interprets information from graph to provide correct answers. Provides accurate explanation of how conclusions were drawn, but explanation is incomplete and requires interpretation.

3: Interprets information from graph to provide partially correct answers. Provides partially accurate explanation of how conclusions were drawn, but includes faulty reasoning. Explanation may also be incomplete and require interpretation.

2: Interprets information from graph to provide partially correct answers. Explanation, if offered, consists of faulty reasoning and does not support correct conclusions drawn.

1: Provides incorrect answers. Explanation, if offered, represents faulty reasoning.

Task-Specific Rubric for Interpreting a Graph

5: Has all five points on the graph labeled correctly. Indicates that Graham and Paul ride their bikes to school. Provides accurate and complete explanation of how those conclusions were drawn. Indicates that Susan walks and Peter takes a car as a part of the explanation.

4: Has four or five points on the graph labeled correctly. Indicates that Graham and Paul ride their bikes to school. Explanation of reasoning is correct but incomplete and requires interpretation. May indicate that Susan walks and Peter takes a car as a part of the explanation.

3: Has three points on the graph labeled correctly. Indicates that Graham or Paul rides a bike. Chooses the incorrect mode of transportation for the other. Explanation of reasoning is partially correct but also includes faulty reasoning. Explanation may indicate that information about Susan or Peter was interpreted incorrectly.

2: Has one or two points on the graph labeled correctly. Indicates that Graham or Paul rides a bike. Chooses the incorrect mode of transportation for the other. Explanation of reasoning, if offered, is incomplete and incorrect. Explanation may ignore information about Susan and Peter or have interpreted it incorrectly.

1: Has no points on the graph labeled correctly. Indicates incorrect mode of transportation for Graham and Paul. Explanation of reasoning, if offered, is faulty.

Source: Chappuis, Jan; Stiggins, Rick J.; Chappuis, Steve; Arter, Judith A., *Classroom Assessment for Student Learning: Doing It Right–Using It Well,* 2nd Ed., ©2012, pp. 184–185. Reproduced by permission of Pearson Education, Inc., Upper Saddle River, NJ.

2: An explanation of some of the main ideas or important events in the passage—may have extraneous information included

1: An explanation that recounts details rather than main ideas or important events in the passage

It would be difficult to break this into two different categories to make it an analytic rubric, and it would serve no purpose. Holistic rubrics can be appropriately used for complex learning targets as well as simpler ones when the assessment purpose is summative; that is, you will be making an overall judgment at the close of instruction about students' level of mastery. They are often used in large-scale assessments.

Analytic Example

If the learning target has several independently varying components, such as "Give an effective oral presentation," an analytic rubric is a better choice. This learning target has several components: the content of the speech, its organization, the speaker's delivery, and the speaker's use of language. Each component can be done well or poorly, each can be taught, practiced, and assessed. An analytic rubric, with a separate scoring scale for each component (remember, these are the *criteria*) is well suited to formative use: to diagnose, to focus instruction, to offer feedback, and to serve as a self-assessment and goal-setting instrument for students, one criterion at a time. For more on focused instruction with rubrics, see Chapters 5 and 6.

Figure 2.14 summarizes the characteristics of scoring rubrics that function well as formative assessment. See the Chapter 2 DVD files for examples of such rubrics. For more information on types of rubrics and rubric quality, see Chappuis et al. (2012, pp. 226–244).

Developing a Student-Friendly Rubric

Once you have found (or created) a suitable rubric, you are ready to create a student-friendly version. Here are the steps in the process (Arter & Chappuis, 2006):

Figure 2.14

Rubrics Suited to Formative Use

This	Not This
General—can be used to judge quality across similar tasks. You can use the same one for different assignments.	Task specific—can only be used on one task. You need a different one for each assignment.
Descriptive—includes language that explains characteristics of work or performance at increasing levels of quality.	Evaluative—uses language that repeats the judgment of the particular score point. Quantitative—uses language that counts or measures number of instances.

Source: Arter, Judith A.; Chappuis, Jan, *Creating and Recognizing Quality Rubrics,* ©2006. Reproduced by permission of Pearson Education, Inc., Upper Saddle River, NJ.

1. Identify the words and phrases in the adult version that your students might not understand.

2. Discuss with colleagues the best wording for your students. It is sometimes helpful to look these words up in the dictionary or in textbooks for ways to rephrase them.

3. Rewrite the rubric in student-friendly language in the first person (from the student's point of view).

4. Try the rubric out with students. Ask for their feedback. Revise as needed.

When designing or revising rubrics for formative use, it is helpful to create a bulleted list of the features of quality embedded in each criterion. The entries on the list are known as *indicators* and summarize the features in each criterion. For example, the Six-Trait Writing Rubric has six separate scoring scales, one for each trait (criterion): *Ideas and Content, Organization, Voice, Word Choice, Sentence Fluency*, and *Conventions*. The bulleted lists (indicators) for the traits, shown in Figure 2.15, can be used to guide diagnosis, instruction, feedback, and self-assessment.

A rubric's criteria and indicators can be posted on the wall. Although targets on the wall are not targets in the head, it can be handy to walk over to the posters and point to the "Narrow focus" bullet under *Ideas and Content*, and say:

> "We are learning how to write opinion pieces, how to express a point of view and support it with reasons and information. This week we will be working on *Ideas and Content*, specifically on how to craft a tightly focused opinion statement."

In this example, "How to craft a tightly focused opinion statement" is the learning target; "narrow focus" is the place it shows up in the rubric.

The example in Figure 2.16 is the list of criteria for a mathematics problem-solving rubric designed for fifth- and sixth-graders. The rubric has three traits, or criteria—three separate scoring scales: *Mathematical Knowledge: Concepts and Procedures, Problem Solving*, and *Communication*. Each criterion is followed by a bulleted list of characteristics (indicators) that help students understand its content.

Figure 2.15

Six Traits of Good Writing

Ideas and Content . . . a clear message

- Narrow, manageable focus
- Rich detail
- Details are interesting, important, and informative

Organization . . . the internal structure

- Introduction hooks the reader
- Purposeful sequencing of ideas
- Controlled pacing
- Transitions link ideas
- Conclusion leaves the reader feeling satisfied

Voice . . . the person behind the words

- Brings the topic to life
- Engaging
- Written to be read

Word Choice . . . simple language used well

- Vivid verbs
- Precise nouns
- Words and phrases paint a picture in the reader's mind

Sentence Fluency . . . easy to read aloud

- Rhythm and cadence
- Purposeful sentence beginnings, varied sentence length
- Sentence structure supports and enhances meaning

Conventions . . . looks clean, edited, and polished

- Capitalization
- Usage/Grammar
- Punctuation
- Spelling

Figure 2.16

Mathematics Problem-Solving Criteria

Mathematical Knowledge: Concepts and Procedures

- Understands the mathematical ideas and operations selected
- Performs appropriate computations
- Chooses the right operations and does them correctly

Problem Solving

- Translates the problem into mathematical terms
- Chooses or creates a strategy
- Uses a strategy to solve the problem
- Checks solution to make sure it makes sense in the problem

Mathematical Communication

- Explains the strategy and processes used
- Explains why what was done was done
- Explains why answer works

Source: Used with permission of Central Kitsap School District: Silverdale, WA.

Introducing the Concepts of Quality in the Rubric to Students

Handing out a student-friendly rubric and reviewing it with students is not generally the most effective way to get students to understand the concepts of quality represented. We can "teach" the rubric much in the same way we teach for conceptual understanding in any context, as demonstrated in the following protocol. In the protocol, you first ask students what they already know about the characteristics of quality and then compare what they say to features the rubric describes (the bulleted list), before distributing it. This activity accesses prior knowledge; it allows students to "hook" the concepts in the rubric to what is already in their long-term memory and to notice what is not yet part of their understanding of quality—what is to be learned. The protocol also generates interest in the rubric and a reason to pay attention to it.

The first example is the "default" protocol, which can be used to introduce any rubric. The second example is a mathematics example, showing a few

> ⚠️ **Match to Targets**
>
> The content of your rubric should match your learning targets. When you are considering a rubric for possible use, ask yourself if it includes the dimensions of quality specified in your content standards. If not, revise the rubric or find a different one that matches the elements of quality you and your district, state, or province believe are important.

variations on the default version. The third example is a series of four lessons that can be used to introduce the notion of criteria and then a set of criteria from a rubric to primary students. With each of these protocols, you will need copies of the rubric written in language your students will understand (at the primary level, this may be a few words combined with pictures or symbols) and a list of the traits or criteria with indicators for each.

Example 1: The "Default" Protocol

Step 1: Ask students what they think a good _____ (whatever it is the rubric describes, e.g., oral presentation, science report, hypothesis, etc.) looks like. Record all responses on chart paper. Keep this list in their language—don't paraphrase it.

Step 2: Share one or more examples of the product or performance (oral presentation, opinion piece, science report, hypothesis, etc.) that have definite strengths. They can also have a few weaknesses, which can generate an interesting discussion. You can present examples by saying something like, "Let's look at an example. What do you notice this example does, or doesn't do, that is important to quality?" You can have students discuss with a partner or in small groups prior to sharing as a class, or just conduct this as a large-group activity. Add their responses to the chart paper from Step 1. Again, record what they say, using their language. Don't worry at this step if extraneous ideas show up.

Step 3: If time permits, keep the list open for a few days. Continue having them discuss anonymous student examples or samples of the product or performance from published sources. You can also show two examples of anonymous work at different levels of quality and ask them to decide which is better. Add their reasons to the chart. You are ready to move to the next step when the class list includes some of the features described by your rubric.

Step 4: Tell students that this is a good list and that they have done exactly what teachers and other content area experts do when they are creating a rubric to judge the quality of _____ (the learning target at the heart of your rubric). Let them know that their list includes many of the same characteristics on the experts' list.

Step 5:   Introduce the "expert" list by saying that the experts came up with lots of ideas just like they did. There were so many, they knew no one could keep all of them in their head at one time, so they grouped their ideas into categories, which are called *criteria* or *traits* (you decide which term you will use). Then show the list of criteria represented in your rubric.

Step 6:   Show the bulleted list of indicators one criterion at a time. While showing each criterion's indicators, ask students to check for a match to the class's list. If they find one, write the criterion next to the word or phrase on their chart. If there are no matches, tell students they will be learning more about that criterion later. Do the same for all of the criteria in your rubric. In going through this process, students identify what they already know, link their descriptions of quality to the language of the rubric, and leave the lesson with a sense that "I think I can do this."

Step 7:   Hand out your student-friendly version of the rubric. The rubric will not seem so daunting after steps 1 through 6. We want students to leave their first encounter with the rubric thinking "I already know some of this and I think I'll be able to learn the rest of it."

Example 2: The Protocol with a Mathematics Rubric

Step 1:   Ask students what good math problem solving looks like. Record all responses on chart paper. Keep this list in their language—don't paraphrase it.

Step 2:   Have them solve a multistep mathematics problem, one that requires reasoning, applying a strategy, and communicating about what they did. Then ask students to think about what they tried to do while they were solving the problem. Should other characteristics go on the list? Record what they say, using their language. Don't worry at this step if extraneous ideas show up.

Step 3:   If time permits, keep the list open for a few days. Add to it as students practice problem solving with different examples. Or show two examples of anonymous student work at different levels of quality on one of the problems they have solved, and ask them to decide which is better. Add their reasons to the chart. You are ready to move to the next step when the list includes some of the features described by your rubric.

Then, follow the default protocol for Steps 4–7.

Examples From Grade Levels You Don't Teach

Try not to dismiss or skip over an example that applies to a grade level or subject you don't teach. Even though it is tailored to a specific context, chances are it will include ideas that you can modify to work with your students.

Example 3: Four Lessons for Introducing Criteria to Younger Students

With primary students, when the learning is clearly developmental, you can modify the previous protocol by using the following series of lessons to introduce the concept of *criteria*, to help them develop criteria for key classroom behaviors, and then to introduce criteria you will be using to evaluate their learning.

Lesson 1: Introducing the Concept of Criteria

In this first lesson, you will be introducing the word *criteria* and the idea that we make choices based on criteria.

Key Understanding:

People use criteria to think about choices and to make decisions.

Materials:

- Read-aloud book about a family. The book should describe different aspects about the family such as members, home, and so forth. The family does not need to be human (e.g., Mercer Mayer stories).

- Three or more pictures of common pets (e.g., dog, cat, fish, gerbil, hamster, bird, snake). Choose animals so that some are more suited to this family than others.

Process:

Introduce the story by saying, "People make choices every day. How do people make *good* choices? We will talk about steps people use when they make choices. The first step many people make is thinking about what they want and don't want. For example, many families have pets. There are many different types of pets. How do families decide what type of pet they want? To make this choice a family needs to think about what would make a good pet for their home and family. What would a family need to think about to select the best pet for the family?"

Then say, "I am going to read a story to you about a family. When I finish reading, we will talk about the family and what they might like or need to think about when they are choosing a pet (or adding another pet to their family)."

Make a chart listing the ideas students generate about what would make a good pet for the family from the read-aloud. Give it a title such as, "Criteria for Choosing a Pet for the _____ (family)." After the list is complete, show students the pictures of pets one at a time. Review the criteria list for each pet, asking students to decide whether each criterion is present.

Say, "Using our criteria for a good pet for the family, and our thinking about each pet, which pet would make the best pet for them?" Let students make a choice and give reasons why. Guide them to use the criteria list for their reasons.

Closure:

Say, "The ideas on the list we created and used to choose a pet are called *criteria*. People use criteria to help them make decisions or choices. We will use the word *criteria* all year as we talk about making good decisions or choices."

Lesson 2: Creating Criteria for Making Choices in Familiar Situations

In this example, students work in small groups to generate criteria for making choices in familiar situations at home.

Key Understanding:

Having clear criteria helps us make good choices.

Materials:

A collection of three pictures for each of the following categories: restaurants, sports, clothes to wear, family fun activities, games to play, TV shows, or other situations in which students have had experiences making choices.

Process:

1. Assign one category to each small group. Tell students they are going to make a list of criteria for deciding which is the best choice in their category. Model doing this with a category you haven't assigned. Then ask each group to make a list of three to five criteria for deciding what the best of their given category would be for their group. If possible, one student in each group records the list for the group. If necessary, circulate and assist with the writing.

2. Tell students they are going to use their criteria to evaluate choices. Model this with three pictures from the category you used to demonstrate creating criteria in Step 1. Then distribute the pictures for their category. Ask students to evaluate each picture

against the list. Which criteria are present in each picture? Which picture would be the best choice for their small group, according to their criteria list?

3. Have small groups take turns sharing their category, the criteria they developed, and their "best" choice from their given pictures. Ask the class to think about other possible choices that would fit the group's criteria, and choices that would not fit the group's criteria. Encourage students to justify their decisions by referring to the small group's criteria.

Closure:

Say, "People make many decisions every day. When making decisions, it is important to think about how the best choice or decision will be determined. Creating a list of criteria is a good way to help us make decisions about different choices."

Lesson 3: Bridging from Home Examples to School Examples
In this lesson, students will shift from thinking about criteria for choices in their home environment to thinking about criteria in the school environment, beginning with a familiar desired school behavior. In this example, students work in small groups to generate criteria for working in small groups.

Key Understanding:

Having clear criteria helps us make good decisions about what to do in school.

Materials:

One T-chart with columns labeled "Looks Like"/"Sounds Like" for each small group, plus one for the whole group.

Process:

1. Say, "You're good at choosing things because you have ideas about what makes them good. Now we're going to use that same kind of thinking on something here at school—working in a small group. We're going to think about what it *looks* like and what it *sounds* like when it's done well."

2. Assign students to small groups of three or four. Have them discuss what a group of students *looks* like when they are working well together. What would someone see while *watching* that group? You may need to give an example to get their thinking

started, or you may want to begin this as a whole-group activity for the first one or two descriptors and then let them continue in their small groups. Ask them to come up with three to five words or phrases describing what working well together looks like and list them on their group's T-chart. If necessary, circulate and assist with the writing.

3. Ask students to discuss with their small group what a group of students *sounds* like when they are working well together. What would someone hear while *listening* to that group? Ask them to come up with three to five words or phrases describing what working well together sounds like and list them on their group's T-chart. If necessary, circulate and assist with the writing.

4. Once all groups have finished their lists, create one class T-chart, titled "Criteria for Working in a Group." Tally any criteria identified by multiple groups. Reinforce the idea that what they have listed are *criteria*—descriptors of quality. Ask students to share which they think are most important and why. Have the class vote on the three to five criteria from each list ("Looks Like"/"Sounds Like") they think should be used to judge effectiveness of groups when working together throughout the school year.

Closure:

Say, "We use criteria in school to know what is expected for behavior and for school work. We will use criteria throughout this year so you know what is expected of you in class and in your work. An important responsibility you have as a student is to be sure you know what the criteria will be for the work you are doing. When you are not sure what is expected, you can ask me and I will clarify the criteria."

Extension:

Students can follow this process to create a list of criteria for quality for any number of desired behaviors, such as walking in the hall, lining up for lunch, or getting ready to go home. You can model some good and not-so-good behaviors to help their thinking along. You may want to keep the list open and ask them to add to it after especially successful or problematic experiences. When you are satisfied with the criteria list, tell students they can use this list to know what they are doing well and what they need to improve.

Lesson 4: Introducing Preexisting Criteria

In this lesson, students apply their criteria-making skills to an academic learning target that will be measured by a scoring guide or developmental continuum describing stages of proficiency. The learning target used as the example is "Gives a presentation."

Key Understanding:

Knowing the criteria in advance helps us perform better.

Materials:

- Chart paper

- Your own short presentation or speech, prepared in advance

Process:

1. Say, "Today we're going to think about the criteria for giving a presentation. You've all seen people give presentations. What does it sound like when we do it really well?" Put "Criteria for a Good Presentation" (or whatever statement describes your oral presentation learning target) as the title on chart paper. Write down what students say.

2. Say, "I'm going to give a short presentation and then we are going to add to our list of criteria things we didn't think of at first. So, watch me and listen to me and think about what I'm doing well." Give a short presentation, modeling for them the characteristics you will teach, such as eye contact, volume, and enunciation. Invite them to add to the list.

   In the case of this learning target, you could also give a short presentation modeling the not-so-good, such as turning your back to the audience, holding a book up in front of your face, and mumbling. (By doing this, you are acting as a "just beginning" oral presentation giver. Be sure you introduce this in such a way that no child will think you are making fun of him or her.) Ask, "What did I do that time?" Let them respond. Then ask, "What could I have done instead to make it better?" Add responses to the list.

3. When your students have come up with a list that has at least some of the criteria you want them to know, tell them, "This is a good list. You have said some of the same things that experts say. Would you like to see the experts' list?" Share the "expert" list—a list of the criteria represented in your scoring guide that you will

be teaching them to master. This list can use terms they either already understand or will learn to understand.

4. As you present each criterion, ask students if it is similar to anything on their list. Mark the similarities. (Any extraneous ideas they may have come up with can offer you information about misconceptions to address as you help them develop oral presentation skills.) When you finish, be sure to show them how much they already know by reviewing the similarities between their list and the "expert" list.

Closure:

Hand out a rubric or checklist that is suited to your students' reading and comprehension levels. Tell them that you all will be using this "expert" list of criteria to help them practice and become experts at giving presentations.

Co-Creating Criteria with Students

Many teachers find it instructionally powerful to co-create criteria with the class. The protocol for doing so is similar to the one for introducing criteria to students.

- Ask students what they think constitutes quality and list their responses. At this step, make sure students are focused on the learning target and not just on the activity. For example, if they will make a poster to illustrate the interrelationships in a food web, direct their attention to accuracy and completeness of information rather than to the number of colors used, neatness, or other features of a poster that don't relate to the learning to be demonstrated. If you also want to teach how to present information effectively visually, make that its own learning target and generate separate criteria for it.

- Share some examples that illustrate specific strengths and weaknesses in quality relative to the intended learning target. Let students discuss the samples and offer additions to the list.

- Compile their brainstormed lists. Look for patterns and characteristics that go together. Also have in mind your own criteria for quality. At this point you will be able to see if they have missed anything of importance to successful execution of the learning target.

- If they have missed important features, you can either share one or two samples chosen to highlight the missing characteristics and guide them to noticing those additional features, or you can let students know that you will be combining their thoughts with those of experts to create the rubric.

- Turn the list of features into a rubric that accurately describes levels of quality, adhering to guidelines described in this chapter. Share the rubric with students.

Video 2.5: Co-Creating Criteria with Students

Watch Video 2.5 to hear a high school student describe co-creating criteria.

When to Share the Learning Target

The point at which you communicate the target can vary. Sometimes you'll do it as a part of the anticipatory set for the lesson or unit (or whatever content "chunk" you are teaching): "Today we're going to learn how to write a hypothesis." Other times, such as when a rubric captures the elements of quality, you will want to let the definition unfold over several days or weeks.

Yet another point is when you have created an activity that causes the learning target to reveal itself during the course of the lesson, such as when students engage in discovery learning, a series of explorations structured to develop understanding of the intended learning. In this case, you probably will not want to post the target in advance. Just make sure students can describe the intended learning *before* you ask them to engage in sustained independent practice and *before* they are preparing for the summative assessment.

However you structure it, make sure that at the appropriate time during the learning, students know what they are aiming for: "We are learning to _____," or "I am practicing being able to _____." And before students engage in a summative assessment—when you will ask them to show what they have learned for their grade—they definitely need to be able to articulate the intended learning: "In this assessment, I am demonstrating my level of understanding of/ability to/proficiency with _____."

Checking for Awareness of the Intended Learning

Periodically, check to see that students can articulate the learning target. This is different from checking their level of mastery of the target. At this point, you just want to determine whether all students know what they are to be learning.

You might walk around the room while they are engaged in a task and ask, "Why are we doing this activity?" You might hear task-completion goals such as, "to get a grade," "to do all of the problems," or "so we can get out early." Or you might hear comments like "to get better at choosing words that paint a picture in the reader's mind" or "to learn the differences between physical and chemical changes." If you hear the former, redirect students with the question, "What are we learning?" If they can't answer it, the learning targets may not be clear enough to them yet, and their subsequent work is less likely to be productive with respect to learning.

One strategy for providing a window into students' understanding of the intended learning is to have students complete an "exit slip," a short note students use as their ticket out the door at the end of the lesson or period. Exit slips have been used for years as a way to achieve closure to a lesson. To focus exit slips on learning targets, you can ask students to write down what they think they were to learn in the lesson (Harlen, 2007), or respond to the question, "Why did we do _____ (activity) today?" followed by a quick assessment of where they are.

Video 2.6: Revisiting the Learning at the End of the Lesson: Kindergarten

It is also a good idea at the end of a lesson to check where students are on their mastery of the learning target. One idea is to begin the lesson by phrasing the learning target as a question that students should be able to answer at the end of the lesson ("How do you find the lowest common denominator for a pair of fractions?" "What is the Pythagorean Theorem and what is it good for?"). Have students write a response to the question on an exit slip before they leave (Wiliam & Lee, 2001). You can then read through the exit slips to identify misconceptions and fine-tune your plans for the next lesson.

Video 2.7: Revisiting the Learning at the End of the Lesson: Grade 1

Middle school teacher Laura Grayson uses two cooperative learning strategies, "Think, Pair, Share" and "Give One, Get One," to help students check their own understanding of the concepts and learning targets they are working on (Figure 2.17).

Watch Videos 2.6, 2.7, and 2.8 for other ways teachers revisit the learning at the end of the lesson.

Video 2.8: Revisiting the Learning at the End of the Lesson: Grade 3

Strategy 2: Use Examples and Models of Strong and Weak Work.

One of the hallmarks of the Common Core State Standards is that across disciplines emphasis is placed on teaching students to express an opinion, defend their reasoning, and critique the reasoning of others. Strategy 2 strengthens

Figure 2.17

From the Classroom

Strategy #1: Give One, Get One

What We Do

To help students check their understanding of the learning they are working on, I often use two cooperative learning strategies, "Think, Pair, Share" and "Give One, Get One." With "Think, Pair, Share," students have a minute or two to process the information on their own, then they turn to a neighbor and share their thoughts. When it is time to share with the whole class, I ask students to share what their partners said. This activity helps develop their ability to process their own thoughts, to listen actively to their partner's thoughts, and to succinctly summarize and share what they heard. With "Give One, Get One" students write down several thoughts about what we have been discussing, reading, or learning on an index card. Then they form small groups and each "give one" of their ideas. Group members "get one" by adding it to their lists if they don't already have it.

After students have practiced with these strategies, I use them in all academic areas to focus attention on the learning. Both can be used without advanced preparation so it is easy to use them at any teachable moment or when it is clear that students need time to process information. Sometimes I collect the Give One, Get One index cards as an exit ticket. Other times, the index cards function as a self-created study guide that students take home.

Impact on Learning

Students often ask for these strategies as they have become used to using them to process information. Both of these strategies help students compare their own thinking with that of their peers, which helps deepen their own understanding. In follow-up class discussions, I see evidence that their thinking has changed and grown. The impact also shows up when students complete an independent exit ticket, a written assignment, or a summative assessment, and they are able to explain their thinking.

What My Students Say

I have heard students say things such as "I hadn't thought about that in that way; thank you for sharing." "Give One, Get One helps me to review and prepare for upcoming tests." They can give specifics such as "I thought this _____, and after talking to _____, I realized that I could add that to my understanding."

Source: Used with permission from Laura Grayson, middle school teacher, Kirkwood School District: Kirkwood, MO. Unpublished classroom materials.

students' evaluative thinking by letting them practice making judgments about accuracy or level of quality with carefully chosen assessment items and examples. The goal is to help students come to hold an understanding about accuracy and quality similar to yours before they engage in extended practice with the target. This strategy has several different possible applications, depending on the kind of learning target you are teaching and assessment method you will use.

> "The features of excellent work should be so transparent that students can learn to evaluate their own work in the same way that their teachers would."
>
> *Frederiksen & Collins, 1989, quoted in Shepard, 2001, p. 1092*

Strong and Weak Examples with Selected Response Items

As we saw earlier in this chapter, for many knowledge and some reasoning learning targets, selected response assessment works well both for formative assessment uses (for diagnosis and practice) and for summative assessment uses (for assigning a mark or grade). In a well-constructed multiple-choice item, the wrong answers, called *distractors*, will represent typical misconceptions, incomplete understanding, or flaws in reasoning. In other words, for any given knowledge or reasoning learning target, there is often more than one way to get it wrong, and good multiple-choice items include those typical wrong answers in their set of answer choices. A simple way to use multiple-choice items as strong and weak examples is to have students work in pairs to identify an answer choice they know to be wrong and then explain why it is wrong. They can do the same thing for the right answer, but they generally have more fun with the wrong answers, and they learn just as much, if not more, trying to figure out what the problem with an answer is. (See Chapter 5 for a discussion of creating distractors and Chapter 6 for more in-depth teaching ideas with selected response items.)

Strong and Weak Examples with Written Response Items

If you teach beyond the primary level, chances are you will often use written response exercises to assess conceptual understanding and reasoning. Again, there are typical, often predictable ways that an answer can go off-track for any given learning target. It can be quite useful to let students examine these pitfalls on the path to mastery as a part of teaching the learning target.

Strong and Weak Examples with Rubrics

When you will be using a rubric to assess a reasoning, skill, or product target, you can use work samples illustrating a range of quality to teach students

Figure 2.18

FAQ: Is It a Good Idea to Use Weak Examples?

It seems reasonable to worry that sharing weak examples will confuse students and perhaps cause them to produce similar work. The protocol for analyzing sample work helps avoid this potential problem in the following ways:

1. You are selecting samples that illustrate typical problems they already have.

2. When they read the rubric, students will notice that it describes a range of quality, not just the top level, and you can point out that they will be working with samples that represent all levels.

3. When students themselves independently decide whether an example is strong or weak for the descriptors listed in your rubric and then discuss their judgment with a small group, it raises awareness of features of quality in their own work that might need attention.

"'That's a 5. I don't know what it means. I've got it on some of my work. I think it's a grade thing.'"

Harlen, 2007, p. 126

to differentiate what it looks like when it's done well and what it looks like when it has weaknesses. This "pre-work" thinking helps students avoid many typical problems they generally begin with, thereby causing their initial work to come in at a higher level of quality. It also prepares them to understand your feedback when they receive it. In addition, sorting through examples of strong and weak work acts as guided practice for offering feedback to peers and for self-assessment. (See Figure 2.18 for an explanation of the rationale for using weak examples.)

Anonymity

When providing examples for students to practice evaluating, use only anonymous work not done by anyone in the class. Letting students practice evaluating work with the student present, even if no one knows whose work it is, is risky. You are better off not taking the chance of risking harm to any of your students.

Selecting Samples

To implement Strategy 2 with a performance assessment, begin by finding (or creating) anonymous samples of strong work as well as work that exhibits one or more problems you want students to begin noticing and correcting in their own work. This helps them attend to both the strengths you want them to demonstrate and typical problems they come with. Use only examples from students *not* in the class that will be using them and keep them anonymous (Figure 2.19).

Figure 2.19

Gathering Anonymous Samples

- Find annotated samples on state or provincial websites.

- Ask students for permission to use their work as a teaching example and then save it for next year, trade with another teacher, or use it with a different class. (Students own their work, so be sure to ask for permission before you use it or trade it.)

- Create your own examples, inserting the kind of errors students typically make.

Keep in mind that this is not yet an exercise in offering peer feedback; rather, it is practice for being able to assess their own and others' strengths and weaknesses accurately.

Teaching Students to Evaluate Anonymous Samples

To maximize the chances that all students will engage in the evaluative thinking required to internalize the rubric's concepts, we can use a protocol to guide their discussion of the anonymous samples you have collected. If you are working with an analytic rubric, select one criterion to focus on at a time. To determine which you will focus on first, consider what students will need to know first. For example, using the mathematics problem-solving rubric, you may decide to focus on the trait of *Problem Solving* before moving to the trait of *Mathematical Communication*, because if they don't first learn how to choose an appropriate strategy and work it through to completion, they won't have much to communicate.

Next, select one or more samples that you would judge according to the rubric to be in the strong range, the weak range, and the middle range. If you are working with an analytic rubric, select samples in each range for each criterion. The same sample can often be used for multiple criteria—sometimes in the same range and sometimes in different ranges for different criteria—just be sure to note which range for each criteria with a few words as to why you put it there. When first introducing this protocol, use samples in the strong range and the weak range. When students have had some practice and are starting to understand the kind of thinking they need to do (evaluative reasoning), you can begin using some midrange samples. Prepare the samples so that everyone can see them clearly, either for display on a screen or for distribution to each student.

Begin Simply

Keep your examples fairly uncomplicated the first few times, while students are learning the protocol.

Beginning with a strong sample, follow this protocol, which is set up for use with a five-point rubric:

1. Display, show, or distribute the sample. Read it aloud as well, if appropriate. In many cases, reading aloud either won't be useful or won't be possible. For example, reading aloud isn't useful with learning targets such as *Accurate Display of Data* in science, *Problem Solving* in mathematics, or *Conventions* in writing. With products learning targets that don't call for writing such as demonstrating use of perspective in a drawing and with all performances (e.g., playing a musical instrument or dribbling a basketball), reading aloud obviously is not possible. And in some cases, as with mathematics problem solving, students will need to carry out the task before viewing samples for evaluation.

2. Ask students to engage independently in the following thought process:

   - Read the rubric. (Don't show or hand out the sample until all students have read the rubric.)

   - Read the sample and decide whether you think it is strong or weak for the criterion we are focusing on. Mentally put in one pile or the other: Strong or Weak.

   - If you think it is strong, begin reading the rubric at the 5 level. If the words and phrases for 5 describe it, give it a 5 (or whatever level is the highest on your rubric).

   - If you think it may not be quite that strong, read the 3. (On a four-level rubric, they read the next-to-the-highest level.) If the 3 describes it completely, give it a 3 (or whatever level is next to the highest on your four-level rubric).

   - If you think the sample has some strengths from the 5 and some problems from the 3, mark the phrases that apply in each level and give the sample a 4. (With a four-level rubric, they will have to work with half-points, or half-levels, if it is possible for a sample to represent a mixture of features from adjacent levels on your rubric.)

   - If you think the sample is weak, begin reading the rubric at the 1. If the words and phrases from the 1 describe it, give it a 1 (or whatever label applies to your rubric's low end).

   - If you think it may not be quite that weak, read the 3. (On a four-level rubric, they read the next-to-the-lowest level.) If the

3 describes it completely, give it a 3 (or the next-to-the-lowest level on your rubric).

If the sample has some weaknesses from the 1 and some strengths from the 3, mark the phrases you think apply in each level and give the sample a 2. (Again, with a four-level rubric, they will have to work with half-points, or half-levels if you are not using points, if it is possible for a sample to represent a mixture of features from adjacent levels on your rubric.) (See Figure 2.21 for an explanation of the number of rubric levels.)

3. After students have had the opportunity to settle on a score individually, ask them to work in small groups to discuss their judgments and the reasons why, using the language of the scoring rubric. Using the rubric's language and concepts is crucial to the effectiveness of this activity because its purpose is to deepen their understanding of the rubric. As they are discussing, walk around the class reinforcing students' use of the rubric's language and concepts to support their judgments.

4. Next, ask students to vote as a class. Tally their choices: How many gave this a 1? a 2? a 3? a 4? a 5? Then, ask for volunteers to share what they gave it and why. Listen for use of the rubric language. Do not worry if student opinions differ at first. During this stage of the activity, encourage them to respond to each other. Consider refraining from expressing your opinion at this point; comment only on their use of the concepts in the rubric to justify their scores: "Good job of using the language of the rubric to justify your score." If a student justifies a score with a reason not in the rubric, you might say, "Can you find language in the rubric that supports your score?" or "You noticed something that is actually described in a different trait. We'll be getting to that later."

5. You can share the score that you (and other raters, if you are using samples that have been rated and annotated by others) would give it, but rather than give a lengthy explanation, you may wish to let them repeat the process with another example, this time a much weaker one, so they can explore and internalize how degrees of quality manifest themselves.

6. Repeat this process until students are familiar with the language and concepts of the scoring rubric. As they get better at differentiating between strong and weak work, begin using midrange samples.

Figure 2.20

Table Protocol for Analyzing Work Samples

Students working in small groups can follow this protocol to work through the process of analyzing samples for one or more criteria on the scoring rubric. They can take turns around the table acting as moderator.

1. Everyone reads the scoring guide for _____ (specify criterion) in this order: the highest level, the lowest level, and then the middle level or levels.
2. The moderator reads the sample paper aloud or shows the sample.
3. Everyone else thinks, "Strong or weak for _____ (specified criterion)?" while listening to the paper or viewing the sample.
4. Everyone (including the moderator) silently and independently reads the high or low level of the rubric corresponding to their own judgments of "strong" or "weak." If the high or low level doesn't describe the sample well, then read the middle level (or levels progressing toward the middle) until you find the phrases that accurately describe the quality of the sample. Everyone writes down their score.
5. When all are ready, the moderator conducts the vote and tallies the scores.
6. The moderator conducts the discussion—"What did you give it and why?"—encouraging the use of the scoring rubric's language and concepts.

Video 2.9: Using Strong and Weak Models: Kindergarten

After students have engaged in this activity several times, you can turn more responsibility over to them in small groups. Figure 2.20 shows a table protocol—instructions you can give students, where one student in each group becomes the moderator of the discussion, the role you played while they were learning how to score. If the job of moderator rotates among the group, each person also gets the opportunity to listen for use of the language of the rubric to justify scores.

Watch Videos 2.9, 2.10, 2.11, 2.12, and 2.13 for examples of how teachers and students use strong and weak models in the classroom.

Video 2.10: Using Strong and Weak Models: Grade 1

Using Classwork as Strong and Weak Models

When you have established a classroom environment in which students view making a mistake as a natural part of learning, you may be able to use their own work as a teaching example. Asking for volunteers to work

Figure 2.21

FAQ: How Many Levels Should a Rubric Have?

The number of levels depends on the learning target being assessed and the intended use of the information the rubric provides. Although you will often see rubrics with an even number of levels (usually four), an odd number of levels (three or five) can work well in formative applications.

Some simpler learning targets can truly only be divided into three levels of proficiency, so it makes sense to only have three levels if the purpose of the rubric is to describe proficiency accurately either for formative or summative use. Others can be divided easily into five levels.

Any rubric having several separate indicators in the same category is more accurately evaluated with a five-point rubric. Here's why. On typical five-point rubrics, only three levels are defined—Level 5, Level 3, and Level 1. It is often the case that a student's performance contains some descriptors from Level 5 and some from Level 3, or some descriptors from Level 3 and some from Level 1. With these rubrics, when a performance falls between two score points, you can highlight the phrases that describe it from each of the defined levels and then assign it the intermediate score, e.g., 4 or 2.

This way, the descriptors at the score level you assign will always accurately represent the strengths and problems of the student's work. Rubrics that don't accurately describe strengths and problems cannot be used effectively to plan further instruction, to offer feedback to students, or to guide student self-assessment.

Source: Arter, Judith A.; Chappuis, Jan, *Creating and Recognizing Quality Rubrics,* 1st Ed., ©2006. Reproduced by permission of Pearson Education, Inc., Upper Saddle River, NJ.

a problem from homework, to share a draft of a response to a prompt or to a piece of writing, or to return to any other work they have done that may not demonstrate mastery can be a strong instructional experience for the volunteers and for the rest of the class. However, caution is in order. Even in a supportive learning environment, students can feel uncomfortable making mistakes in full view of their peers. For that reason, it is a good idea to only use volunteers and to plan carefully how you will respond to what they share or demonstrate. The person volunteering is offering to let the class learn from his or her thinking. Help the class understand that we can learn from each other's mistakes as well as each other's strengths. For an example of this strategy done well, watch the video "My Favorite No," from the Teaching Channel, which shows an eighth-grade math teacher selecting mistakes to teach with (https://www.teachingchannel.org/videos/class-warm-up-routine).

Video 2.11: Using Strong and Weak Models: Middle School Science

Video 2.12: Using Strong and Weak Models: High School Science

Also watch Video 2.14 for a discussion of how students benefit.

Video 2.13: Using Strong and Weak Models: AP Calculus

Video 2.14: Using Classwork as Strong and Weak Models: AP Calculus

Examples of Strategies 1 and 2 with Elementary Students

The following scenario, transcribed from a demonstration teaching lesson, is an example of how you can use a student-friendly version of a reasoning learning target as the basis of a lesson. In this case, the teacher is introducing fourth graders to the reading learning target, "Makes inferences based on what is read." As you read through the scenario, look for Strategy 1, introducing the definition of *inference*, and Strategy 2, using strong and weak examples.

Inference Scenario

TEACHER: Have any of you ever known what you're getting for a present before you opened the package? (*Hands wave in the air.*) What was it? Luke?

LUKE: It was a basketball.

TEACHER: How did you know it was a basketball? Did it say 'To Luke— Basketball' on the tag?

LUKE: Noooo. I knew it was one because I asked for it, and it was round, and it bounced.

TEACHER: So you made a guess, based on clues.

LUKE: Yeah.

TEACHER: How about you, Sarah?

SARAH: It was a bike.

TEACHER: What were your clues?

SARAH: Well my mom said it was a pony, but I knew it was a bike.

TEACHER: How did you know it wasn't a pony?

SARAH: It was too skinny.

(*The teacher then asks for other examples ("What did you get?" "How did you know?"), reiterating the concept that students made correct guesses based on clues.*)

TEACHER: You all made guesses and you were right because you had some clues. When we make a guess based on clues, we call that an *inference*.

(She writes the word *inference* and the definition, *a guess based on clues,* on a piece of chart paper.) Let's practice inferring some more. (She walks up to a student wearing a turquoise sweater.) I'm going to make an inference that Maria's favorite color is turquoise. Maria, is your favorite color turquoise?

MARIA: Well, no.

TEACHER: What happened here? I made a guess and I based it on a clue. What went wrong?

STUDENT: You didn't have enough clues.

ANOTHER STUDENT: Just because she's wearing a turquoise sweater today doesn't mean she loves it.

A THIRD STUDENT: Maria hardly ever wears turquoise.

TEACHER: What would I have to see in order to make a confident guess that her favorite color is turquoise?

STUDENT: All her pencils would be turquoise.

A DIFFERENT STUDENT: The mirror in her locker would be turquoise.

ANOTHER STUDENT: She would wear turquoise every day.

TEACHER: So it's not enough to have one clue to make a good inference. I might need three or four clues.

JAMAL: Well if she wore turquoise every day, that's just one clue, but it happens over and over.

TEACHER: So we could call that a repeated clue? An inference, to be a good one, needs to be based on enough clues—more than one piece of evidence or the same evidence repeated over and over?

JAMAL: Yeah.

TEACHER: Let's call this a level 3 inference. (Under the definition of inference, she writes: 3 = *A guess based on enough clues.*) Now, think about the guess that Maria's favorite color is turquoise. Let's call that a level 2 inference. How would we define that? It's a guess, but what's wrong with it?

JAMAL: It doesn't have enough clues.

(The teacher writes 2 = *A guess, but not enough clues.*)

TEACHER: Okay. Now what if I guessed that Jerome's favorite color is orange. What would you call that? Is it an inference? It's a guess, isn't it? (Jerome is not wearing any orange.)

STUDENTS: Yeah but you don't have any evidence.

TEACHER: What kind of an inference is it?

STUDENTS: A bad one.

TEACHER: So, we could call a poor inference a *wild* guess because it's not based on any clues. Let's call this a level 1 inference. (The teacher writes: 1 = *Wild guess—no clues*.)

In this example, the teacher is guiding students in developing a simple scoring rubric for quality inferences by using strong and weak examples to help them get a clear vision of exactly what constitutes a high-quality response to an inference question. Figure 2.22 shows the inference rubric they developed, along with the posters she used to illustrate the definition. Contrast this short lesson with telling students that to *infer* means to "read between the lines." That definition itself requires an inference to understand.

Primary Application of Strategies 1 and 2

Primary teacher Amy Meyer used Strategies 1 and 2 to introduce the learning targets for a writing project (Figure 2.23). Here is her description of what she did and what happened with students as a result (personal communication, 2008):

> I introduced each writing target, one by one, in a minilesson. I provided examples and models of each writing piece so students could see what I wanted their work to look like. As a group we looked at strong and weak examples. The students had a clear vision of what they needed to do for their writing project. Using models and the specific targets helped students understand more clearly what I expected. Their work was much better than what they had done in a previous activity without the targets and models.

Secondary Application of Strategies 1 and 2

High school science teacher Stephanie Harmon works with her students to create criteria describing strong and weak work. They use the criteria to evaluate anonymous samples of student work and then use what they have learned to offer each other feedback and to self-assess. Figure 2.24 is her explanation of what she does and the impact it has had on her students.

Figure 2.22

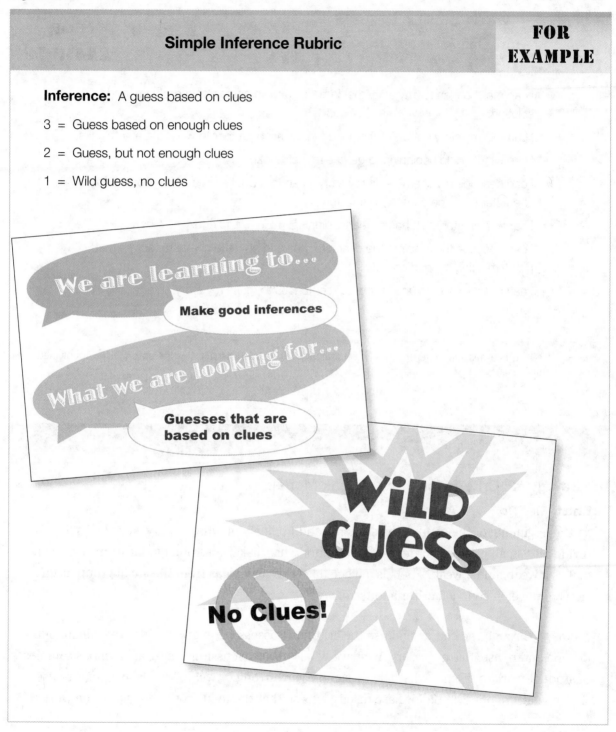

Simple Inference Rubric

FOR EXAMPLE

Inference: A guess based on clues

3 = Guess based on enough clues

2 = Guess, but not enough clues

1 = Wild guess, no clues

We are learning to...

Make good inferences

What we are looking for...

Guesses that are based on clues

WILD GUESS

No Clues!

Figure 2.23

How Can I Make a Story Enjoyable to Read?	FOR EXAMPLE

- I can make a plan for my story that includes a main character, a problem, and a solution.
- I can talk my story out or tell it out loud to a writing partner to work out any "clunks."
- I can write a bold beginning to get the reader hooked.
- I can describe my character in my story. I can tell about appearance (looks) and character traits (personality) in my story.
- I can write a story that has a clear beginning, middle, and end.
- I can describe the problem the character has and how the character solves that problem using supporting details.
- I can use juicy words and "showing" sentences to make my story entertaining to the reader.

Source: Used with permission from Amy Meyer, Olentangy Local School District: Lewis Center, OH. Unpublished classroom materials.

Figure 2.24

From the Classroom

Strategy #2: Criteria for Strong/Weak Models

What We Do

At the beginning of the course, the students and I talk about what quality work looks like. We divide into small groups and develop criteria for what makes a strong model strong and what makes a weak model weak. Then as a whole class, we use ideas from the small group discussions to develop common criteria for strong/weak models.

As we go through the course and use the criteria to assess our work, we also reevaluate our criteria and revise it as necessary. We have whole-class discussions using anonymous samples of student work to discuss whether the samples are strong or weak. We make a point to use the language of our criteria in these discussions so that the focus is the quality of the work.

Impact on Learning

Students take ownership of this process. They become proficient in self-assessing and peer-assessing work samples. They make insightful comments, and the quality of their work has improved. They use what I call the "language of quality" from the language we used in our class criteria for strong models. This is evident in their feedback comments and also their self-assessments.

Figure 2.24 (continued)

What My Students Say

"I used to think that peer-assessing was about making my friends feel better about the work they did. Now I know it isn't about how we feel but is the work meeting what the task requires and how can we help each other do that. Looking at other people's work helps me improve my work—not because I'm copying but because I have to think more about what it takes to be good. Using the criteria for strong models doesn't mean everyone's work has to be alike but there are certain features that everyone should have in common." Brian M., 11th grade student

---

Source: Used with permission from Stephanie Harmon, science teacher, Rockcastle County High School: Mt. Vernon, KY. Unpublished classroom materials.

Conclusion

By making the learning targets clear to students from the outset, we build student confidence and increase the chances that they will master the target. With Strategy 1, we provide students with descriptive statements of the intended learning in language they can understand. With Strategy 2, we engage them in evaluating examples representing a range of quality to help them recognize the differences between "strong" and "needs work." Both Strategies 1 and 2 are necessary for students to internalize a vision of where they're headed—the vision that will drive their effort from practice to the final test. If you had to choose one thing to do from all the recommendations in this book, it would be most profitable to start with an activity in this chapter.

Understanding and Applying the Content of Chapter 2

End-of-chapter activities are intended to help you master the chapter's learning targets and apply concepts to your classroom. They are designed to deepen your understanding of the chapter content, provide discussion topics for collaborative learning, and guide implementation of the content and practices taught in the chapter. Forms and materials for completing each activity appear in editable Microsoft Word format in the Chapter 2 DVD file. Each form needed for an activity is listed after the activity directions and marked with this symbol: ◎

Chapter 2 Learning Targets

1. Know how to share different types of learning targets with students so they have a clear vision of the intended learning
   - Convert learning targets into student-friendly language
   - Identify rubrics suited for formative use
   - Convert rubrics to student-friendly language
   - Introduce the concepts of quality represented in a rubric to students
2. Know how to monitor student awareness of the intended learning
3. Know how to use strong and weak examples effectively to deepen conceptual understanding and to make standards of quality clear

Chapter 2 Activities

Discussion Questions (All learning targets)

Activity 2.1   Keeping a Reflective Journal (All learning targets)

Activity 2.2   Clarifying Learning Targets (Learning target 1)

Activity 2.3   Sharing Learning Targets (Learning target 1)

Activity 2.4   Converting Learning Targets to Student-Friendly Language (Learning target 1)

Activity 2.5   Revising Rubrics for Formative Use (Learning target 1)

Activity 2.6   Developing a Student-Friendly Rubric (Learning target 1)

Activity 2.7   Selecting a Strategy 1 Application (Learning target 1)

Activity 2.8   Monitoring Student Awareness of the Intended Learning (Learning target 2)

Activity 2.9   Assembling Samples of Student Work (Learning target 3)

Activity 2.10 Practicing with the Table Protocol for Analyzing Samples (Learning target 3)

Activity 2.11 Selecting a Strategy 2 Application (Learning target 3)

Activity 2.12 Adding to Your Growth Portfolio (All learning targets)

Chapter 2 Discussion Questions

Discussion questions are also explored in depth in the activities listed in parentheses.

Questions to Discuss Before Reading Chapter 2

1. How do you communicate the intended learning of a lesson, activity, task, project, or unit to students? When does this occur? (Activities 2.3 and 2.7)

2. What do you currently do to check for understanding of the intended learning of a lesson? (Activity 2.8)

3. How do you use models and examples with students? What do you do? What does it help students do? (Activities 2.10 and 2.11)

Questions to Discuss After Reading Chapter 2

4. Are your learning targets clear to you as written? If not, what do they need? Discussion with colleagues? Deconstructing? Clarification from an outside expert? (Activity 2.2)

5. Which of your learning targets will be clear to students "as is"? Which may need to be rephrased or converted into student-friendly language? (Activities 2.3 and 2.4)

6. Of the rubrics you use, which will need conversion to student-friendly language? (Activities 2.5 and 2.6)

7. How will you make sure that students know which learning target(s) they are working on at any given time? (Activity 2.8)

8. Which of your learning targets would benefit from a Strategy 2 activity? Where might you find strong and weak examples? (Activities 2.9 and 2.11)

9. How will you engage students in analyzing samples? How much class time might you devote to this? (Activity 2.10)

10. What activities from Chapter 2 did you try in the classroom? How did they work? What successes did you notice? What modifications might you make? (Activities 2.7, 2.8, 2.11, and 2.12)

Activity 2.1

Keep a Reflective Journal

This is intended as an independent activity. If you choose to do it, you may want to discuss the thoughts you record with your learning team.

Keep a record of your thoughts, questions, and any implementation activities you tried while reading this chapter.

Activity 2.1 Chapter 2 Reflective Journal Form

Activity 2.2

Clarifying Learning Targets

This is intended as an independent activity. If you do it independently, you may want to discuss the results with your learning team.

After reading through the section titled "Prerequisites: Clear Learning Targets," use the form on the DVD to list each learning target for a given unit or marking period. Then decide for each: Is it clear as is? Do you need to discuss it with colleagues or get outside clarification? Does it need to be deconstructed into lesson-level learning targets?

Activity 2.2 Clarifying Learning Targets

Activity 2.3

Sharing Learning Targets

This is intended as an independent activity. If you do it independently, you may want to discuss the results with your learning team.

After reading the section on Strategy 1, use the form on the DVD to list each clear learning target for a given unit or marking period. Then decide for each: Will I share as is? Rewrite it in student-friendly language? Define it with a student-friendly rubric?

Activity 2.3 Sharing Learning Targets

Activity 2.4

Converting Learning Targets to Student-Friendly Language

This is intended as a partner or learning team activity.

Working with a partner or your learning team, select one or more learning targets that would benefit from being rephrased for students. Use the form on the DVD to follow the process described in this chapter to create a student-friendly definition.

Activity 2.4 Converting Learning Targets to Student-Friendly Language

Activity 2.5

Revising Rubrics for Formative Use

This is intended as a partner or learning team activity.

Collect the scoring rubric or rubrics you will use for a given unit or marking period. Working with a partner or your learning team, compare each to the characteristics described in the section, "Prerequisite: A Suitable Rubric." Use the form on the DVD to note any changes needed to make your rubrics function well as formative tools. Then revise the rubrics so that their content and structure will support effective formative assessment use. For further guidance on restructuring rubrics, refer to the Rubric for Rubrics in Chappuis et al. (2012), Chapter 7.

Activity 2.5 Revising Rubrics for Formative Use

Activity 2.6

Developing a Student-Friendly Rubric

This is intended as a partner or learning team activity.

Once you have found or created a rubric suited to assessment for learning applications, work with a partner or your learning team to follow the steps for developing a student-friendly version described in this chapter, using the form on the DVD.

Activity 2.6 Developing a Student-Friendly Rubric

Activity 2.7

Selecting a Strategy 1 Application

This is intended as an independent activity. If you do it independently, you may want to discuss the results with your learning team.

After reading the section explaining Strategy 1, choose one way to share learning targets. After having tried it with students, use the form on the DVD to reflect on the activity: what you tried, what you noticed as a result, and what, if any, actions you have taken or will take on the basis of the experience. If you are working with a learning team, consider sharing your reflection with them.

Activity 2.7 Selecting a Strategy 1 Application

Activity 2.8

Monitoring Student Awareness of the Intended Learning

This is intended as an independent activity. If you do it independently, you may want to discuss the results with your learning team.

After reading the section titled "Checking for Awareness of the Intended Learning" and Figure 2.17, select one strategy described and use it "as is" or modify it to suit your context. After having tried it with students, use the form on the DVD to reflect on the activity: what you tried, what you noticed as a result, and what, if any, actions you have taken or will take on the basis of the experience. If you are working with a learning team, consider sharing your reflection with them.

Activity 2.8 Monitoring Student Awareness of the Intended Learning

Activity 2.9

Assembling Samples of Student Work

After reading the section explaining Strategy 2, work with a partner or team to make a collection of numbered anonymous samples that illustrate one or more strengths and problems as defined by your rubric. Make sure the strengths and problems link directly to phrases on your rubric. If your samples relate to an analytic rubric (two or more criteria evaluated separately), identify the criterion that the sample illustrates. Use the chart on the DVD to keep track of your selections. If you are including your own students' work, remember to ask for written permission for their work to be shown as an anonymous teaching example and then make sure not to use it with their class.

Activity 2.9 Assembling Samples of Student Work

Activity 2.10

Practicing with the Table Protocol for Analyzing Samples

This activity is intended to give your learning team practice with the table protocol that students can use to evaluate samples of anonymous work. It can also help your team become familiar with running the protocol as a whole-class activity. This activity works best when all team members are familiar with the scoring rubric used.

1. After reading the section explaining Strategy 2, practice using the table protocol described in Figure 2.20 by doing the following:

    -   Select two or three samples of student work and make copies of each for each learning team member.

    -   Make a copy of the scoring rubric for each team member. If it is an analytic rubric, select one criterion to focus on. You only need to make copies of that criterion, but it is a good idea to have one copy of the complete rubric to refer to in case people have questions about other features of the samples that are not addressed in the selected criterion.

Variations

-   One or more team members can provide samples, all relating to the same scoring rubric.

-   Different team members can bring samples relating to different rubrics.

2. As a team, review the section titled "Teaching Students to Evaluate Anonymous Samples."

3. Follow the protocol described in Figure 2.20. Allow a different person to act as table moderator for each sample of student work. You can use the form on the DVD to track your responses.

4. Discuss how you might use the whole-class protocol and/or the small-group protocol with your students. If you have already used one or both, discuss what you did and changes you noticed in students' understanding of the characteristics of quality as a result.

 Activity 2.10 Practicing with the Table Protocol for Analyzing Samples

Activity 2.11

Selecting a Strategy 2 Application

This is intended as an independent activity. If you do it independently, you may want to discuss the results with your learning team.

After reading the section explaining Strategy 2, choose one context in which to use strong and weak examples as teaching tools: with selected response items, with written response items, or with rubrics. After having tried it with students, use the form on the DVD to reflect on the activity: what you tried, what you noticed as a result, and what, if any, actions you have taken or will take on the basis of the experience. If you are working with a learning team, consider sharing your reflection with them.

Activity 2.11 Selecting a Strategy 2 Application

Activity 2.12

Adding to Your Growth Portfolio

This is an independent activity.

Any of the activities from this chapter can be used as entries for your own growth portfolio. Select activities you have completed or artifacts you have created that will illustrate your competence at the Chapter 2 learning targets. If you are keeping a reflective journal, you may want to include Chapter 2's entry in your portfolio. The portfolio entry cover sheet provided on the DVD will prompt you to think about how each item you select reflects your learning with respect to one or more of the chapter's learning targets.

 Activity 2.12 Chapter 2 Portfolio Entry Cover Sheet

Where Am I Now?

Effective Feedback

Strategy 3

Offer regular descriptive feedback during the learning.

> Formative assessment *does* make a difference, and it is the
> quality, not just the quantity, of feedback that merits our
> closest attention. By quality of feedback, we now realise
> we have to understand not just the technical structure of
> the feedback (such as its accuracy, comprehensiveness and
> appropriateness) but also its accessibility to the learner
> (as a communication), its catalytic and coaching value,
> and its ability to inspire confidence and hope.
>
> —*Sadler, 1998, p. 84 [emphasis in original]*

W hen learning to play a sport, athletes practice regularly, with feedback, before they are expected to play in the game that counts for the record. Coaches don't teach their sport by scheduling 20 games and then pulling players out during the game to point out errors. They schedule as many practices as possible, in which athletes learn the fundamentals, practice the fundamentals in drills and scrimmages, and get immediate feedback on what they are doing right and what they need to change. Effective feedback in the classroom operates in much the same way: its role is to help students improve while they are engaged in practice.

In the first section of this chapter we'll examine characteristics of feedback that make it more and less effective in impacting learning in the classroom. In the second section, we'll delve into options for offering feedback and streamlining the process. In the third section, we'll look at how to prepare students to offer and act on peer feedback.

Chapter 3 Learning Targets

At the end of Chapter 3, you will know how to do the following:

1. Understand the characteristics of effective feedback

2. Offer feedback effectively and efficiently

3. Select feedback options suited to students' grade level and the kind of learning to be addressed

4. Prepare students to give each other effective feedback

The Impact of Feedback Done Well

The benefits of feedback extend beyond its impact on immediate learning. Done well, it produces long-term effects in students: a solid sense of self-efficacy—that is, a faith in themselves that they can and will succeed, given enough effort—and the commitment to continue trying. Feedback done well or poorly shapes attitudes toward learning and molds students' identities as learners. It has the power to nurture self-awareness, responsibility, and self-regulation. The type of feedback we offer can change our classroom culture so that students think and act like learners, rather than like grade grubbers or homework-completion machines.

Effective feedback, then, can be thought of as feedback that encourages students to think and act like learners and results in deeper learning.

Cautions

"If feedback has all these benefits, let's give more feedback." Unfortunately, it's not that simple. Strategy 3 encompasses more than the act of providing feedback. *Giving* feedback does not cause improvement. *Acting* on it does. Learning well requires both consciousness and intentionality from the student. In an analysis of more than 130 studies on feedback, researchers Kluger and DeNisi (1996) found that in approximately one-third of the studies, feedback worsened subsequent performance levels; in one-third of the studies, feedback had no measurable impact on subsequent performance levels; and only in one-third of the studies did feedback cause improvement consistently. A significant factor differentiating feedback that led to greater achievement from feedback that worsened achievement was whether it focused students' attention on the self or on learning-centric features of their work (Shepard, 2008, pp. 284–285).

Thinking back to the goal-orientation research discussed in Chapter 1, negative-impact feedback leads to an ego-involved orientation, while positive-impact feedback leads to a learning orientation. As Sadler (1998) reminds us, feedback's power comes from its "catalytic and coaching value and its ability to inspire confidence and hope" (p. 84). In other words, if the feedback we offer causes students to give up, to quit trying, it has catalyzed action in the wrong direction.

Characteristics of Effective Feedback

Hundreds of studies on feedback suggest a multitude of nuances in effective feedback-giving. However, several commonalities emerge from meta-analyses, which are presented here under an umbrella of five characteristics (Figure 3.1). The first and most significant characteristic is that it directs attention to the intended learning, pointing out strengths and

> "Feedback is effective when it consists of information about progress, and/or about how to proceed."
>
> *Hattie & Timperley, 2007, p. 89*

offering specific information to guide improvement. To be effective, feedback must provide accurate guidance so students' efforts do indeed result in better work. If the feedback doesn't relate directly to the learning, it is not likely to offer the type of direction needed. Equally significant is the second characteristic: Feedback is most effective when it occurs during the learning, while there is still time to act on it. Three additional characteristics contribute to feedback's ability to positively impact learning: It is most effective when it addresses partial understanding, does not do the thinking for the student, and limits corrective information to the amount of advice the student can act on.

Figure 3.1

Characteristics of Effective Feedback

1. Directs attention to the intended learning, pointing out strengths and offering specific information to guide improvement

2. Occurs during learning, while there is still time to act on it

3. Addresses partial understanding

4. Does not do the thinking for the student

5. Limits corrective information to the amount of advice the student can act on

1. Effective Feedback Directs Attention to the Intended Learning

Feedback that directs attention to the intended learning does so by focusing on pertinent features of the work the student has done or on features of the process used. It points out what the student has done well (*success* feedback) and gives specific information to guide improvement (*next-step* or *intervention* feedback). See Figure 3.2 for a summary of options for success and next-step feedback.

Figure 3.2

Success and Next-Step Feedback Options

Success Feedback Options	• Identify what is done correctly. • Describe a feature of quality present in the work. • Point out effective use of strategy or process.
Next-Step Feedback Options	• Identify a correction. • Describe a feature of quality needing work. • Point out a problem with strategy or process. • Offer a reminder. • Make a specific suggestion. • Ask a question.

Success Feedback

All students need to know when they are doing something well or right. Even finding relative success ("the strongest part of your solution is . . .") will work as long as it's accurate and specifically linked to the intended learning. This is particularly helpful for lower-achieving students or for any students who are in early stages of developing proficiency. Success feedback identifies what was done correctly, describes a feature of quality that is present in the work, or points out effective use of a strategy or process. For example:

- "You got all of the questions on parallel and perpendicular lines right."

- "The information you found is important to your topic and answers questions the reader is likely to have."

- "The table you drew really helped solve the problem."

- "I see that while you were revising, you noticed you needed to gather more information about censorship cases before going on. I think that will improve your argument."

- "You have made your pencil marks so they line up exactly with the marks on the ruler."

Praise as Success Feedback

Although many students enjoy praise and many teachers want to provide it, if the praise is directed to characteristics of the *learner* rather than to characteristics of the *work* or the *process used*, it appears to be less effective both as a motivator and as an agent for improved achievement. In general, praise as a motivator is unpredictable and often counterproductive.

Praise can have a negative effect on learning because it directs students' attention away from the learning and onto what the teacher thinks of them: "The teacher thinks I'm smart/not smart." "The teacher likes me/doesn't like me." In studies comparing ego-oriented and learning-oriented feedback, learning-oriented feedback in all cases was far more powerful in effecting change in achievement (Ames, 1992; Black & Wiliam, 1998a; Hattie & Timperley, 2007; Shepard, 2008). Too often, praise does not provide information of value either to reinforce the learning or take action to change it. In addition, students' responses to praise vary widely, influenced by past experiences and self-concepts. Learning-oriented feedback does a much better job of developing a learning-goal orientation in students, which fosters a belief that effort will lead to success and results in a commitment to putting forth effort.

> "Enhancing student motivation, however, is not about enhancing self-concept of ability. . . . Enhancing motivation means enhancing children's valuing of effort and a commitment to effort-based strategies. . . ."
>
> *Ames, 1992, p. 268*

Praise for intelligence can have some surprisingly negative results. In a study contrasting the effects of praise for effort and praise for intelligence on learners' persistence and achievement, Blackwell, Trzesniewski, and Dweck (2007) found that recognizing effort ("Look how hard you tried!"), which students see as a variable within their control, is much more beneficial than praising intelligence ("Look how smart you are!"), which students tend to see as a personal attribute they cannot change. The researchers describe students who believe that getting better is within their control as having a *growth mindset* and those who believe that getting better is a function of ability as having a *fixed mindset*. Dweck (2007) explained

> [For students with a fixed mindset,] mistakes crack their self-confidence because they attribute errors to lack of ability, which they feel powerless to change. They avoid challenges because challenges make mistakes more likely and looking smart less so. [They] shun effort in the belief that having to work hard means they are dumb. [Students with a growth mindset] think intelligence is malleable and can be developed through education and hard work. They want to learn above all else. After all, if you believe that you can expand your intellectual skills, you want to do just that. Because slipups stem from a lack of effort, not ability, they

can be remedied by more effort. Challenges are energizing, rather than intimidating; they offer opportunities to learn. (p. 2)

 Praise and Intrinsic Motivation

A student's level of effort may be driven by an internal desire to achieve, and not the desire to get a reward, such as praise or a high grade. We want to be careful that we don't reduce a student's intrinsic motivation—the desire to do something for its own sake, or because of an internal drive—by assuming that an extrinsic motivator—reward or praise—will reinforce it. Extrinsic motivation can reduce students' desire to do something they initially had intrinsic motivation to do. We can make students dependent on rewards, which can harm learning, even though our intention is to help it.

Figure 3.5 found later in the chapter on page 105 presents a summary of the Blackwell et al. (2007) study.

Recognition for effort, on the other hand, can direct students' attention back to their work, by helping them make the link between what they tried and where they experienced success as a result: "This time is better than last time because you...." When student effort doesn't produce success, use feedback that offers "direction correction" to maximize the chances that continued effort will produce satisfactory results. You may be able to offer a thought ("Consider this..."), a suggestion for further learning ("Read this..."), or information ("Add this...").

Effort feedback should be genuine. It is important to keep in mind that the student is the only person who truly knows how much effort went into any task. You may want to acknowledge effort with a statement such as, "It looks to me like you put a great deal of effort into this. Tell me what you did." Although there can be a fine line between *recognition* for effort and *praise* for effort, it is one worth drawing. "You tried so hard—great job!" may not be as motivating to the student as an invitation to think about what he did try.

"I Like the Way You..."

Many of us have heard or used success feedback statements that begin with the phrase, "I like the way you...". The problem with this beginning is that it may lead students to infer that pleasing the teacher is the key to quality. If your students repeatedly ask, "Is this what you want?" it's possible they have internalized the formula "quality equals pleasing the teacher." Sure, quality does please us, but the best use of our feedback is to offer information that helps students internalize the aspects of quality that make their work good. Also, prefacing learning-focused remarks with a praise statement can reduce the effectiveness of the information that follows. Students are likely to remember "I did a good job"

Comments emphasizing learning goals have been repeatedly shown to lead to greater learning gains than comments emphasizing self-esteem.

Ames, 1992; Butler, 1988; Hattie & Timperley, 2007

or "the teacher likes it," but less likely to remember the feature of quality we had intended to reinforce.

As you think about your own practices in the classroom, be careful about using praise in a way that labels the student, such as "You are excellent." If honest expressions of praise are a natural part of your dialogue with students, direct praise statements to the work the student has produced and include features of the work that make it praiseworthy: "Your math solution is excellent because . . ."

Next-Step Feedback

Next-step feedback, also called *intervention feedback*, identifies areas in need of improvement and provides enough information so that the student understands what to do next. It, too, is most effective when linked to the intended learning targets. Next-step feedback can do one or more of the following: identify a correction, describe a specific feature of quality that needs work, or point out an ineffective or incorrect use of strategy or process. In addition, it points the way to further action by offering a reminder, making a specific suggestion, or asking a question that opens up a course of action for the student. For example:

- "You had some trouble with the differences between isosceles and scalene triangles. Reread page 102 and try these again."

- "Remember what we have learned about converting mixed numbers to improper fractions. Try using that process before subtracting."

- "The meaning of the paraphrased information in paragraph 3 does not come through clearly enough yet. Try underlining the key ideas in the original and then rewriting them in your own words. Then try the paragraph again."

- "The drawing you made didn't seem to help you solve the problem. Try drawing a Venn diagram and placing the information in it."

- "Try putting your arguments into the graphic organizer for persuasive writing and look for holes."

- "You have to make your pencil marks so they line up exactly with the marks on the ruler, or the lines you draw won't be parallel."

- "This ruler is too short to draw the lines you need. Try using a 12-inch ruler."

Notice that in the previous examples, students are given information that prompts an action. We don't always need to offer the whole solution, however. Often, we can help students think about what to do by asking a question:

- "The meaning of the paraphrased information in paragraph 3 does not come through clearly enough yet. What might you do to make it clearer?"

- "The drawing you made didn't seem to help you solve the problem. What other kind of drawing might work?"

If next-step feedback isn't clear to students, it can cause a whole host of problems. For example, what is missing from the following attempts at corrective feedback, and what might be the impact on student effort?

- Try these again

- Incomplete

- Keep studying

- More effort needed

In their synthesis of research on effective feedback, Hattie and Timperley (2007) summarized the dangers:

> There can be deleterious effects on feelings of self-efficacy and performance when students are unable to relate the feedback to the cause of their poor performance. Unclear evaluative feedback, which fails to clearly specify the grounds on which students have met with achievement success or otherwise, is likely to exacerbate negative outcomes, engender uncertain self-images, and lead to poor performance (p. 95).

If students don't understand our feedback or know how to act on it, it can undermine their sense of *self-efficacy*—their belief that effort can lead to success—and prevent them from developing a commitment to effort-based strategies. The key question is, "Can *this* student take action on the basis of *this* comment?"

Figure 3.3 gives more examples of success and next-step feedback. The comments link directly to learning targets. They relate either to the work the student has produced or the process used, pointing out strengths and offering specific guidance for next steps. Notice the kinds of interventions in each: reminders, suggestions, and/or corrections. When we say that feedback needs to be *specific*, this is what it means.

Figure 3.3

Success and Next-Step Feedback Comments

FOR EXAMPLE

Social Studies:

Let's say your content standard is "Understands ways in which native and immigrant cultures have contributed to form American culture," and you have translated that into a series of "I can" statements, one of which is "I can describe similarities and differences between people in the English settlements and those in the French and Spanish settlements." When students do an assignment that addresses this target, the assignment itself might specify that you are looking for accurate information about each culture, important details about each culture, and accurate categorization of information into similarities and differences.

Feedback emphasizing these learning targets then relates to one or more of the features you asked students to include: "All of the information you gave about the English settlements is accurate." Or "Please recheck your facts. Some of the information you gave about English settlements is not true for all English settlements" (suggestion + correction).

Science:

Let's say the content standard you are teaching to is "Understands how to plan and conduct scientific investigations," and as a part of making that content standard clear, you have introduced a rubric for scientific inquiry that includes creating a good hypothesis as a component. Specifically, it states that a strong hypothesis includes a prediction with a cause-effect reason.

Feedback emphasizing the learning target can use that language: "What you have written is a hypothesis because it is a prediction about what will happen. You can improve it by giving a reason explaining why you think that will happen" (success + suggestion).

Mathematics:

Let's say your content standard is "Uses a problem-solving strategy to construct a solution," and you have introduced a scoring rubric that includes Mathematical Problem Solving as one of its traits.

You can use that language to offer feedback: "Your strategy worked for part of the problem, but it didn't lead to a correct solution because it fell apart right here. What other strategy could you use to deal with this remaining group of people?" (success + correction + suggestion elicited from the student).

For primary students, success and next-step feedback can take the form of "That's good!" and "That's next!" For example: "I see you have . . ." (that's good). "Now let's see you . . ." (that's next). See Figure 3.4 for samples of feedback with younger students.

Establishing a Forward-Looking Stance Toward Learning

By using the terms *success* and *next-step* to describe kinds of feedback, we can steer students away from interpreting feedback as "positive" or "negative." Even though we often hear success feedback referred to as *positive*, try to avoid calling it that because it gives a negative connotation to the next-step feedback. Children learn about opposites early and tend to apply this concept liberally: If one type of feedback is positive, the other must be negative. Because the "not-success" feedback concerns what students need to work on next, it doesn't benefit anyone if students perceive that as negative. For example, you may notice that a student is using a comma to separate two complete thoughts in a sentence. Your next-step feedback can be, "You're ready for semicolons," which is a forward-looking stance toward a mistake, or in this case, perhaps a new learning. The role of next-step feedback is to offer information—a reminder, a suggestion, or a correction—or to pose a question, so that further effort will bring the student closer to successful achievement. The intent is to motivate, not discourage, continued effort.

With that in mind, not every feedback comment must include reference to a strength to be effective. Nor does all feedback need to include both success and next-step remarks. Your comments needn't come across as artificial or formulaic; you will want to use your own judgment, taking into account what *this* student needs at *this* point in his or her learning.

Additionally, there is no rule that feedback must be limited to commenting only on the specific learning target of the lesson. If students are practicing what they learned in a lesson, it is often a good idea to stick to the focus of the lesson in your comments, so students can take full advantage of the opportunity to improve. However, when students are in the process of preparing a final performance or product, it is appropriate to give success or corrective comments relating to concepts or skills previously taught. Rely on your professional judgment. Just be careful that the feedback does not focus undue attention on trivia unrelated to the learning targets.

Grades as Feedback on Practice Work

One of the problems of expecting marks or grades to act as feedback on practice work is that they do not communicate details about what students

Figure 3.4

Success and Next-Step Feedback with Younger Students

FOR EXAMPLE

How might this work with younger students? It can be as simple as pointing out which of their letter "J"s matches the standard: "This is a good letter 'J.' Do you know what makes it a good one?" Or you can identify which is their best one and then give a pointer for making it better: "This is a good 'J' because you have the hook going in the right direction. For your next 'J,' see if you can get it to sit on the line."

Or, let's say you are teaching students to use details in their writing. For the first-grader who wrote "The Tent" (see accompanying figure), feedback emphasizing the learning target may sound like this: "Look at those details! I can tell you've examined how zippers work because you have drawn all the teeth at an angle. Good writers notice details others might overlook, just like you did." Contrast this descriptive feedback with feedback that praises the work without giving any specific information: "Wow! What a great story!"

Or, if you'd like to describe a success and offer a next step: "We've been reading stories that have a beginning, a middle, and an end. I see you've included a beginning and a middle in your story, just like good writers do. Next, see if you can write (or draw) the end." The feedback refers to the learning targets, in this case by using the language of quality ("We've been reading stories that have a beginning, a middle, and an end"); it shows the student what she has done well ("You've included a beginning and a middle in your story, just like good writers do"); and it offers a suggestion for the next step, also related to the learning targets ("Next, see if you can write [or draw] the end").

understand or don't understand. Grades are not really feedback; they are summary evaluative judgments about the level of achievement. They don't describe the quality of the work. Does a C alone tell a student what she has done well? Does it show her which parts of the learning she still needs to work on? To help students understand why a grade is not helpful feedback on practice work, you can initiate a class discussion by doing the following:

- Distribute half-sheets of scrap paper. Ask students to write the phrase "To me, a C means _____" at the top and then complete the sentence with whatever this grade means to them. This should only take a few minutes.

- Collect the slips and read them all aloud anonymously.

- Ask students to share the thoughts and questions they had while listening to the responses.

- Use their comments as a springboard to ask what kinds of feedback work best when they are practicing something they are not yet good at.

- Introduce the policy you will use for marking practice work, along with the requirements for turning it in and the consequences (not involving a lowered grade) for not doing so, if appropriate.

It might be tempting to think that offering comments along with grades on practice work will solve the problem. However, studies have shown that attaching evaluative grades to work while students are in the midst of learning can cause problems for both high- and low-achieving students (Black & Wiliam, 1998a). In one interesting and often-cited study, Butler (1988) found that assigning normative grades to practice work (grades that were computed on a curve to show students where their performance ranked against others in their class) inhibited further learning and that students ignored comments when they were accompanied by these normative grades. Your own experience may confirm that many students pay more attention to the evaluative mark or grade than to the comments, even on practice work. When the purpose of the assignment is formative—to help students improve—it can be a waste of feedback and of a learning opportunity to insert a summative mark or grade.

Some alternative suggestions include:

- Consider not putting evaluative marks or grades on practice work until the feedback has been acted on.

- Write the evaluative mark or grade in pencil, their "would-be" grade. Tell students they can erase it by acting on the feedback. It is the grade they would have received if they stopped here, but because they're not finished learning, it's not their final grade. Then write the final evaluative mark in pen on the finished work. You can also use the "pencil/pen" system for keeping formative and summative scores separate in your record book.

- Identify another way to motivate work completion for practice work, along with opportunities for students to come before or stay after school to complete practice work as needed.

Video 3.1: Effective Feedback Focused on the Learning Targets: Middle School Students

Initially, many of our students will not do work unless it counts toward the grade. See the section in Chapter 6 titled "Grading Too Soon" for examples of how teachers have addressed this motivation problem with learning-focused strategies.

Watch Video 3.1 to hear middle school students describing the feedback they receive.

Figure 3.5

RESEARCH SNAPSHOT

"Implicit Theories of Intelligence Predict Achievement Across an Adolescent Transition: A Longitudinal Study and an Intervention"—*Blackwell, Trzesniewski, & Dweck, 2007*

Hypothesis:

Adolescents who believe intelligence is malleable (can be developed through education and hard work) will demonstrate persistence in the face of setbacks and will outperform those who believe intelligence is a fixed trait (you are born with a certain amount).

Who Was Involved:

Students entering seventh grade each year for four years (for a total of 373 students), followed over the course of their seventh- and eighth-grade years in an urban junior high school. Students were described as "moderately high achieving."

Figure 3.5 (continued)

What They Did:

At the beginning of their seventh-grade year, students were identified as having either an *incremental theory of intelligence* (growth mindset) or an *entity theory of intelligence* (fixed mindset) by responding to a questionnaire with statements such as "Your intelligence is something very basic about you that you can't really change" and others regarding their beliefs about whether intelligence is something they can change or not. They also answered questions designed to measure their learning goals, effort beliefs, and response to failure (failure attribution and subsequent strategy selection).

Students' baseline achievement in mathematics was determined by a standardized mathematics achievement test taken in the spring of their sixth-grade year. Seventh-grade fall and spring term grades and eighth-grade fall and spring term grades served to measure achievement during the study. (All students in the study within the same grade had the same curriculum and the same teacher.)

What the Researchers Found:

At the outset of the study, "growth mindset" and "fixed mindset" students' achievement scores in mathematics were comparable. At the end of the first semester, the growth mindset students' mathematics grades were higher than those of the fixed mindset students. The gap between the two groups' mathematics grades widened over the two years. Students with a growth mindset also were found to hold more positive motivational beliefs than did students with the fixed mindset. Characteristics of a growth mindset included valuing learning over getting good grades; believing that the more you work at something the better you can become; and in the face of a setback, such as a disappointing grade, studying harder or attempting a different strategy. Characteristics of a fixed mindset included valuing looking smart over learning; believing that if you have to work hard, it means you have low ability; and in the face of a setback, such as a disappointing grade, studying less, avoiding taking the subject again, and considering cheating on subsequent tasks.

Source: Summarized from L. Blackwell, K. Trzesniewski, & C. Dweck, Implicit theories of intelligence predict achievement across an adolescent transition: A longitudinal study and an intervention. *Child Development 78*(1), 2007, pp. 246–263.

2. Effective Feedback Occurs During Learning

In my first year of teaching I set out to post a sign that said, "It's okay to make mistakes in this room." When I copied it out on a sentence strip, I ran out of room for the word "room." I wrote it two more times, each time getting only one more letter squeezed in. I hung the third version, with the last letters running up the side, because it showed what it told (Figure 3.6).

Figure 3.6

It's okay to make mistakes in this ro°m.

Even though we say to students, "We learn from our mistakes," very few of them view an error as their friend. In the words of a panicked high school freshman, "I'm doomed. In that class *all* of my mistakes count against me." How do we *show* students that it's not only okay to make mistakes, but that when they occur, they are to be welcomed as information about what to tackle next?

"If assessment insights are to be used to move learning along rather than merely tally how much learning has occurred so far, then assessment has to occur in the middle of instruction, not just at the end points . . ."

Shepard, 2001, p. 1086

We cultivate this growth-oriented mindset when we offer feedback with opportunities to improve *during* the learning. Feedback is most effective in improving achievement if it is delivered while there is still time to act on it, which means *before* the graded event. If practice work counts toward the mark or grade, mistakes "count against" students. When students take a quiz, for example, the score does not have to be used for marking/grading purposes; rather it can serve you and the students as information about what they understand and what they need to improve. You, and they, can record the score, but including it as evidence of final achievement penalizes those students who have not yet reached mastery. If you want the results to increase learning, students are better served by looking at the quiz and asking, "What does this tell me I know? What do I still need to work on?" Chapter 4 provides examples of how tests and quizzes can be set up so students can use them to self-assess and set goals for further learning.

In Figure 3.7, high school science teacher Stephanie Harmon discusses her approach to differentiating practice work from summative assessment.

Figure 3.7

From the Classroom

Differentiating Practice Work from Summative Assessment

I assign numeric grades for summative items and give feedback rather than numeric grades on formative items. The intention is that the feedback helps the student improve before taking the summative assessment. For some practice assignments, students self-assess with an answer key and then come to me with questions. Several times each week, I set up a question desk where students can come for individual assistance. They can also bring items on which they have received feedback to clarify what the feedback means if it isn't clear to them.

I communicate with parents as much as possible so they understand what is happening in my classroom. I try not to get too wrapped up in the jargon of school, but I want them to understand what they are seeing when they read a progress report from my class and what it means for their student.

Clear, specific feedback is so important to this process. I have also found that I spend less time marking papers when I am focused on providing descriptive feedback than years ago when I tried to assign points fairly to all work. When I focus on helping students understand and build quality into their work, it makes the learning process more productive for all of us.

Source: Used with permission from Stephanie Harmon, Rockcastle County High School: Mt. Vernon, KY.

Feedback can encourage students to view mistakes as a natural part of the path to excellence if you plan time for students to take the actions suggested, before asking them to demonstrate their level of achievement for a mark or grade. The time we spend giving feedback may be wasted if we do not build in time for them to act on it. The question here is, "Where is the practice?" The answer points us to the optimum place for feedback. Chapter 6 focuses on providing a variety of practice opportunities for students.

3. Effective Feedback Addresses Partial Understanding

Offering feedback is not always the appropriate instructional intervention to use. It is most effective when it addresses faulty understanding, rather than a total lack of understanding. For example, think about this comment:

"Remember, a generalization is a statement that's accurate for the evidence at hand and also applies to a broader array of instances.

Your generalization doesn't take into account the characteristics of all meat-eating plants. How do you think you will need to change it?"

If a student is lost in the content, he is not likely to understand the direction given in this intervention feedback; it can even cause him to feel worse because he has failed twice: "I don't know how to do this, and I don't understand what you're telling me to do about it."

Look at the two samples of student mathematics solutions in Figure 3.8. Both students attempted to use the strategy of drawing a picture: one drew a canteen and the other drew stick figures. Which one shows partial mastery? Which one is struggling with the basics and does not understand that the problem-solving strategy *draw a picture* does not mean illustrate the problem? Which one would benefit from feedback? Which one probably needs further instruction to move ahead? The student who drew three rows of eight people and then circled groups of five has a strategy that is working up to the end, at which four people will suffer mightily from thirst. Feedback to this student can look like this: "Your strategy worked for most of the problem, but it didn't lead to a correct solution because it fell apart right here. What other strategy could you use to deal with this remaining group of people who will have no water?" However, the student who drew the canteen did not have an even partially workable strategy. Although you could begin to solve the problem by dividing 12.5 by 5, it doesn't appear that he had a grasp of what to do next, and so trying to help him through offering feedback will not work. He needs more instruction.

Be ready to reteach if student work does not show at least partial mastery of the concepts—if there is nothing you can offer success feedback on—or if you find yourself offering the same corrective feedback repeatedly to large numbers of students. Reteaching saves time in the long run and avoids the risk that your feedback will turn into fruitless nagging.

"Corrective feedback can be ignored by students if it is poorly presented or if the student's knowledge is insufficient to accommodate additional feedback information."

Hattie & Timperley, 2007, p.100

4. Effective Feedback Does Not Do the Thinking for the Student

Next-step feedback, if overdone, can reduce the cognitive challenge of a task so far that students are no longer required to think at all—their only next step is to follow directions. When this happens, we have removed the rigor instead of helping students to work through the rigor.

Figure 3.8

Student Mathematics Solutions	**FOR EXAMPLE**

Problem: A group of eight people are all going camping for three days and need to carry their own water. They read in a guide book that 12.5 liters are needed for a party of 5 people for 1 day. Based on the guide book, what is the minimum amount of water the 8 people should carry all together? Explain your answer.

Sample 1

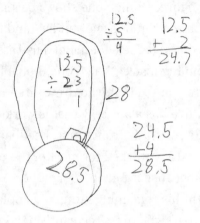

Sample 2

Imagine saying to a child at home, "Please clean up your room." And then, "Clean up your room, please." And then, "Clean up your room, *now*." And finally going in and doing it for her. We usually don't clean the room ourselves for a very good reason: If we do, we'll train her to wait us out. How does this example relate to feedback? Do we ever remind students of what to correct and then when they do an incomplete job, we take over and finish the work for them? In my early teaching years, I did this with student writing. I would ask students to edit their papers for spelling, capitalization, and punctuation. They would turn in papers with some of the errors fixed, and then I would fix the mistakes they didn't catch. I was "over-feedbacking"—instead of pointing the way to success, I was doing their work for them. This is a lot like me cleaning my teenager's bedroom. The more I do, the less she will do, which I know from experience. Figure 3.9 shows three versions of feedback on a piece of tenth-grade writing. The first shows over-feedbacking through marking every error,

Figure 3.9

Three Versions of Feedback

FOR EXAMPLE

Version 1:

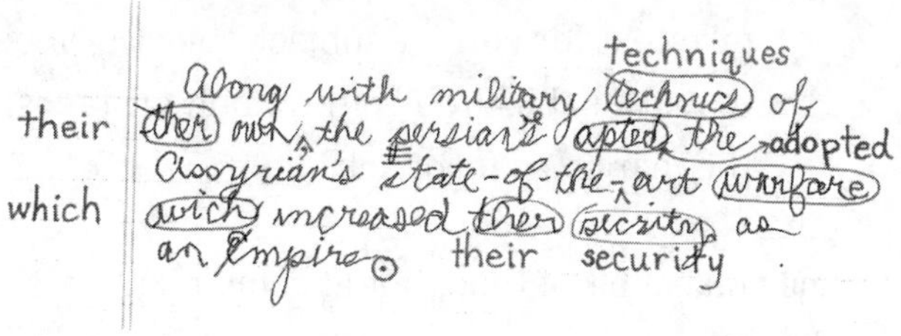

Version 2:

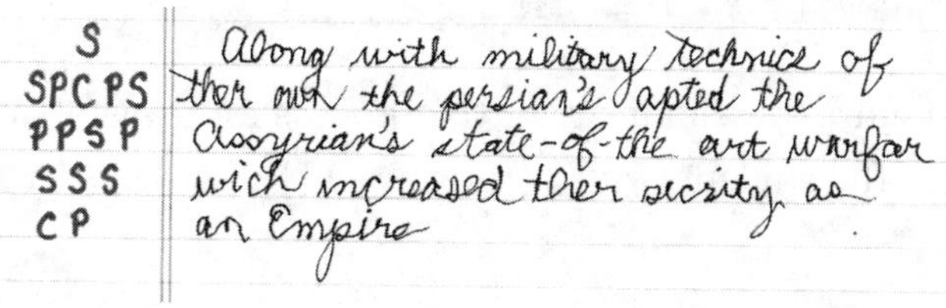

Version 3:

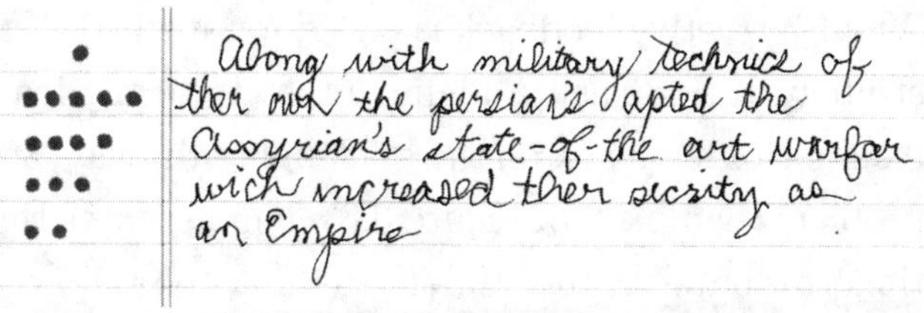

the second shows the use of codes to offer feedback, and the third shows use of dots in the margin as feedback. Using codes or dots in the margin helps us pull back from doing all the work for the student, while still offering guidance on next steps. Both strategies are explained further in the second section of this chapter.

As a prerequisite, it is crucial to make sure students understand the learning target and have had practice with it prior to expecting them to act on feedback. Here is an example of a lesson for the learning target "Use subject and object pronouns correctly" in which practice is followed by feedback:

- Teach what subject and object pronouns are.

- Give students practice at identifying subject and object pronouns until they can do it without having to look them up.

- Teach the rules for using each correctly in sentences.

- Give them practice in applying the rules.

- Give them text with embedded subject/object pronoun errors and ask them to work with a partner to identify and correct the errors.

- When they can do this, hold them accountable for editing their own text for correct subject/object pronoun usage. If they continue to make subject/object pronoun mistakes, use a code or a dot in the margin as feedback.

This may take a bit of time, but at some point in later elementary grades, it would be worth it to never hear "Me and Robin went to the store" or "Give the tickets to her and I" again.

Figure 3.10 summarizes the process for transferring editing competence to the student.

Feedback by Questioning

When corrective feedback is called for, instead of offering a solution or a strategy, you can ask students if they have an idea of what to do. The earlier example of feedback on the stick figure drawing as a solution to the camping problem (Sample 2 of Figure 3.8) demonstrates this: The teacher points out the error but asks the student to think about how to correct it. Then, if the student draws a blank or describes a nonproductive path, the teacher can provide a suggestion.

Figure 3.10

Transferring Editing Competence to the Student   **FOR EXAMPLE**

Editing for correctness requires two things: knowing how to do it correctly and developing the ability to notice it when it is wrong. You can take the following steps to transfer to students the skills and responsibility of error-hunting: teach your students whichever conventions you want them to demonstrate; teach them editor's symbols as a way to identify errors; and then give them practice at using those symbols to hunt for convention mistakes, first in isolation as they learn each one and then together with the conventions they have previously learned.

Post a list titled, "Conventions We Have Learned" (or, in the case of older students, "Conventions We Have Had Opportunity to Learn," if you have moved beyond teaching "capital letter at the beginning of a sentence" and "terminal punctuation at the end," but still want to put these targets on the list). Once students have shown they understand the rule for use of the convention and have had practice at error-hunting for it, add it to your list and hold them responsible for finding that problem in their own writing.

If they miss correcting one or more conventions on the next paper they turn in, rather than doing the error-hunting yourself, offer feedback by placing a dot in the margin on the line for each unmarked error and ask them to try again.

This is an example of feedback that points the way to success without going too far: the person who holds the editor's pen does the learning.

To maximize learning, after you have identified an error or problem in students' thinking or work, let them explore how to correct or solve it, before (or instead of) sharing your correction or solution. If their thinking or work demonstrates partial understanding, they may have an idea of what to do about the error or problem. The only intervention they may truly need is a carefully crafted question or two to guide their thought processes.

Feedback in Discovery Learning Tasks

Not all tasks require an external intervention to guide the learning. Some tasks, especially in science, are set up as a series of discovery learning events in which correctives are built into the experiences. The only feedback needed may be

---

⚠ Learning from Errors

Do not use feedback to shortcut learning from errors if a task is structured so that students can analyze their own mistakes and determine a course of action to correct them.

---

a question or two designed to help students investigate mismatches between prior understanding and present experience. Such questions can be directed to an individual or offered for the class to discuss.

A hallmark of good feedback is that it spurs thoughtful action. It should result in learning, not just following directions or copying someone else's ideas. We are "over-feedbacking" whenever students would benefit from engaging in the thinking that we have done for them in our comments.

Video 3.2: Offering Effective Feedback: Kindergarten

Watch Video 3.2 to see a kindergarten teacher offering feedback that guides the learning without doing all of the thinking for the student.

5. Effective Feedback Limits Correctives to What Students Can Act On

When pointing out areas for improvement, first check to see that students know what to do with the next-step guidance they receive. Then, think about how many pieces of advice they can reasonably be expected to act on in the time given. More information than that is overkill. How much feedback is too much is a matter of professional judgment. Some students can respond to lots of corrective direction without giving up. This recommendation only asks that you differentiate between providing all of the directions for improvement that would make the work of highest quality and providing as much next-step feedback as the individual student can reasonably act on.

Offering Too Little Corrective Feedback

Do not underestimate students' capacity for taking action and thereby *"under-feedback"*; offer as much corrective feedback as you think they can act on in the time given. (Just keep in mind that identifying *every* problem is not always the most helpful approach for struggling students.)

If student work exhibits a daunting number of problems, you may want to limit the focus of the feedback to one criterion or aspect of quality at a time. This narrows the scope of work for both you and students. We sometimes offer a great deal of corrective feedback to struggling students, but if the feedback refers to things they don't know how to do or if it offers too many next steps, it will not be effective. If pointing out every problem along with suggestions for how to fix it will overwhelm students, limit the scope of correctives. Also consider giving students further guided practice opportunities.

Video 3.3: Offering Effective Feedback: Grade 3

Watch Video 3.3 to see a third-grade teacher offering effective feedback.

Suggestions for Offering Feedback

Sometimes quick feedback is all that is needed, but other times a more labor-intensive process may be in order. The suggestions that follow offer time-saving strategies that adhere to the requirements for effective feedback.

Picture or Symbol Cues

A picture, symbol, or graphic representation creating a metaphor may help cue your students in how to use your feedback. The following four options include examples of elementary and secondary applications.

1. Stars and Stairs

This is an example of using a metaphor—stars and stairs—represented by a graphic to offer feedback. You can copy a form such as the one in Figure 3.11. Describe what the student did well in the "star" area and offer specific intervention feedback in the "stairs" area. You can also draw the star symbol and the stairs symbol next to success and next-step feedback as you write it on their work. Figure 3.12 shows teacher Amy Meyer's system for remembering the "stars and stairs" comments she has given to her second-grade reading class. With her third graders, Mrs. Meyer (personal communication, 2013) uses a free iPad application to accomplish the same thing:

> I now use "Evernote" to create a notebook for each student. I can take pictures of their work and record their voices and they will be saved as notes in their notebooks. I use these observations often in conferencing with students to give feedback, in thinking about where students are in their learning, and where they need to go. The information and visuals in students' notebooks are also very helpful during parent teacher conferences to discuss progress and show growth.

Figure 3.11

Stars and Stairs

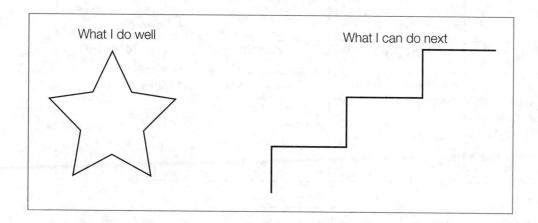

What I do well

What I can do next

Figure 3.12

Mrs. Meyer's Reading Observations	**FOR EXAMPLE**

⌐ *Stair—goal to work on* ★ *Star—something you do well*

Gabriela	**Zoe**	**Keegan**	**Chaim**
Rereading chapter book for better comprehension	★ *Rereading, Jr. books* ⌐ *Try some new books*	⌐ *Picking "too easy" books* ★ *fluency, retelling*	*sequel → Mouse & Motorcycle* ★ *Great book choices* ★ *Great fiction* ⌐ *Capital letters at beginning of story.*
Gael	**David**	**Brendan**	**Colin**
★ *Chunking a word up* ★ *Getting stuck in a book, recording important facts down in NF* ⌐ *What makes sense?*	★ *Asking ?'s in my head* ⌐ *Stretching out a word—using a stategy* ★ *Good fluency expression!*	★ *Staying with a chapter book, asking ?'s, inferring* ⌐ *Recording thinking, reading assignments*	*Discussed determining importance in NF*
Aisha	**Charlie**	**Carmen**	**Eli**
★ *Reading different genres—great pic books* ★ *Asking ?'s* ⌐ *Writing down different thinking*	★ *Excellent inferences and use of comprehension skills*	★ *fluency, expression, asking ?'s while I read* ⌐ *Skipping over unknown words, trying a strategy*	⌐ *Reread when it doesn't make sense* ★ *Great expression Talks like the characters.*
Oscar	**Katherine**	**Marcos**	**Julian**
Geronimo Stilton *Getting recommendations from Chaim*	*Lots of nonfiction webs to record data*	★ *Recording new learning from NF* ⌐ *Tricky words in NF (" pronunciations help")*	★ *Seeing what makes sense Using strategies!* ⌐ *Continue to work on expression* ⌐ *Reread books for fluency*
Abby	**Sophia**	**Austin**	**Peter**
⌐ *I genre* *Miley/High School Musical* ★ *Great comp., fluency*	*What character traits does Amber Brown have?*	★ *Decoding and comprehension improving!* ⌐ *Fluency, expression*	*NF firefighters* ★ *Rereading*

Source: Adapted with permission from Amy Meyer, Worthington City Schools: Worthington, OH. Unpublished classroom materials.

2. That's Good! Now This

Record success and next-step feedback on a form such as the one in Figure 3.13, Example 1. If students are resubmitting their work, you may want to use a form such as the one in Example 2. Students revise their work based on your feedback and then reattach the form to their revision with a comment about what they did and a suggestion for what they'd like you to pay particular attention to. This helps you track how they are interpreting your comments and what they have changed from draft to draft.

Figure 3.13

That's Good! Now This:

Example 1

That's good!   Now this:

Example 2

MY TEACHER'S COMMENTS:
    That's good!
 	
    Now this:
 	
MY COMMENTS:
    What I did:
 	
    Please give special attention to:

3. Codes

You can develop codes to cue corrections, which you write in the margins of student work to indicate what needs fixing. For example, world languages teachers may want to make a list of common errors, create a code, and post it on the wall (e.g., G = gender, T = tense, P = plural, WO = word order). Language arts teachers may want to use an acronym such as CUPS (Capitalization, Usage, Punctuation, and Spelling), explained in Figure 3.10. To develop a code in your subject area, list errors students commonly make for which a reminder will serve as sufficient direction. Identify a key word in each error type and see if your key words will conveniently arrange themselves into a pronounceable acronym. If not, create an easily drawn and remembered symbol for each, or use the first letter of the key word. Post a chart or distribute a key so students can quickly interpret the letter or symbol.

4. Immediate Feedback for Younger Students

Preschool teacher Susan Luengen makes laminated charts to test her students on learning targets such as recognizing numbers, shapes, and colors (Figure 3.14). Above each number, shape, or color on the chart, she has affixed a Velcro® dot in a row labeled "Right!" She sits directly across from a child and hands him a Velcro-backed smiley face when he provides a correct response. He then gets to attach the happy face above the number, shape, or color in the "Right!" row. Then she takes a picture of each child and his or her chart with all of the happy faces for the Math Center page in their portfolios. Mrs. Luengen reports that her children request to do this activity and want to do it over and over, an indicator of how motivating it is for them to watch themselves grow. Her colleagues also use these charts successfully with special education preschool children and with kindergartners.

Figure 3.14

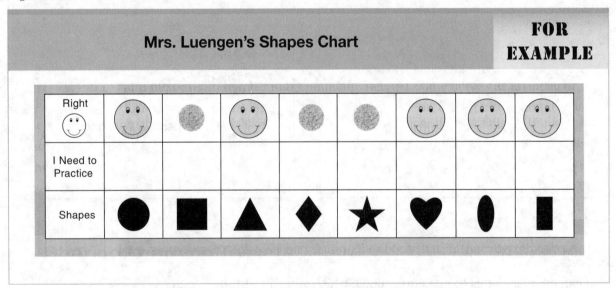

Source: Adapted with permission from Susan Luengen, Central Oahu School District: Mililani, HI. Unpublished classroom materials.

Assessment Dialogues

The previous suggestions are all relatively quick forms of feedback. When you are teaching to reasoning, skill, and product learning targets, the feedback process can consume a great deal more of your time. You can make this process more efficient by asking students to self-diagnose *before* offering your thoughts. Then you can limit your comments to the amount of guidance they truly need. Engaging in this form of assessment dialogue cuts down the time you spend formulating feedback because you only need point out successes or problems they overlooked. The three options for assessment dialogues described here include written comments, two-color highlighting, and a three-minute conference.

Written Comments

The following written assessment dialogue is structured for use with a performance assessment task and rubric. It refers to two feedback recording forms, Figure 3.15 for elementary students and Figure 3.16 for secondary students.

1. Identify a focus for the feedback. Select one or more elements of quality represented on the scoring rubric for the content standard students are working on, based on what you have been teaching. (Remember, it is generally not productive to give feedback on skills or processes students have had no practice with.) In some cases, if you have been teaching several facets of quality, you may want to let students determine which one or ones they are ready to receive feedback on.

2. Students self-assess by using the scoring rubric to identify their successes (aspects of quality they see in their explanation, performance, or product) and one or more aspects of quality that are missing or that need work. Encourage them to use the language and concepts of the scoring rubric.

3. Students complete the "My Opinion" portion of the form on Figure 3.15 or Figure 3.16 and turn it in with their work.

4. Review their work and write your feedback in the "Feedback" space, also using the language and/or concepts of the scoring rubric. If you agree with students' self-assessments, you can write "I agree," but it's always a plus when you can find something they didn't notice to add to the "strengths" comment. You may want to hold a personal conference with or plan a small-group lesson for those students whose judgments differ significantly from yours.

5. After receiving your feedback, students take their own judgments and your comments into account and decide what to do next, creating a specific plan for further work focused on ideas or strategies that will improve the paper, product, or performance.

119

Figure 3.15

Elementary Assessment Dialogue Form

Name: _____ Date: _____

Assignment: _____ Feedback Focus: _____

MY OPINION

★ My strengths are _____

_____

⌐ What I think I need to work on is _____

_____

_____

MY TEACHER'S FEEDBACK

★ Strengths: _____

_____

_____

⌐ Work on: _____

_____

_____

MY PLAN

💡 What I will do now: _____

_____

_____

_____

Figure 3.16

Secondary Assessment Dialogue Form

Name: _____   Date: _____

Assignment: _____   Feedback Focus: _____

MY OPINION

My strengths are _____

_____

What I think I need to work on is _____

_____

_____

FEEDBACK

Strengths: _____

_____

_____

Work on: _____

_____

_____

MY PLAN

What I will do now: _____

_____

_____

_____

_____

Source: Based on Chappuis, S., Stiggins, R., Arter, J., and Chappuis, J. *Assessment FOR Learning: An Action Guide for School Leaders,* Second Edition. Pearson Assessment Training Institute: Portland, OR.

Some students will be able to complete it on their own; others will need your help, at least at first.

6.   If your students tend to set large, nonspecific, task-completion, or grade-based goals instead of identifying next steps ("My plan is to do better" or "My plan is to get an A"), redirect them to your intervention feedback comments if they offer next-step guidance, or provide additional suggestions.

Two-Color Highlighting

Another possibility (Shannon Thompson, personal communication, 2008) is to dispense with the assessment dialogue form and have students mark with a yellow highlighter the phrases on the scoring rubric they think describe their work. They turn the highlighted scoring rubric in with their work, and you mark with a blue highlighter the phrases that you believe describe it. Where you and the student are in agreement, the phrases are green. Phrases that remain yellow and blue represent areas where you and the student differ.

Then you can offer additional written comments for those students whose judgments vary significantly from yours, or you can meet with them individually or in small groups, depending on the instruction they need. Students can also highlight a developmental continuum or other graphic display that describes elements of quality, as long as the wording is suitable for their use (they understand the terms and the document does not use negative evaluative labels, such as "failing" or "far below standard").

The Three-Minute Conference

You can use the assessment dialogue process to provide oral feedback to one or more students individually. Some teachers, particularly in the primary grades, structure time to meet with each student regularly. If you do not have the opportunity to do this, you may still want to meet with certain students while others are working independently or engaged in peer conferences. To minimize the time an individual conference can take, have the student self-assess prior to the conference, filling out the "My Opinion" portion of the Assessment Dialogue form (Figures 3.15 and 3.16).

At the beginning of the conference, ask the student to share her thoughts. Then share your feedback. If appropriate, point out a strength the student overlooked. If needed, add to or modify what the student said she needs to work on. After you have shared your comments, have the student summarize them by writing on the Assessment Dialogue form.

This final step of directing students to summarize your feedback in writing helps ensure that they have understood your comments. Letting them know beforehand that they will be the ones writing your comments helps them pay attention while you are talking.

Regardless of how you deliver descriptive feedback, consider asking students to engage in self-assessment prior to receiving your feedback. Students' reflecting on their work increases the likelihood that they will understand your feedback and act on it. This is an example of *accessing prior knowledge*, which helps students make sense of new information and retain it longer. In addition, it communicates that they have an equal responsibility in thinking about quality. It teaches students that their opinions are welcomed and respected. And, when students speak first, you are better able to identify misconceptions and target comments to what they can't figure out for themselves. Finally, when students think about their work first, feedback conferences often can be successfully completed in three minutes or less.

Offering Feedback with a Scoring Rubric

Make sure you have introduced the language of the rubric (Strategy 1) in advance of using it to offer feedback. Students will understand your comments better if you have also given them practice with Strategy 2, evaluating strong and weak anonymous samples, which helps them internalize the concepts of quality described in the rubric.

If your students aren't used to expressing their thoughts about their work before hearing from you, let them know in advance that you will be asking them to do so. Some students don't like surprises—you want this to be a challenge they are comfortable attempting. See Figure 3.17 for an example of a form that Amy Meyer uses in feedback conferences with her third-grade students.

Peer Feedback

In a study of the effects of peer- and self-assessment on science achievement, White and Frederiksen (1998) found that the process of coming to understand the criteria by which their work would be judged and learning to apply it to their own and to others' work benefited all students and worked to narrow the achievement gap between low- and high-achieving students. (See Figure 4.1 in Chapter 4 for a research snapshot of White and Frederiksen's study.)

Figure 3.17

Third-Grade Personal Narrative Conference Form	FOR EXAMPLE

_____'s Personal Narrative

I can write a narrative to develop real or imagined experiences or events using effective technique, descriptive details, and clear event sequences.	My Score	Mrs. Meyer's Score
My story is focused on one event or small moment that happened to me.		
My story is organized. I introduced the characters and setting at the beginning. The events of what happened are in order, or in sequence.		
I have used descriptive details that tell about the "big moment" or "heart" of my story. I included my thoughts and feelings about the event.		
I used dialogue correctly in my story.		
I used transition words or phrases to signal event order (sequence).		
My ending provides a sense of closure (lets the reader know the story is over).		
I have used complete sentences that 1. _____ Make sense and sound right 2. _____ Use capital letters correctly 3. _____ Use punctuation correctly 4. _____ Have correct spelling (demonstrate knowledge of rules and patterns)	1. _____ 2. _____ 3. _____ 4. _____	1. _____ 2. _____ 3. _____ 4. _____

Source: Used with permission from Amy Meyer, Worthington City Schools: Worthington, OH.

Although finding time for students to give feedback to each other can be challenging, several learning advantages make it worth the effort.

1. When students practice constructing descriptive feedback for their peers, they deepen their own understanding of quality.

2. If students are trained to recognize and describe features of quality, they can offer valuable constructive critiques to each other, which maximizes feedback opportunities for all.

3. Some students are more relaxed and receptive to feedback from a peer, who is not in the position of "evaluator" that you occupy.

4. Because they themselves are engaged in completing the assignment, students can often come up with strategies for tackling problems their peers are struggling with.

5. After conferring with a peer, they are more likely to attempt to view their work through another's eyes, which can trigger new thoughts and insights into what to rework.

6. Peer feedback activities tap into the advantages that social interaction contributes to learning.

White and Frederiksen (1998) described two prerequisites to engaging students in peer feedback activities, based on their studies of reflective assessment (peer feedback and self-assessment) in the science classroom:

1. All participants must understand that it is performance that is being rated, not people, where performance is what you actually do, not what you are capable of doing.

2. Students must be given the means to understand how to do well in their performances; otherwise performance ratings may be damaging to students (p. 80).

White and Frederiksen explained that these requirements address a serious issue:

> If the process of producing a high-quality project is mysterious to students, they are likely to fall back on an ability attribution for the assessment results, that is, on the belief that they are not "smart enough" to do well in science. There is a clear equity issue here as well, because failure to provide both an understanding of the assessment criteria and of how to perform well may be particularly damaging to less-advantaged students who, without a clear understanding of how highly-rated work is produced, are likely to invoke the damaging theory of performance as a reflection of their ability. So, reflective assessment [peer feedback and self-assessment] should not be added on to a curriculum, rather it should be an integral part of a curriculum that scaffolds the development of the skills being assessed (p. 80).

Scaffolding a Peer Feedback Conference

You can teach students to give feedback to each other by having them practice in a controlled setting. Limiting the variables scaffolds the experience so they can focus on mastering the process before using it with their own work.

One way to accomplish this is to have them engage in a three-minute conference simulation with a partner, in which they take turns playing the roles of student and teacher. Select two anonymous samples of student work that each fall in the midrange of quality, illustrating strengths and areas needing attention for the aspect or aspects of quality you are focusing on. Label the samples "Student A" and "Student B." If students do not already have a copy of the scoring rubric, prepare a copy for each one. They will also each need a copy of the Assessment Dialogue form in Figure 3.15 or 3.16 and scratch paper. Then follow this process:

1. Ask students to find a partner. The person with the longer fingers is "Partner A." The other person is "Partner B." Tell students that for the first activity, "Partner A" is the student and "Partner B" is the teacher.

2. Hand out (or ask them to take out) the scoring rubric. If it is an analytic rubric, direct their attention to the criterion they are to focus on. Tell them they will be using the rubric to give each other feedback in this simulation and give them a few minutes to review it.

3. Hand out the sample labeled "Student A" and tell them Partner A has just completed this piece of work. Then tell them to take a few minutes independently to read through the sample, compare it to the rubric, and find words and phrases they think describe what they see. Give them enough time to read the sample and review the rubric. Partner A writes his thoughts on the Assessment Dialogue form (Figure 3.15 or 3.16). Partner B writes her thoughts on scratch paper. Or, you can let Partner B tick off the rubric phrases on the scoring rubric.

4. When all are ready, have them conduct a three-minute conference with their partners. Partner A (the "student") speaks first. When it's Partner B's (the "teacher's") turn to speak, the "student" writes the "teacher's" comments on the Assessment Dialogue form.

5. Time their conferences—give them a two-minute reminder and then let them know when three minutes are up. Ask them to thank their partners at the end of the three minutes.

6. If they have enough time during the three minutes—it's surprising that they often do—ask partners to discuss what the student could do next, working together to fill out the "My Plan" portion of the Assessment Dialogue form.

7. While they are talking with each other, walk around the room and look for students who are using the language of quality and students who seem to be struggling. Make note of where problems seem to be if they don't quite have the hang of it yet.

8. When the three minutes are up, if you noticed any problems with the process, conduct a whole-class debrief discussion, addressing the problems in general terms: "I noticed some struggles with _____. What did you notice?"; "How might we solve that problem? What are some things you can do?"

9. You can also conduct a large-group exploration of strategies that might improve the work.

10. Have them reverse roles and repeat the process with the second sample, labeled "Student B," where Partner B is the "student" and Partner A is the "teacher."

11. Debrief the process by engaging the class in discussing questions such as these:

   • What was easy about this? What was hard?

   • What did you discover when you were being the student? What did you learn when you were being the teacher?

   • What did this teach you about (the elements of quality they were focused on)?

   • How would you describe the characteristics of useful feedback?

In certain contexts, such as mathematics problem solving, before conducting the three-minute conference simulation, students should attempt to solve the problem themselves. Then they put their own work aside and participate in the simulation with anonymous samples. At the conclusion, they can review their own solutions and make any changes they think of after having discussed the two samples.

What does engaging in the simulation do for students? It introduces or reinforces the idea that they might think first about their work before asking someone else to look it over. It prepares them to give accurate, useful feedback to others, and it causes them to think more deeply about the elements of quality they are learning.

Students can then use the same process to seek and offer feedback from one another. The peer conference version of the Assessment Dialogue form on the DVD includes a line in which they can request further feedback either from a specific person or choose between "teacher" and "peer" (where you assign the partners), depending on your preference.

Evidence suggests that in peer feedback situations, struggling learners benefit from heterogeneous pairing or grouping, while stronger students do well in either homogenous or heterogeneous groups (White & Frederiksen, 1998). Consider assigning heterogeneous partners or groups of three or four members, at least until the struggling students are performing more successfully.

About Peer Editing

If you have students edit each other's work for issues of correctness, consider requiring that they first have reviewed their own work and have found all the errors they are capable of finding. The argument for peer editing (and it is valid, in my opinion) is that in life beyond school, we ask others to check over our work when correctness counts. However, consider structuring peer editing so that it mirrors life-beyond-school practice: We don't ask others to do our work for us. We check it ourselves first. To let students hand over the complete editing task to someone else encourages a bad habit—expecting someone else to do their work. After students have made all the corrections they can find, they can exchange their work with a partner and use editors' symbols, the feedback codes you use, or the "dots in the margin" strategy to mark errors on one another's papers. Be sure to hold the original author responsible for making the changes.

Making Sure Students Understand the Language of Quality

If students are not comfortable with the concepts included in your scoring rubric (or other definition of quality you will ultimately use to judge their work), they won't be able to give each other useful feedback reliably, so make sure they have engaged in some version of Strategies 1 and 2 prior to engaging in this Strategy 3 activity.

Peer editing is not appropriate in some circumstances. When teaching students to master writing conventions, you will need to evaluate each student's proficiency with spelling, punctuation, grammar/usage, and capitalization periodically within the context of their writing. If students peer-edit in this context, you will not have an accurate read of their individual achievement. If you teach English, keep in mind that there are times in life beyond school when we have to produce the best version of error-free text we are capable of, independent of others. Help students develop this capability by teaching them to edit solo. When mastery of writing conventions is not the focus of the achievement to be demonstrated, encourage students to use peer editors.

Peer Response Groups

You may want to broaden the peer feedback experience by expanding from partner feedback to small-group feedback. Think of peer feedback in group settings as assessment conversations that students have with one another. Set the stage for these conversations by establishing norms or guidelines for how they will take place: what protocol students are to follow, what kinds of comments are likely to be most helpful, how to offer feedback, and how to respond when receiving it. Groups of three or four members generally function best; they are large enough to provide some diversity of opinion and small enough to complete the process in 20 to 45 minutes (depending on the scope of the feedback requested).

Prior to beginning, determine how students will share their work samples with the group. If the learning target is demonstrated through a piece of writing, it is recommended that students read their own writing aloud to the group, which helps the group pay attention to the ideas. If the learning target is demonstrated through another artifact, such as a diagram, a problem solution, or a type of product, then have students exchange artifacts. If the learning target is demonstrated through a performance, have the students either perform it live or share a recording (video or audio).

The following procedure is based on how a writing response group functions and includes adaptations for groups responding to work samples in any content area.

1. All members come prepared to share their work in progress. For a written sample, this means they are prepared to give it a good interpretive reading to showcase the ideas as clearly as possible. For an artifact, this means the artifact is legible enough, crafted well enough, or labeled clearly enough so another person can understand it well enough to provide feedback. If possible, there should be one copy of the artifact for each group member. If it is a three-dimensional object, the group will work with the original. For a recording, this means all can see and/or hear it clearly.

2. Before sharing, each person identifies what aspects of quality he or she would like feedback on. Ideally, they relate to concepts in the scoring rubric or other mutually understood characteristics of quality. What specifically should members attend to?

3. For a written product, when one person is reading, everyone else listens. For an artifact, all group members work independently to review the same artifact. When the group is watching and/or listening to a recording, all attend to the same recording.

4. For a written product, the author reads through once. Other group members listen without commenting. At the end of the reading, group members take a few minutes to jot down thoughts. For an artifact, each group member reviews the artifact without commenting aloud and writes his or her feedback down for sharing when all have finished their review. For a recording, follow the procedure for a written product, substituting watching and/or listening to the recording for reading aloud.

5. For a written product, the author reads through a second time. Group members take notes, focusing on the feedback requested. For a recording, the group will watch and/or listen to it a second time and then craft their feedback individually in writing at this point. For an artifact, you can skip this step.

6. Group members can either share their thoughts orally or in writing. They can offer their feedback after each group member has shared or save it until all have finished sharing. Figure 3.18 shows a sample peer response recording form.

Figure 3.18

Peer Response Feedback Form

Date: _____

Author: _____

Title: _____

Feedback requested: _____

My response: _____

_____

*Suggestions for Students Receiving Feedback
in Peer Response Groups*

Here are some suggestions for what you might tell students when they are receiving peer feedback (derived in part from Spandel, 2009):

1. Think about what you want the group to pay attention to—what do you want feedback on? Let your group know. For example, if you have questions about how to narrow an idea or where to take it, ask for suggestions.

2. If you are reading your work aloud, give it the best reading you can so that your group can really visualize what you are saying. If you are exchanging work samples instead of reading them aloud, make sure your sample is legible. If you are sharing a recording, make sure it is visible and/or audible to all group members.

3. Don't apologize. You want the group to offer honest responses about your work. Remember, the goal of your group is to provide feedback you can use to improve your work. With a writing sample, "Just plunge in. . . . Be brave. Read your text with confidence so that the feedback you get will be more about your writing and less about you" (Spandel, 2009, p. 360).

4. Thank group members for their comments. Don't argue with them. It's okay if you don't agree with them, but you don't have to tell them that. Think of their comments as gifts—some gifts you use and some you put away, but you always thank the giver. You are in charge of your work, so you get to decide which comments to act on. Even if you don't think you will use the comment, say thank you.

*Suggestions for Students Offering Feedback
in Peer Response Groups*

Here are some suggestions for what you might tell students when they are giving feedback:

1. Use your best listening skills. Listen to what the author wants feedback on and then keep that in mind as you formulate your comments.

2. Remember to refer to the language and concepts of quality that we have been practicing in your success and next-steps feedback comments. Link your comments to specific instances in the writing, artifact, or performance.

3. You are offering the author the gift of an audience response to her ideas or work. Success feedback isn't always praise. Sometimes it's an honest response that shares what her ideas or work caused you to see, to understand, to feel, or to think differently about.

4. If you have next-step feedback—a question or a suggestion to offer—point out the feature you are referring to and phrase your thoughts as an "I" statement. Examples:

    *   "I felt confused when . . ." (or "This confused me . . .")
    *   "I wondered why . . ."
    *   "I wanted to know more about . . ."

    If your first thought begins with "You need to," you have come up with a solution to a problem. Think about the *question in your mind* that triggered your solution idea and offer the *question* as feedback. Comments that help the author figure out what needs work can be even more valuable than comments that tell the author what to do (unless that is what he or she has asked for).

5. Remember that the author is in charge of the quality of the writing, artifact, or performance. Your feedback doesn't have to fix everything. Your role is to offer your thoughts respectfully.

Figure 3.19 describes how a high school English department conducts peer feedback sessions, and Figure 3.20 gives subject-specific suggestions for structuring peer feedback opportunities.

Tips for Timing

It's helpful to think carefully in advance about how much time you will allow for students to participate in peer response groups. To make the process as efficient as possible, consider these suggestions:

*   Students don't need to share the whole piece of writing if they only need or want feedback on a portion of it. Or, you can ask them to limit their feedback to one or a few dimensions of quality.

*   Keep feedback groups fairly small—three to four students per group. This process takes time and the more students in a group, the longer it will take.

*   Give students a time frame for each portion of the process. How long should each member spend presenting his or her work? How long for group members to compose their responses? How long for sharing their responses?

Figure 3.19

Peer Review in High School English Class

FOR EXAMPLE

In grades 9–12 (in our school), individual teachers tend to have their own way to handle peer review, but there are some universal trends. Typically, peer review is used to create student learning conversations during the middle phase of the writing process. For some teachers, once students have working drafts, they meet in partnerships or small teams to review their work. The review process is focused on ideas and content, organization and structure, and voice. Many teachers adapt the 6+1 trait rubric so that it can be used by the kids to formatively assess the work of their peers.

After providing time in class to review, students use the comments to revise their drafts. At this time, many teachers formally collect the revised drafts (or specific paragraphs) to offer their comments. When the paper is returned, students use the teacher's comments (and writing conferences) to start working on their final drafts. Several days before the due date, students get back in their peer review partnerships/groups and look at their essays again. This time grammar and conventions are evaluated along with the other traits. Throughout the process, students complete metacognitive reflection tasks that ask them to think about the strengths and weaknesses of their drafts. Our Creative Writing class uses a workshop approach that involves one full week per unit devoted to peer review.

Source: Used with permission from Michael L. Doman, Naperville Community Unit School District 203: Naperville, IL.

Figure 3.20

Subject-Specific Peer Feedback Applications

FOR EXAMPLE

Mathematics: Students can critique each other's extended problem solutions. Let them read through each other's solutions and explanations and then offer comments on whichever aspects of quality you (or they) select as the focus. They can use a student-friendly scoring rubric to guide their critiques. For example, if the focus is Mathematical Communication, they can give feedback on clarity and completeness of the explanation and correct usage of mathematical terms.

Science: Students may be working on a project that demonstrates their mastery of the inquiry process. Depending on the requirements of the task, they may either read their work aloud or exchange work with another student for feedback on one or more characteristics of quality. They also will need a student-friendly scoring rubric or explicit list of criteria to guide their critiques (e.g., formulating an hypothesis; designing and conducting an investigation; gathering, analyzing, and interpreting data; communicating results [National Research Council, 1996]).

Figure 3.20 (continued)

Social Studies: Students may be working on a paper that compares and contrasts two religions they are studying. It will be very important here as well that they have a student-friendly scoring rubric or explicit list of criteria that offers a clear notion of what constitutes quality as it relates to social studies knowledge and reasoning learning targets (e.g., presents accurate factual information, chooses appropriate things to compare, chooses appropriate characteristics on which to base comparisons, identifies similarities and differences accurately, explains similarities and differences with sufficient detail [Marzano, Pickering, & McTighe, 1993]).

Writing: Younger students can begin by looking or listening for one thing: a phrase that sparks their imagination, a surprising word, a catchy beginning, a rhythmic sentence. Model this for them by first pointing out characteristics of good writing in what you read aloud to them: "I noticed. . . ." Invite them to offer their own observations: "What did you notice?" Then move to identifying those characteristics in examples of student writing (not from them). Ask them for suggestions of what they might notice in their classmates' writing and what they might like to have others notice in theirs. Let them practice on anonymous student work, before trying it with a partner. Debrief by asking them what they learned from the experience.

Video 3.4: Peer Feedback: Kindergarten to High School

Watch Video 3.4 to hear teachers and students talk about peer feedback.

Conclusion

Teaching students to see their work in school as opportunities to improve is at the heart of learning. When we offer feedback effectively, students greet assessment information warmly, because it builds a hopeful vision: "I think I can do this," rather than establishing a dreaded, fatalistic sense: "Here I go again, down the drain grade-wise for another year." We can model an open, forward-looking stance to learning through how we respond to their work and then we can show them how to look at their own work in the same way. Providing feedback takes time—time to give and time to act on—so we want to make sure that (1) we're offering the right kind of feedback, and (2) students will use it to improve.

Understanding and Applying the Content of Chapter 3

End-of-chapter activities are intended to help you master the chapter's learning targets and apply concepts to your classroom. They are designed to deepen your understanding of the chapter content, provide discussion topics for collaborative learning, and guide implementation of the content and practices taught in the chapter. Forms and materials for completing each activity appear in editable Microsoft Word format in the Chapter 3 DVD file. Each form needed for an activity is listed after the activity directions and marked with this symbol:

Chapter 3 Learning Targets

1. Understand the characteristics of effective feedback
2. Know how to offer feedback effectively and efficiently
3. Know how to select feedback options suited to students' grade level and the kind of learning to be addressed
4. Know how to prepare students to give each other effective feedback

Chapter 3 Activities

Discussion Questions (All learning targets)

Activity 3.1 Keeping a Reflective Journal (All learning targets)

Activity 3.2 Assessing Your Own Feedback Practices (Learning targets 1 and 2)

Activity 3.3 Giving Success and Next-Step Feedback (Learning target 2)

Activity 3.4 Turning Summative Events into Feedback Opportunities (Learning targets 1 and 2)

Activity 3.5 Preparing for a Three-Minute Conference (Learning target 2)

Activity 3.6 Selecting and Modifying Feedback Forms (Learning target 3)

Activity 3.7 Planning a Peer Feedback Activity (Learning target 4)

Activity 3.8 Selecting a Strategy 3 Application (All learning targets)

Activity 3.9 Adding to Your Growth Portfolio (All learning targets)

Chapter 3 Discussion Questions

Discussion questions are also explored in depth in the activities listed in parentheses.

Questions to Discuss Before Reading Chapter 3

1. What types of feedback do students in your class typically receive? (Activity 3.2)
2. When do students in your class receive feedback on their progress? (Activity 3.2)
3. What do you expect students to do with feedback information? (Activity 3.2)

Questions to Discuss After Reading Chapter 3

4. How do you give success feedback to your students? What forms of next-step feedback do you give? (Activity 3.3)
5. Which feedback options will work best in your context (grade, subject, and learning goals)? (Activities 3.3, 3.5, 3.6, and 3.7)
6. Could any of your marked/graded assignments or quizzes be turned into purely feedback events? If so, what actions do you want students to take on the basis of the feedback they receive? What changes would you have to make to the assignment or quiz to make the results serve the intended actions? (Activity 3.4)
7. What preparation will your students need to give effective (accurate and useful) feedback to each other? (Activities 3.5 and 3.7)
8. What activities from Chapter 3 did you try in the classroom? How did they work? What successes did you notice? What modifications might you make? (Activities 3.6 and 3.7)

Activity 3.1

Keeping a Reflective Journal

This is intended as an independent activity. If you choose to do it, you may want to discuss the thoughts you record with your learning team.

Keep a record of your thoughts, questions, and any implementation activities you tried while reading Chapter 3.

 Activity 3.1 Chapter 3 Reflective Journal Form

Activity 3.2

Assessing Your Own Feedback Practices

This is intended as an independent activity. If you do it independently, you may want to discuss the results with your learning team.

Use the form on the DVD to determine the extent to which each of these characteristics is in place in your current practice.

1. My feedback to students links directly to the intended learning.

2. My feedback points out strengths and offers information to guide improvement linked to the intended learning.

3. My students receive feedback during the learning process.

4. I have paced instruction so that students have time to act on the feedback they receive.

5. I don't use written feedback as instruction unless the student's work exhibits at least partial understanding.

6. My feedback encourages students to take action likely to lead to further learning. My next-step feedback doesn't do all of the thinking for students.

7. My next-step feedback limits correctives to the amount of advice the student can act on in the time given.

After completing the feedback inventory, determine which of the characteristics is your highest priority for continued learning.

 Activity 3.2 Assessing Your Own Feedback Practices

Activity 3.3

Giving Success and Next-Step Feedback

This is a partner and learning team activity.

After reading the Chapter 3 section titled "Characteristics of Effective Feedback," bring a collection of student work to your next team meeting. Also bring a description of the pertinent learning target(s) or the scoring rubric. Number the student work samples you have brought. If more than one person brings student work, number the samples consecutively. Then follow the steps for either Option A or B to practice giving success and next-step feedback.

Option A

1. Working alone or with a partner, identify each sample's strengths and areas needing additional work. You may want to refer to the text for suggestions on success and next-step feedback options. Use the form on the DVD to record your comments.

2. Compare your judgments to those of others in your group, one sample at a time. Discuss and attempt to resolve discrepancies by referring to the definition of quality (description of the learning target or scoring rubric).

3. Discuss with your team which students might need reteaching and which students would be able to move forward on the basis of the feedback given. Also discuss what types of lessons might be needed by those requiring reteaching.

Option B

1. Bring a collection of colored index cards to the meeting. You will need a different color for each person on the team and enough cards of each color to correspond to the number of samples you are using (e.g., five samples requires five cards for each person).

2. Each of you numbers your cards to correspond to the sample numbers, one card per sample, and then draws a star on one side of each card and a set of stairs on the other side.

3. Independently, write your success and next-step feedback for each sample on your cards.

4. After everyone has completed their cards, assign one sample and its pile of index cards to one person and have that person read aloud all of the success comments and then all of the next-step comments. Discuss and attempt to resolve discrepancies for each sample by referring to the definition of quality (description of the learning target or scoring rubric).

5. Assign another sample and its pile of index cards to another person and repeat the process in Step 4.

6. Discuss with your team which students might need reteaching and which students would be able to move forward on the basis of the feedback given. Also discuss what types of lessons might be needed by those requiring reteaching.

You can follow this activity by having your students do either version, using only anonymous samples not from their class. Share with your colleagues your observations about the effects of the activity on your students' motivation and understanding of quality.

 Activity 3.3 Giving Success and Next-Step Feedback

Activity 3.4

Turning Summative Events into Feedback Opportunities

This is a partner or learning team activity.

After reading through the Chapter 3 section titled "Characteristics of Effective Feedback," focus on the second characteristic: *Occurs during the learning.* Bring a paper copy of a page from your grade book or assignment and assessment records to your team meeting and discuss the following questions.

1. Which of your assignments are intended to be used for practice? Mark them with the letter P.

2. Is the number of practice opportunities sufficient to prepare students to perform well on the summative assessment? Which of your students would have benefited from more practice before being held accountable for mastery of a given learning target?

3. Could any of your marked or graded assignments or quizzes be turned into purely practice events, where students receive success and next-step feedback instead of a mark or grade? If so, which ones?

4. What actions do you want students to take on the basis of the feedback they receive? What changes, if any, would you have to make to the assignment or quiz to make the results serve the intended actions?

5. What changes might you need to make to the pacing of your instruction to accommodate further practice?

Activity 3.5

Preparing for a Three-Minute Conference

This is a partner and learning team activity. It begins with a simulation, followed by a discussion.

After reading the Chapter 3 section titled "Assessment Dialogues," have each person on your team find an example of student work (a sample performance or product) that demonstrates partial mastery, and bring two copies to your meeting along with two copies of the scoring rubric and one copy of either the elementary or the secondary Assessment Dialogue form (on the DVD).

1. Review the explanation of the three-minute conference in the text. Then partner up. Decide who will be "Partner A" and who will be "Partner B."

2. In this simulation Partner A, you are the student. Partner B, you are the teacher. Begin with the work sample Partner A brought. You should each have a copy of the student work and the scoring guide.

3. Partner A and Partner B, spend about five minutes independently to determine what the sample's strengths and needs are, using the language and/or concepts from the scoring rubric. If you are working with an analytic rubric, decide in advance which criterion to focus on. Don't share your thoughts with your partner yet. In this simulation, you want the student to think independently of the teacher before the conference.

4. Partner A (the student), write your judgments about the sample's strengths and needs on the Assessment Dialogue form. Partner B (the teacher), write your judgments on scratch paper or tick off phrases on the rubric that describe the features you see in the sample. Make sure that you both use the language and/or concepts of quality represented on the rubric.

5. Conduct a three-minute conference with your partner. Let Partner A (the student) speak first. When Partner B (the teacher) talks, the student writes the teacher's comments on the Assessment Dialogue form.

6. Switch roles: Partner B, you become the student, and Partner A, you become the teacher. Follow the same protocol using the work sample that Partner B has provided.

7. At the end of three minutes, discuss with your partner: What does this protocol do for the student? For the teacher?

8. Discuss as a team:

    • Which of the five characteristics of effective feedback were present in the three-minute conference?

    • How might you use the three-minute conference in your classroom?

    • What modifications to the protocol might you make?

9. Discuss if the protocol revealed any changes you might want to make to your rubric to make it more suited to formative use. Refer to Chapter 2 for suggestions.

Activity 3.5a Elementary Assessment Dialogue Form   Activity 3.5b Secondary Assessment Dialogue Form

Activity 3.6

Selecting and Modifying Feedback Forms

This is a partner or learning team activity.

1. After reading the Chapter 3 section titled "Suggestions for Offering Feedback," look over the feedback forms in the Chapter 3 DVD file with a partner or your team. Identify those that could be used in your context (grade, subject, learning targets) to help students understand and act on feedback. Select or modify one and make a plan to use it by deciding the following:

   • Which unit of study you will use it with

   • What learning target(s) will be the focus of the feedback

   • At what point(s) in the instruction you will offer feedback

   You can use the form for this activity on the DVD to keep track of your decisions.

2. Use the form you have selected or modified to offer feedback to your students. Bring a few samples of your feedback to your next team meeting to share. If some students were more successful than others in acting on the feedback, bring a sample of successful and unsuccessful student attempts.

3. Discuss possible revisions to the process or the form to make it work well for all students. You can also use the following checklist to determine students' readiness to understand and act on feedback.

Feedback Readiness Checklist

☐ Does the student have a clear vision of quality (what's expected)?

☐ Can the student describe the intended learning?

☐ Can the student differentiate between strong and weak examples and/or levels of quality?

☐ Has the student practiced using the language of quality to describe attributes of strong and weak examples?

4. If the answer to one or more of the questions on the Feedback Readiness Checklist is "no," then you may want to revisit Strategy 1 and Strategy 2 activities before offering further feedback.

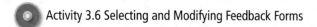
Activity 3.6 Selecting and Modifying Feedback Forms

Activity 3.7

Planning a Peer Feedback Activity

This is a learning team activity.

1. Try one of the options explained in the Chapter 3 section titled "Peer Feedback" with a class.

2. As students are engaged in offering and receiving feedback, walk around the room to look and listen for successes and problems they encounter. Record your observations.

3. Meet with your team to share the option you tried, the successes you noticed, and any problems or glitches your students encountered.

4. Discuss ways to solve the problems or remedy the glitches. If some students had trouble giving effective feedback, you may want to spend more time with Strategy 2 activities, or engage them in the three-minute conference simulation described in Activity 3.5.

Activity 3.8

Selecting a Strategy 3 Application

This is intended as an independent activity. If you do it independently, you may want to discuss the results with your learning team.

After reading Chapter 3, choose one activity to use with your students. Then use the form on the DVD to reflect on the activity: what you tried, what you noticed as a result, and what, if any, actions you have taken or will take on the basis of the experience. If you are working with a learning team, consider sharing your reflection with them.

Activity 3.8 Selecting a Strategy 3 Application

Activity 3.9

Adding to Your Growth Portfolio

This is intended as an independent activity.

Any of the activities from this chapter can be used as entries for your own growth portfolio. Select activities you have completed or artifacts you have created that will illustrate your competence in the Chapter 3 learning targets. If you are keeping a reflective journal, you may want to include Chapter 3's entry in your portfolio. The portfolio entry cover sheet provided on the DVD will prompt you to think about how each item you select reflects your learning with respect to one or more of the chapter's learning targets.

 Activity 3.9 Chapter 3 Portfolio Entry Cover Sheet

Where Am I Now?

Self-Assessment and Goal Setting

Strategy 4

Teach students to self-assess and set goals for next steps.

> One of the problems with self-assessment is that lots of students aren't very good at it, and if they're not good at it, it doesn't do them much good.

"*H*ow'm I doin'?" "Well, it looks FINE to me." "I AM done." "Is this what you want?" No doubt, students' self-assessment can be a shot in the dark and the goals they set can be off the mark, trifling, or overwhelming. We avoid these problems through the preparation provided in the first three strategies: making the learning targets clear to students (the basis of their self-assessment and goal setting); letting them practice evaluating anonymous examples of varying quality; offering descriptive feedback (modeling the kind of thinking they are to do when they self-assess); and having them practice self-assessment as you give feedback. With sufficient preparation, the transition to evaluating the strengths and weaknesses of their own work accurately will be easier and quicker.

"Formative assessment requires that pupils have a central part in it . . . . Unless they come to understand their strengths and weaknesses, and how they might deal with them, they will not make progress."

Harlen & James, 1997, p. 372

Chapter 4 Learning Targets

At the end of Chapter 4, you will know how to do the following:

1. Understand the impact of self-assessment and goal setting on student motivation and achievement

2. Understand the conditions that maximize the impact of self-assessment and goal setting

3. Know how to teach students to self-assess accurately with a focus on learning targets

4. Know how to prepare students to create specific and challenging goals

Impact of Self-Assessment on Student Achievement

Finding any extra time during instruction for students to self-assess and set goals can be challenging, but the benefits to learning are worth it. Research results repeatedly confirm that when students are required to think about their own learning and articulate what they understand and what they still need to learn, achievement improves (Black & Wiliam, 1998a; Hattie, 2009).

Effects of Linking Feedback and Self-Assessment

Feedback and self-assessment are not always conducted as discrete events, as we have seen in Chapter 3. New Zealand researcher Terry Crooks (2007) described their relationship as symbiotic. He suggested that students will respond more positively to feedback if we first ask them to describe what they have done, where they think they have succeeded, and where they think they have not. As we saw in Chapter 3 in the three-minute conference, treating feedback and self-assessment as a reciprocal event helps teachers know what guidance to provide as it strengthens students' abilities to self-assess.

Effects of Peer Feedback and Self-Assessment

We looked at peer feedback strategies in Chapter 3 as a logical extension of teacher-generated feedback, but researchers often call it peer *assessment* and study it together with self-assessment. One study described by Black & Wiliam (1998a) compared the impact of three formative assessment practices—teacher feedback, peer feedback, and self-assessment—on special education students. In the study, elementary students with learning difficulties received one of three forms of feedback on their oral reading rates: feedback from the teacher, feedback from their peers, or self-generated feedback (self-assessment). Black & Wiliam summed up the impact of each as follows:

> The largest gains, measured by comparison of pre- and post-test scores over the programme's period of nine weeks, were achieved by the self-monitoring group, whilst all three did better than a control group who had no formative feedback. . . . The peer and self-monitoring methods were preferred (by teachers and students) and one benefit of both was that they reduced the amount of time that the special education teachers had to spend on measurement in their classroom. (p. 27)

In another study, with middle school science students, White and Frederiksen (1998) tested the effects of what they call "Reflective Assessment," a cycle of peer- and self-assessment activities throughout the course of a unit focused in part on scientific inquiry skills (Figure 4.1). They found the following:

> Students' learning was greatly facilitated by Reflective Assessment. Furthermore, adding this metacognitive process to the curriculum

Figure 4.1

RESEARCH SNAPSHOT

"Inquiry, Modeling, and Metacognition: Making Science Accessible to All Students"—*White & Frederiksen, 1998*

Hypothesis:
Students' ability to engage in scientific inquiry will be enhanced by the addition of a metacognitive process in which students reflect on their own and each other's learning.

Who Was Involved:
Twelve urban classes of students in grades 7 through 9, classified as high achieving or low achieving on the basis of their combined CTBS verbal and quantitative test scores.

What They Did:
The researchers first developed a program using the scientific inquiry cycle to teach middle school students to design and create causal models of force and motion (the ThinkerTools Inquiry Curriculum). Participating classes

Figure 4.1 (continued)

were divided into two groups—a "Reflective Assessment" group and a control group. Both groups received the same instruction and completed the same activities, engaging in the inquiry cycle through seven modules scaffolded to develop understanding of how forces affect motion. They all completed two inquiry research projects, one after the third module and the other after the seventh. Students were free to choose their partners in working on the research projects—some research groups were composed of high-achieving students, some were composed of low-achieving students, and some were a mixture of both.

The "Reflective Assessment" group participated in a cycle of reflective peer and self-assessment. They were first introduced to a set of criteria for good scientific research at the beginning of the curriculum. Then, at the end of each phase of the inquiry cycle in each module, students evaluated their work using the most relevant criteria. At the end of each module, they evaluated the work for all criteria. In addition, when they presented their research projects to the class, they evaluated their own and gave each other feedback orally and in writing.

What the Researchers Found:

- In the Reflective Assessment classes, the gap between low-achieving and high-achieving students' performance on research projects and inquiry tests was significantly narrower than it was in the control classes (p. 34).

- On a test of inquiry skills, the average gain for students in the Reflective Assessment classes was three times that of the control classes. An analysis of subscores reveals the greatest gains came from the most difficult aspects of the test (pp. 48–49).

- Low-achieving students (CTBS composite <60) in the Reflective Assessment classes performed almost as well on their research projects as high-achieving students (CTBS composite >60) in the control classes (p. 51).

- Low-achieving students in Reflective Assessment classes benefited from heterogeneous grouping when working with a partner (p. 38).

Source: Summarized from B. Y. White & J. R. Frederiksen, "Inquiry, Modeling, and Metacognition: Making Science Accessible to All Students," *Cognition and Instruction, 16*(1), 1998, 3–118.

was particularly beneficial for low-achieving students: performance on their research projects and inquiry tests was significantly closer to that of high-achieving students than was the case in the control classes. Thus, this approach has the valuable effect of reducing the educational disadvantage of low-achieving students while also being beneficial for high-achieving students. (p. 4)

Providing students with opportunities for a combination of peer feedback and self-assessment can cause them to achieve at significantly higher levels, without more instruction. This combination is especially beneficial to special education students and to low-achieving students, the populations we might think are least prepared to offer and receive peer feedback or to self-assess.

Linking Self-Assessment to the Intended Learning

In concluding remarks to his synthesis of over 800 meta-analyses of classroom practices, Hattie (2009) emphasized the importance of challenging learning targets, which he calls both *learning intentions* and *learning goals*, to higher achievement. This is good news for all who are faced with implementing more rigorous content standards in the immediate future. As has been shown in many studies, students will work harder and bring to bear more of their brain power when given a challenging learning target. "The rate of learning is a direct function of goal difficulty, as is the level of persistence over time to attain difficult goals" (p. 246).

Two studies examining the impact of making the intended learning clear to students at the outset of instruction coupled with the practice of self-assessment showed that "emphasizing to students that their goal is to learn (to add fractions) can raise their self-efficacy for learning and motivate them to regulate their task performance and work diligently" (Schunk, 1996, p. 377). Additionally, when students self-assessed during the learning, their achievement improved. However, Schunk issued a caution regarding self-assessment worth paying attention to:

> The present results must be qualified because students were acquiring skills and their self-evaluations were positive. Self-evaluation may not always have desirable effects. Asking students to periodically assess their capabilities on a task they repeatedly have failed to master might lower, rather than raise, self-efficacy and motivation, because after many negative attempts, students might conclude they are incapable of learning. . . .
> To be effective, self-evaluation must be linked with instruction so students learn and perceive they are making progress. (p. 378)

Self-assessment is beneficial when students are demonstrating improvement. When they aren't yet progressing, time is better spent on instruction to move learning forward. As they begin to improve, self-assessment works to nurture a sense of self-efficacy ("my effort causes results") and the ownership of responsibility for improving that strong learners possess. It teaches students to *become* better learners.

Concerns with Accuracy of Self-Assessment

In a 2013 review of research on self-assessment, Brown and Harris examined studies on the degree of accuracy of student self-assessment and found that although there is a positive correlation between student self-assessment and external measures such as teacher ratings, several factors appear to make student judgments more or less accurate. Younger children tend to skew positive in their self-assessments, whereas older students' judgments tend to be more realistic and in line with their teachers' ratings. Higher-performing students tend to be more accurate than lower-performing students. More difficult tasks were associated with lower levels of agreement between student and teacher ratings. And students who received feedback on clearly defined criteria and who based their self-assessments on those criteria were more closely aligned with external measures such as teacher ratings than those who did not (pp. 384–387).

All of these problems can be mitigated. We can increase the accuracy of student self-assessment by taking the following actions:

- Making sure that students understand the learning target at the focus of their work

- Providing guided practice in evaluating anonymous work samples using the rubrics that will define quality for the more complex learning targets

- Offering accurate feedback that models the kind of thinking students are to engage in when they self-assess

- Having them self-assess before providing feedback to help them "norm" their thinking to standards of accuracy (represented by your judgment)

Psychological Safety

An additional factor influencing accuracy noted by Brown and Harris (2013) is that of *psychological safety*—whether the student feels emotionally safe enough to render an accurate judgment. Studies they reviewed suggest that student judgments may skew low out of fear of being seen as overly prideful or for cultural reasons, such as when self-effacement is a cultural expectation. On the other hand, student judgments may skew high with students who want to avoid being embarrassed in front of peers or parents.

You can take several actions to help make self-assessment psychologically safe. First, explain to your students what self-assessment is, why we are doing it, and who will see the information. Do not make the information public unless students are comfortable doing so and there is a good reason to do so. Second, make sure they are using a description of the learning target as the basis for their self-assessment, rather than just giving themselves a grade, a mark, or a rating. Third, model healthy self-assessment through feedback that doesn't label mistakes as failures, but rather as ways to figure out what is next to learn. Fourth, help students attribute their current status to a mixture of what they have learned and what they have yet to learn, as opposed to attributing it to a level of intelligence. Fifth, be vigilant about eliminating sayings, posters, and motivational practices that send the message that some people are smart and others aren't or the message that grades are the most important reason to do their work. In short, make your classroom an environment that nurtures and values learning behaviors.

Self-Assessment, Justification, Goal Setting, and Action Planning

Strategy 4 has four parts: self-assessment, justification, goal setting, and action planning. When students self-assess, they make judgments about their current achievement status against a standard of correctness or quality. This is different from self-grading in that it is not the mark or grade that is as important as the descriptive information about level of attainment of the intended learning. Self-assessment is also more than self-monitoring, where students keep track of what they have accomplished. "While self-monitoring is very effective, it is not as high as self-evaluation, suggesting that self-monitoring in itself (such as ticking off completed tasks) can be much improved if taken further, where the learner actually evaluates what they have monitored" (Hattie, 2009, p. 190). In many instances, it is also a good idea to ask students to justify their judgment by identifying

 Directing Attention to the Learning

Self-assessment and goal-setting processes and forms should direct attention to improving features of the work as they relate to the learning targets (a learning goal), rather than to getting a better score or grade (a performance goal). If students do the learning, the grade will follow.

evidence in their work that supports their self-assessment, because self-assessment by itself is an act of offering an opinion. As has been emphasized in the Common Core State Standards, students need to learn how to support their opinions with evidence, which is what justification calls for. When their self-assessment identifies an area of growth, students learn more when they set goals and make a plan of action. They are the ones in control of the effort and the actions required to improve, so it stands to reason that the more intentional they are, the more progress they can make.

All four components of Strategy 4 do not have to be present at all times. It may be most appropriate for students to do only a quick self-assessment, especially for simpler learning targets, and you may be the one planning further action on the basis of their information. Sometimes students will interpret the results of an assessment you have evaluated; other times they will be doing the evaluation themselves. Or, you may want to have students move to goal setting and action planning based on your feedback or feedback from peers without a formal self-assessment step. In the following sections, you will see activities that include one or more of the four parts of this strategy in various combinations.

Ten Quick Self-Assessment Ideas

The following ten suggestions are fairly simple to carry out and don't take much time. The first few are suited to primary students, the majority are aimed at elementary and middle school students, and a few apply across grade levels. Quick self-assessments are especially useful when students are at the beginning stages of learning how to self-assess.

1. Checkers, Buttons, and Poker Chips

Young children can move checkers, buttons, or poker chips to track learning. Each time children move a checker, button, or chip, they are celebrating a bit of progress. For young students who require immediate gratification or who haven't yet made the connection between effort and success, simple concrete actions can be helpful. Students can put a button on a string for every spelling word mastered. Or, you can put checkers in a jar, each representing a different learning target, and have students move the checkers into a different jar as they master each learning target. Just be sure students can link the action to the learning they have accomplished (Donna Snodgrass, personal communication, 2008).

2. Learning Chains

Primary students can make learning chains by completing links from a template such as the one shown in Figure 4.2. When students have mastered a learning target, let them complete a link and save it in an envelope or bag. Periodically have students tape their links together and add them to a class chain. Each link makes an equal contribution to the total length of the chain no matter whether the links represent the work of the most advanced student or the work of a student who is just starting to make progress. You can make color-coded chains, with each color representing a subject for a multi-subject class chain or a learning target for a subject-specific chain (Donna Snodgrass, personal communication, 2008).

Figure 4.2

Learning Chains

Reserve for taping   Reserve for taping

Name: _____ Date: _____

I have learned to: _____

_____

Evidence: _____

_____

Source: Reprinted with permission from Donna Snodgrass, Cleveland State University: Cleveland, OH. Unpublished classroom materials.

3. Stars and Stairs

With elementary-age students, if you have used "Stars and Stairs" to offer success and intervention feedback, you can explain self-assessment and goal setting in the same terms:

- "What have I done well? That's my star."

- "What can I do next? That's my stair."

You can help them think through what they are going to write for their "stair" by asking "What's the difference between 'stars' and 'stairs'? The letter *I*. What step am *I* going to take to reach the star?" (Figure 4.3).

Figure 4.3

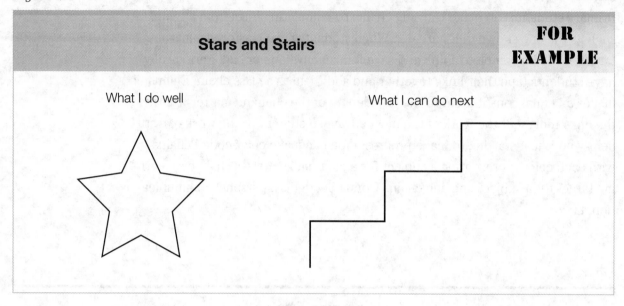

Stars and Stairs

FOR EXAMPLE

What I do well

What I can do next

4. Stamping Stairs

Students can also use a "Stamping Stairs" form such as the one in Figure 4.4, where they stamp and date their progress on one learning target, from "Just beginning" to "Success."

Figure 4.4

Stamping Stairs

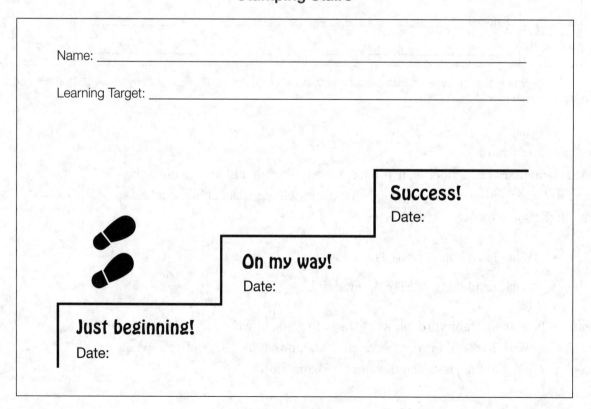

Name: _____

Learning Target: _____

Success!
Date:

On my way!
Date:

Just beginning!
Date:

5. KWL

Use the KWL strategy. At the beginning of a unit, have students draw three columns on a piece of paper, labeled K, W, and L. Ask students what they already *know* about the topic(s) and have them write that in the K column. Then ask them what they *want* to learn and have them write that in the W column. At the end of the unit, ask them what they *learned* and have them write it in the L column. Here is a variation on the KWL activity (Gregory, Cameron, & Davies, 2000):

> Give students a blank sheet of paper (11″ × 17″) before you begin a new unit of study. Have students sketch, write, or diagram anything they think they already know on the topic. Collect these sheets. Partway through the unit, return the sheets to the students and ask them to add information they now know on the topic using a different colour of ink. At the end of the unit, repeat the process. (p. 25)

6. "I am learning to . . ." ⇨ "I can . . ."

If at the outset of a unit you give learning targets to students in the form of "I am learning . . ." statements ("I am learning how other civilizations influenced the development of Greek civilization"), students can write an "I am learning" statement as an "I can" statement when they have mastered the target ("I can explain how other civilizations might have influenced the development of Greek civilization") and staple it to the evidence. This is handy when students are keeping portfolios to track their progress.

7. Checklist of Learning Targets

Students can keep a list of the learning targets for a grading period and regularly mark and date the ones they have mastered. This is also handy as a portfolio entry, especially if the evidence of mastery of each target is included.

8. Exit Task

Students can complete an exit task at the end of a lesson to assess their level of understanding and turn it in before leaving. This closure activity deepens awareness of the intended learning, and you can use the information to inform instruction for the next lesson (Sue Cho and Aaron Mukai, personal communication, 2008). Figure 4.5 shows an example of a mathematics exit task.

Figure 4.5

	FOR EXAMPLE
Diameter-Circumference Exit Task	

Name: _____

Today's Learning Target:
I can explain the relationship between the diameter and circumference of a circle.

Self-Assessment: _____

_____

Evidence:
Samantha was measuring circles around her home. The diameter of her little sister's bicycle wheel is 12 inches. Predict the circumference. **Be sure to clearly explain why you think your prediction makes sense.**

_____

_____

_____

Source: Used with permission from Sue Cho and Aaron Mukai, Mukilteo School District: Everett, WA. Unpublished classroom materials.

9. Note Home

Students can write a note to their parents about a piece of work, explaining where they are now with it and what they are trying to do next. Elementary and middle school students may want to use a version of the stem "That's good! Now this . . ." or a version of the "Stars and Stairs" form as templates for their notes.

10. Traffic Light

Before or during a unit of study, ask students to categorize their understanding of concepts using "traffic light" icons. They mark their work with a green, yellow, or red dot to indicate strong, partial, or little understanding. Students can discuss their judgments in small groups and explain their rationale. Then students with green and yellow dots work together while you conduct a lesson for students with red dots (Black, Harrison, Lee, Marshall, & Wiliam, 2002).

A variation on the traffic light strategy is to highlight learning targets. Either before beginning a unit or a few days prior to a test, have students use green, yellow, and red highlighters to mark the list of learning targets to be taught or the list of targets represented on the test. They mark those they believe they have mastered green, those they think need a little review yellow, and those they are the most unsure of having mastered red. You can use this information to differentiate instruction, or students can create a study plan identifying what they will do for the yellow and red highlighted learning targets.

Self-Assessment and Goal Setting with Selected Response and Written Response Tasks

The following ideas take students more deeply into thinking about their learning. They work well when students are focusing on knowledge and reasoning learning targets and are demonstrating their achievement with selected response items and shorter written response tasks.

Using Pretest Results

With any selected response or short written response pretest, you can prepare a chart that shows which learning target each item on the test measures and then hand out the chart when you pass back the corrected pretests. Next, have students use the chart to identify which targets they already know and which they need to learn based on how they did on each item (Figure 4.6). For the "Simple Error" column on this form, students indicate how many points they missed due to a problem they can self-correct. Then they take into account the balance of right, wrong, and simple mistake points to estimate their level of mastery for each target using a ranking scale such as this one:

1 = I don't know this very well yet.

2 = I need a little review on this.

3 = I know this well.

For this response task to be a valid judgment, you will need to make sure that your assessment samples each target sufficiently. For more information on how to construct accurate selected response tests, see Chappuis et al. (2012) Chapter 5.

Figure 4.6

Self-Assessment Pretest Results						FOR EXAMPLE

Fraction Study Targets:

- I will use factors to rewrite fractions in lowest terms.

- I will use common denominators to compare, order, add, and subtract fractions.

- I will use the relationship between fractions and mixed numbers to add, subtract, multiply, and divide fractions.

Lesson Targets	Pretest Results			Rating		
	# Right	# Wrong	Simple Errors	1 Not Yet	2 Part-Way	3 Got It
Fractions to lowest terms						
Fraction multiplication						
Fractions to mixed #						
Mixed # to fraction						
Order/compare fractions						
Fraction/mixed # addition						
Fraction/mixed # subtraction						
Mixed # multiplication						
Fraction/mixed # division						

Source: Reprinted with permission from Paula Smith, Naperville Community Unit School District 203: Naperville, IL. Unpublished classroom materials.

You can then target instruction with one of the following activities:

- Conduct small-group instruction focused on specific learning targets for students who have identified those targets as areas of need. Other students can work independently on further practice for review or further learning.

- For students needing review, offer suggestions for each learning target: "To review learning target number 1, reread pages 246 to 250 and do problems 1 and 2 on page 251."

Figure 4.7

Properties of a Circle Self-Assessment

FOR EXAMPLE

Self-Assessment Rubric			
4 – Exceeds	3 – Meets	2 – Approaching	1 – Below
I have a complete understanding of the learning target and I can apply and extend the concept to new situations.	I have a complete understanding of the learning target.	I have some understanding of the learning target.	I don't understand the learning target.

Power Standard: Understand the Properties of Circles	
Learning Target	Self-Assessment
I can use the radius to find the diameter of a circle.	
I can use the diameter to find the radius of a circle.	
I can explain the relationship between the diameter and circumference of a circle.	
I can explain why the formula, $C = \text{diameter} \times \pi$ works for finding the circumference of a circle.	
I can use the circumference to find the diameter of a circle.	
I can explain why the formula, $A = \text{radius}^2 \times \pi$ works for finding the area of a circle.	

Source: Reprinted with permission from Sue Cho and Aaron Mukai, Mukilteo School District: Everett, WA. Unpublished classroom materials.

Figure 4.7 shows a variation created by middle school mathematics teachers Sue Cho and Aaron Mukai. Here is how they describe its use and the effects on their students (personal communication, 2008):

> This self-assessment is given at the beginning of the unit along with a pre-assessment that allows students to set goals for the unit. It also helps us plan and modify lessons. Students self-assess again at the end of the unit to reflect on their progress. As a result we have noticed students are better able to understand what they know or what they need to improve. Students strive to achieve their goals by working hard

Video 4.1: Self-Assessment and Goal Setting with Target Tables

to understand the material and asking thinking questions when they are struggling. Our students are now more relaxed and confident on the summative assessments because they know what is expected of them.

High school mathematics teacher Jennifer McDaniel uses a target table (explained in Chapter 2 and illustrated in Figure 2.11) to guide her students' self-assessment and goal setting throughout a unit. Watch Video 4.1 to hear Ms. McDaniel and her students talk about how this practice helps their learning.

Human Bar Graph

In this activity, students estimate their level of mastery for each learning target and then as a class form a human bar graph to show their rankings for each learning target. Conducting the activity with a pretest at the beginning of a unit creates awareness of what will be learned. The "bar graph" also gives a sense of which learning targets may need large-group instruction or review and which may only need small-group work, keeping in mind that the results are based on student self-reporting. Begin by giving a pretest and having students self-assess using a scale such as one of those shown in the preceding section. Then have them follow these steps:

1. Each student numbers a blank piece of paper corresponding to the number of learning targets on the list (e.g., if there are five separate learning targets, they will number from one to five). Students don't put their names on this paper. It is anonymous.

2. They mark their personal rankings for each target on the numbered paper (e.g., "I gave learning target number 1 a ranking of 2—I need a little review on this. So I will write a 2 next to number 1 on my ranking sheet.").

3. When all have finished, they crumple their numbered papers into a ball about the size of a snowball, form a circle, and toss their snowballs at one another. They continue picking up and tossing snowballs until you are certain no one knows who has whose snowball (three or four rounds).

Then do the following:

*   Post the numbers 1, 2, and 3 on the wall in a space large enough for at least two-thirds of your class to line up in front of each number. (If your students used a four-point scale, post the number 4 as well.)

- Have students uncrumple their snowballs. Explain to them they will be representing the person whose snowball they have. For each learning target, they will line up in front of the ranking their person gave that target. They will begin by lining up in front of the number that matches what their snowball has for learning target 1. Count the number of students in each line or have the head of the line count and report. (You can graph this, if you like.) Read the learning target out loud.

- Repeat the process for each remaining learning target. You and the students may notice the distribution shifts one way or the other, sometimes dramatically, as they reline up for each new target.

At the end of the activity, you will have a good idea of which learning targets need the most attention, and so will your students. You can then conduct a whole-class or grouped instruction focused on the needs as identified by the lines—the "bars" on your "graph" for each target.

 Match to Content Standards

The items on a formative quiz or test should match the learning targets you are teaching. If it's not clear which learning target an item is intended to assess, rewrite the item or delete it.

Self-Assessment During an Assignment, Quiz, or Test

While students are completing any assignment that includes multiple-choice or short written response items, you can ask them to explain why they chose the answer they did. This not only gives them a chance to think more deeply about their answers, it gives you insight into misunderstandings and comprehension problems.

Format the assignment, quiz, or test so that after each selected response or fill-in item, students respond to the question, "How do you know your answer is correct?" as illustrated in Figure 4.8. When you review the assignment, quiz, or test with students, discuss common reasons for specific right and wrong choices. You can use their explanations diagnostically to determine which misconceptions to address in subsequent lessons. The information is especially useful when you will use the results of the assignment, quiz, or test formatively to guide your decisions about further instruction or to guide students in setting goals for their own learning needs.

Second-grade teacher Amy Meyer formats the assignment so that each problem begins with a statement of the learning target and has a box in the left margin next to it. While students are completing each problem, they assess their level of understanding by putting one of two symbols in the box: a star for "I think

Figure 4.8

How Do You Know Your Answer Is Correct?	**FOR EXAMPLE**

This reading comprehension question is designed to test students' ability to infer the author's purpose.

Which of the following BEST sums up the author's purpose in writing this article?

a. To explain how the sliding rocks moved.

b. To explain how scientists determined how the rocks moved.

c. To explain how to conduct your own experiments.

d. To explain why the lake bed is called the Racetrack.

How do you know your answer is correct? _____

_____

I know this" or stair steps for "I need more practice with this." Figure 4.9 shows an example of one student's work on two math problems.

Self-Assessment Using the Results of a Formative Quiz or Test

Students often take quizzes and tests without knowing what they measure beyond the most general level. If asked, they might respond that a quiz is testing reading, social studies, or science. However, with clearly identified learning targets, the corrected quiz or test itself can give students the information they need to identify which learning targets they have mastered and which ones they still need to work on. In this activity, you create a test blueprint for a quiz or test that works as a key to the learning represented by each item. After taking the quiz or test, students use the results along with the blueprint to figure out which targets require further effort. This formative assessment strategy works best if there is a later opportunity to demonstrate increased learning for the summative grade. The activity has two versions, a simpler one for elementary and a more complex one for secondary students.

Elementary Process

1. Identify which learning target each item on the quiz or test measures by filling out the first two columns of the form "Reviewing My Results" (Figure 4.10). This becomes your test blueprint.

Figure 4.9

Casey's Math

FOR EXAMPLE

Name _Casey_ # _8_ Date _9-2-08_

As you take this practice test please indicate in the box beside the learning target a symbol to show whether you think the target is a star (something you know how to do) or a stair (something you need more practice with) for you.

 I can write numbers in sequence or in order.

_42_ , 43, _44_ , 45, _46_ , _47_ , _48_

17, 18, _19_ , _20_ , _21_ , _22_ , _23_

_97_ , 98, 99, _100_ , _101_ , _102_ , _103_

I can count the value of coin combinations using quarters, dimes, nickels and pennies.

Write the value of these coins.

D, D, N, P = _26¢_

Q, N, N, P = _36¢_

Q, Q, D, N, P, P = _67¢_

Fantastic Casey! You hit all learning targets and every "bulls-eye" :)

Source: Reprinted with permission from Amy Meyer, Worthington City Schools: Worthington, OH.

Figure 4.10

Reviewing My Results

Name: _____ Assignment: _____ Date: _____

Please look at your corrected test and mark whether each problem is right or wrong. Then look at the problems you got wrong and decide if you made a mistake you can fix without help. If you did, mark the "Fixable Mistake" column. For all the remaining problems you got wrong, mark the "Don't Get It" column.

Problem	Learning Target	Right	Wrong	Fixable Mistake	Don't Get It
1					
2					
3					
4					
5					
6					
7					
8					
9					
10					

2. Administer the quiz or test, correct it, and hand it back to students, along with the form "Reviewing My Results."

3. Have students review their corrected quizzes or tests and mark the appropriate column—"Right" or "Wrong"—for each item.

4. Then have students review the items they got wrong and ask themselves, "Do I know what I did wrong? Could I correct this myself?" If the answer is "Yes," they mark the "Fixable Mistake" column. If the answer is "No," they mark the "Don't Get It" column. Now they have the raw material for determining their strengths and areas of greatest need.

5. Hand out the form "Analyzing My Results" (Figure 4.11) and have students transfer their results to one (or more) of three

Figure 4.11

Analyzing My Results

I AM GOOD AT THESE!

Learning targets I got right:

I AM PRETTY GOOD AT THESE, BUT NEED TO DO A LITTLE REVIEW

Learning targets I got wrong because of a fixable mistake:

What I can do to keep this from happening again:

I NEED TO KEEP LEARNING THESE

Learning targets I got wrong and I'm not sure what to do to correct them:

What I can do to get better at them:

categories: "I am good at these"; "I am pretty good at these, but need to do a little review"; and "I need to keep learning these." Results can go into more than one category if students demonstrate different levels of mastery for different parts of one learning target (e.g., "I'm good at adding fractions with unlike denominators when the denominators are 2 and 5, but I'm not good with other denominators").

6. Guide students to make a plan to improve. The third section of this chapter shows a variety of goal-setting frames you might choose from.

Before conducting this activity for the first time, show students the forms and explain they are going to be using the results of this quiz or test to discover what they are good at and what they still need to learn. Ask in advance what kinds of simple mistakes they might make and what they might do to keep them from happening on this assessment.

Then after the assessment when students are analyzing their results, ask them to think about strategies for avoiding any mistakes they might have made and to write down what they believe will work for them. Students can keep these forms and review them to remember what to avoid prior to taking the next assessment.

Be prepared to offer suggestions for what students can do to get better as they are listing their "Don't Get It" targets. You might want to conduct one or more small-group reviews focused on specific learning targets for students who have identified those targets as areas of need. Or, offer suggestions for each learning target.

Figure 4.12 shows a student's results for a quiz on literary elements in language arts. Lauren answered 9 of 15 problems correctly, for a score of 60%. If she were to receive a grade on this quiz, Lauren would likely get an F. How many students receive an F and think "Gee—look how much I know"? Yet Lauren's "true" score, admittedly self-reported, is an 80%, a B. There is a big difference in students' minds between those two grades, and the failing grade provides no constructive support for students who have not yet reached mastery. When we use quiz results formatively to meet students' information needs, we should dispense with the grade because it is a judgment that has come too soon. While students are still learning, it is more useful for the quiz to show them what they have mastered and what still needs work. Even students who score low, such as Lauren, have mastered a portion of the material, and it is important for them to see that. And for the problems they miss, not all represent a need for reteaching. They may be able to handle some of what needs work on their own ("Oh, I see what I did").

Let's say Lauren's teacher planned to use the quiz results to regroup for reteaching and did not ask students to analyze their results. Lauren would surely be in the reteaching group along with all other students who missed at least several problems. But what does Lauren need help with? Because her teacher is not acting on target-specific data, Lauren may get intensive reteaching on all of the learning targets, when she only needs help with metaphors. Imagine Lauren made no fixable mistakes and only missed the three she truly doesn't understand. With a raw score of 12 of 15, without target-specific data, she may not be in the reteaching group, even though she doesn't yet understand metaphors.

Figure 4.12

Literary Elements Quiz	FOR EXAMPLE

Reviewing My Results

Name: *Lauren B*   **Assignment:** *Literary elements Quiz*   **Date:** *December 10*

Please look at your corrected test and mark whether each problem is right or wrong. Then look at the problems you got wrong and decide if you made a mistake you can fix without help. If you did, mark the "Fixable Mistake" column. For all of the remaining problems you got wrong, mark the "Don't Get It" column.

Problem	Learning Target	Right	Wrong	Fixable Mistake	Don't Get It
1	Identify elements of story—plot	X			
2	Identify elements of story—setting	X			
3	Identify elements of story—characters	X			
4	Identify elements of story—characters	X			
5	Describe a character's actions based on textual evidence		X	X	
6	Describe a character's thoughts based on textual evidence		X	X	
7	Describe events based on textual evidence		X	X	
8	Recognize simple similes in context	X			
9	Recognize simple similes in context	X			
10	Recognize metaphors in context	X			
11	Recognize metaphors in context		X		X
12	Explain the meaning of simple similes in context	X			
13	Explain the meaning of simple similes in context	X			
14	Explain the meaning of simple metaphors in context		X		X
15	Explain the meaning of simple metaphors in context		X		X

Secondary Adaptations

With secondary students you can add a reflective step by having them track their level of confidence for each item while they are taking the quiz or test. The form for this adaptation doesn't tell students which learning target each item is measuring, because they are looking at the form while they are taking the quiz or test and in some cases that information will offer a clue to the correct answer. Instead of writing the learning target itself on the form, you make a separate numbered list and only write the number of the learning target next to each item number. While taking the test, students mark one of the two columns—confident or unsure—for each item after they have answered it. The vertical gray bar on the form visually separates use during the test and use after the test has been corrected.

When you hand back the corrected tests, distribute the numbered list of learning targets and have students mark the columns "Right," "Wrong," "Fixable Mistake," and "Don't Get It," just as with the elementary version. Then students analyze their results on the second page of the form, taking into account also the "Confident" and "Unsure" information they recorded while taking the quiz or test. With the secondary version, they categorize the learning targets as strengths, highest priorities for study, or in need of review. Figure 4.13 shows an example of the secondary form.

Students can develop an action plan to improve their understanding of the learning targets not yet mastered by completing a study plan, using one of the goal-setting frames described in the third section of this chapter. As with elementary students, you can conduct one or more large- or small-group reviews focused on specific learning targets and offer study suggestions for each learning target. Alternatively, students can assign themselves to study groups based on their greatest needs; you can offer suggested activities for each group to be conducted either in or outside of class.

If you are using this process with an end-of-unit test, students can submit a study plan as their ticket to a retake and take a parallel form of the test (same learning targets, different items) a few days later with the new score replacing the previous one. Or, give Form A of the test prior to the time you normally spend reviewing for a test, use the results as the basis for your and their review activities, and use Form B of the test as the summative event.

Middle school mathematics teacher Paula Smith links the pre- and post-test self-assessment activities to keep students in touch with their growth.

Figure 4.13

Reviewing and Analyzing My Results, Secondary Version

Name: _____ Assignment: _____ Date: _____

As you answer each question, decide whether you feel confident in your answer or are unsure about it and mark the corresponding box.

Problem #	Learning Target #	Confident	Unsure		Right	Wrong	Fixable Mistake	Don't Get It
1								
2								
3								
4								
5								
6								
7								
8								
9								
10								
11								
12								
13								
14								
15								
16								

ANALYZING MY RESULTS

1. After your test has been corrected, identify which problems you got right and which you got wrong by putting Xs in the "Right" and "Wrong" columns.

2. Of the problems you got wrong, decide which ones were due to mistakes you can correct yourself and mark the "Fixable Mistake" column.

3. For all of the remaining wrong answers, mark the "Don't Get It" column.

Figure 4.13 (continued)

Name: _____   Assignment: _____   Date: _____

My Strengths

To identify your areas of strength, write down the learning targets for problems you felt confident about and got right.

Learning Target #	Learning Target or Problem Description

My Highest Priority for Studying

To determine what you need to study most, write down the learning targets for problems you marked "Don't Get It" (problems you got wrong, NOT because of a fixable mistake).

Learning Target #	Learning Target or Problem Description

What I Need to Review

To determine what you need to review, write down the learning targets for problems you were unsure of and for problems on which you made mistakes you can correct yourself.

Learning Target #	Learning Target or Problem Description

Source: Chappuis, S., Stiggins, R., Arter, J., and Chappuis, J. (2006). *Assessment* FOR *Learning: An Action Guide for School Leaders*, Second Edition. Pearson Assessment Training Institute: Portland, OR.

In Figure 4.14 she explains what her students do and how it affects their learning. Figure 4.15 shows the forms she uses.

Figure 4.14

From the Classroom

Assessment for Learning Plan

What We Do

At the start of a new unit, students take a pretest. They know that this assessment is not counted as a grade and that it is normal to not know how to solve most of the problems. The test is organized by learning target. We go over the pretest together, and I briefly show how to solve one problem from each target skill so students can determine if they just made simple mistakes. This is all some students need to jog their memory or make a connection to other math skills that can help them with new material. As we correct together, they chart the results on their Assessment for Learning (AfL) plan. I guide them the first time we go through the process, but for future chapters they do the process independently. After reviewing each set of problems covering a specific target, they record the number correct and incorrect, check off if they made simple errors, and make a judgment about overall understanding by checking a thumbs up or thumbs down. Students also record their understanding of key vocabulary terms with a thumbs up or thumbs down. At the end of the analysis, they complete a plan of action for the chapter that includes various reflective questions. I collect the AfL forms and pretests to record the class results for my own use, then return them to the students. I use the results to plan differentiated lessons. This motivates students to try their hardest on the "ungraded" test because they want to be working at their learning level throughout the unit. We refer back to the AfL plans and pretest results often during the study of the unit, especially when they are preparing for their posttest. After the posttest, students repeat the process of recording results, compare them to the pretest results, and complete a reflection.

Impact on Learning

This process is quite powerful for students. It gives them clear targets and clear understanding of where they are before we start a new chapter. They have clear goals for measuring their progress. They have complete control over and responsibility for their learning. The growth students see after charting posttest results is the most motivating experience many have had as students. They are beyond proud to show off their work.

What My Students Say

Student reactions to the use of formative assessment practices in my classroom are always positive. They like knowing what they know and don't know, and they see the power of that knowledge. They confess often how they never have been good at math before and how they

Figure 4.14 (continued)

never liked math before. But now because they see their growth, they see proof that they can do well in math and that makes them like it. Student reflections often include comments about how their confidence has increased and how proud they are of themselves. They also say that they see how things connect and how holes in learning affect overall understanding. They are not bored because they don't have to do busy work when they understand something. One of the biggest differences for them is that they are more confident when they take assessments. They realize that the grade on the test isn't the important thing to take away from a test: It's the learning and growth as a math student.

Source: Reprinted with permission from Paula Smith, Naperville Community Unit School District 203, Naperville, IL.

Video 4.2: Self-Assessment and Goal Setting with Test Corrections

High school teacher Jennifer McDaniel uses a variation of this activity with her AP Calculus students. She returns the test with the problems students missed marked on the form shown in Figure 4.16. For each problem they missed, students determine the reason and check the appropriate column: Simple mistake, Guessed, or Misconception. Then, for each of the wrong answers, students complete a test corrections form with three columns: What I did, What I should have done, and What I used to think . . . but now I know. . . . Figure 4.17 shows an example of a completed test correction form. Watch Video 4.2 to hear Ms. McDaniel and her students talking about test corrections and their impact on learning.

Self-Assessment with Rubrics

The following strategies are designed for use when students are working on reasoning, skill, or product targets and demonstrating their achievement via assessment tasks evaluated by scoring rubrics. There are a number of ways to make self-assessing with a rubric work well, but you first need to make sure that you have a suitable rubric as described in Chapter 2. And then, students should have practiced using the rubric to evaluate anonymous samples (Strategy 2) and had experience receiving feedback based on the rubric (Strategy 3).

⚠ Rubric Prerequisites

The effectiveness of self-assessing and goal setting with a rubric hinges on its structure, content, and language and on students' familiarity with it.

Ways to Format Rubric Text

The words of your rubric describe quality, but you can also make the meaning resonate with students

Figure 4.15

Linear Equations & Functions AfL Plan

Name: _____

Linear Equations & Functions
AfL Plan

Chapter 3 Targets:

- I will write algebraic expressions & equations from sentences.
- I will solve addition, subtraction, & multiplication equations.
- I will graph data to demonstrate relationships.
- I will solve 2-step equations.
- I will find areas & perimeters of figures.
- I will use the *work backwards* strategy to solve problems.

Lesson Targets	Pre-Assessment Results							Extra Help	Post-Assessment Results					
	Problem #s	Total #	# Right	# Wrong	Simple Errors?	👎	👍		Problem #s	Total #	# Right	# Wrong	Simple Errors?	👎	👍
3.1: Expressions & Equations	#1-4	4						p. 674							
3.2: Equations: Add, Subtract	#5-7	3						p. 674							
3.3: Equations: Multiply	#8-10	3						p. 674							
3.4: Work Backwards	#11	1						p. 674							
3.5: 2-Step Equations	#12-14	3						p. 675							
3.6: Perimeter	#15,16	2						p. 675							
3.6: Area	#17,18	2						p. 675							
3.7: Functions & Graphs	#19-22	4						p. 676							

Figure 4.15 (continued)

Pre-Assessment: Plan of Action

1. What is your specific learning target (weakness)?

2. What are two things you will make sure you do during the study of Ch. 3?

3. Who can help you along the way? When?

4. Will you prepare for your Ch3 test the same way you prepared for Ch2 test? Why or why not?

I am feeling _____

I promise I will _____

Post-Assessment: Reflection

1. How did you prepare for this test? Did you follow your *Plan of Action?*

2. Did you reach your target?

3. What would you do differently?

I learned _____

I was surprised _____

Vocabulary	Pre-			Post-		
formula						
equation						
linear equation						
two-step equation						
work backward strategy						
perimeter						
area						
variable						
inverse						
zero pair						
expression						
coefficient						
algebraic equation						
division prop. of equality						

PRE: Parent signature _____

POST: Parent signature _____

Test Grade: _____

Comments:

Source: Reprinted with permission from Paula Smith, Naperville Community Unit School District 203: Naperville, IL. Unpublished classroom materials.

Figure 4.16

Test Reflections and Corrections — FOR EXAMPLE

AP Calculus Test Reflections and Corrections: Implicit Differentiation

Learning Target	Question Numbers	Simple Mistakes	Guess	Misconceptions
I can use implicit differentiation to find the derivative of a function.	1 2 3 4 5			
I can find dy/dx by implicit differentiation and evaluate the derivative at the indicated point.	6 7			
I can find the 2nd derivative in terms of x and y using implicit differentiation.	8 9 10			
I can find equations for the tangent and normal line to the graph at the indicated point.	11			
I can find dy/dx using both implicit and explicit methods and evaluate at a given point.	13 14			
Open Response: I can use implicit differentiation to find the derivative of a function. I can find a point P which the line tangent to the curve at P is horizontal.	14			

Test Corrections

What I did	What I should have done	What I used to think. . . but now I know. . .

Figure 4.17

Student Test Corrections

What I did	What I should have done	Explain it
4) $\int \frac{3}{x}\,dx$ $u=x$ $du=1$ $\int 3\,u^{-1}$	4) $\int \frac{3}{x}\,dx$ $3\ln|x| + c$	I didn't realize the integral was a direct match to $\int \frac{1}{u}\,du$ and tried to solve the problem by finding my u and du
5) $\int \frac{2}{(3x)^3}\,dy$ $u=3x$ $du=3$ $\frac{1}{3}u^{-3}$ $\frac{1}{3}\cdot-\frac{1}{2}$ $-\frac{1}{6}(3x)^{-2}+c$ $\frac{-1}{6(3x)^2}+c$	5) $\int \frac{2}{(3x)^3}\,dx$ $\int \frac{2x^{-3}}{27}$ $\frac{2x^{-2}}{27\cdot-2} = \frac{x^{-2}}{27}-54$	when I was trying to solve the integral the first time I didn't distribute causing me to miss the problem.
10) $y=x^3-1$ from -2 to 2 $\frac{x^4}{4}-x\Big|_{-2}^{2}$ $\left(\frac{2^4}{4}-2\right)-\left(\frac{-2^4}{4}+2\right)$ $2 \quad -4$ $\frac{-4}{4}$ 6	10) $y=x^3-1$ from -2 to 2 $\int_{-2}^{1}x^3-1\,dx + \int_{1}^{2}x^3-1\,dx$ $\frac{x^4}{4}-x \;+\; \frac{x^4}{4}-x$ $\left(\frac{1^4}{4}-1\right)-\left(\frac{-2^4}{4}+2\right) + \left(\frac{2^4}{4}-2\right)-\left(\frac{1^4}{4}-1\right)$ $\left(\frac{7}{4}-6\right) \;+\; (2) \;-\;\left(-\frac{3}{4}\right)$ $\frac{-17}{4} \qquad \frac{25}{4}$ $= 4$	when I first solved this problem it didn't divide it up into 2 parts. And since it is an area problem this caused me to miss the answer.

176

by formatting the concepts as a checklist or by plotting the phrases on a diagram or drawing.

1. **Developmental Continua.** With younger students, where developmental continua phrases are often suited to self-assessment, you can write selected phrases on the "Stars and Stairs" form (Figure 4.18), under the labels, "Just beginning," "On my way," and "Success!" Students can use the form to document progress on individual learning targets represented in the rubric by identifying what in their work matches the rubric steps.

First-grade teacher Melissa Vernon has converted a writing rubric into a developmental continuum that students use as the basis for peer feedback and

Figure 4.18

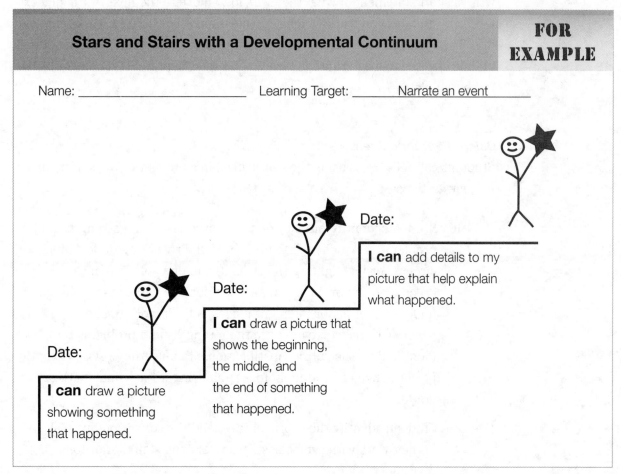

Video 4.3: Peer Feedback
and Self-Assessment:
Grade 1

self-assessment. In Video 4.3, Ms. Vernon's students engage in this activity and talk about the rubric.

2. **Checklist.** As a class, you and your students can convert a rubric into a checklist of descriptive phrases for them to use to look over their work in advance of turning it in. Make sure the phrases on the checklist describe important elements of quality. Figure 4.19 shows an example of a writing checklist for elementary students, derived from the "6+1 Trait™ Writing Assessment Scoring Guide." You can also convert the rubric into a checklist yourself. If students are familiar with the rubric, they will understand the checklist.

3. **Diagram.** Another strategy is to plot the phrases from your rubric on a diagram, such as the example in Figure 4.20. Students can mark or highlight the level that best describes the quality of their current work sample and then write a short statement of what they will do to move to the next or the highest level. Or, students can mark which ring they think their current work sample hits. They can continue to mark and date the same form throughout the period of time devoted to mastering the target. (See the Chapter 4 DVD file for blank target templates.)

Using the Rubric Itself

Students can self-assess using the rubric itself in a number of ways. Here are four suggestions:

1. Students identify phrases on the rubric describing strengths and problems they believe are present in their work by underlining, circling, or highlighting the strengths in one color, such as green, and the problems in another, such as yellow. Next, they underline, circle, or highlight places in their work to show which features correspond to the strengths and problems they identified on the rubric (justification). Finally, they revise their performance or product before submitting it for a final mark or grade.

2. Students identify the rubric phrases and the corresponding places in their work with symbols, such as stars and stairs, prior to revising.

3. Students write the rubric phrase they believe describes a characteristic of their work, followed by a short description of

Figure 4.19

Self-Check for a Story

Ideas and Content

_____ Is my message clear?

_____ Did I stick to one topic?

_____ Did I include details that are interesting and important?

Organization

_____ Does my story have an inviting introduction?

_____ Did I tell things in the best order?

_____ Does my story have a satisfying ending?

Voice

_____ Does this writing sound like me?

_____ Did I say what I think and feel?

_____ Can the reader tell I am interested in my story?

Word Choice

_____ Did I use words I love?

_____ Do my words make sense?

_____ Did I try not to repeat words too many times?

_____ Do my words paint a clear picture?

Sentence Fluency

_____ Are my sentences easy to read out loud?

_____ Do my sentences begin in different ways?

_____ Are some sentences long and some short?

Conventions

_____ Did I show where each paragraph starts?

_____ Did I look up the spelling of words I am not sure of?

_____ Did I use capital letters in the right places?

_____ Did I punctuate dialogue correctly?

_____ Did I use end punctuation (periods, exclamation marks, question marks) correctly?

Figure 4.20

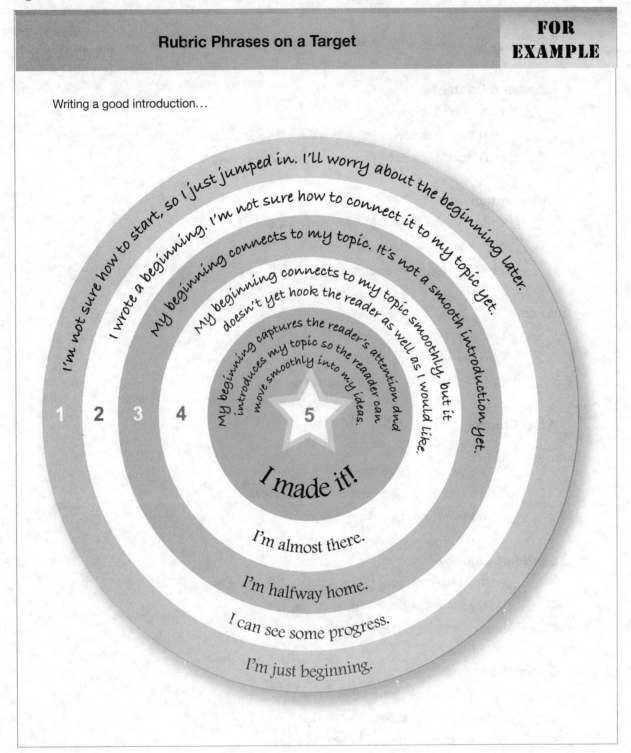

Rubric Phrases on a Target

FOR EXAMPLE

Writing a good introduction…

I'm not sure how to start, so I just jumped in. I'll worry about the beginning later.

I wrote a beginning. I'm not sure how to connect it to my topic yet.

My beginning connects to my topic. It's not a smooth introduction yet.

My beginning connects to my topic smoothly, but it doesn't yet hook the reader as well as I would like.

My beginning captures the reader's attention and introduces my topic so the reader can move smoothly into my ideas.

1 2 3 4 5

I made it!

I'm almost there.

I'm halfway home.

I can see some progress.

I'm just beginning.

the feature in their work that supports their judgment. It can be a strength, a problem, or a combination of both. In the example in Figure 4.21, a student has decided his social studies essay's thesis statement is strong and has copied phrases from a rubric for social studies essays that he believes describe the qualities present in his thesis statement. His next step is *justification*, where he will write down the phrases in his thesis statement that illustrate each feature of quality he is claiming is present.

Figure 4.21

Self-Assessment with Justification	FOR EXAMPLE

Name: *Brad Smith* Date: *Nov. 20*

Criterion: *Clear, analytical, and comprehensive thesis*

My rating: *Strong*

Rubric phrase that describes my work	Feature of my work that illustrates the phrase
Focuses on one specific aspect of the subject	
Makes an assertion that can be argued	
Covers only what I will address in my essay	

Teacher Laura Grayson has her second-grade students complete exit tickets (Figure 4.22) to develop the skill and habit of self-assessment. Here is what she has noticed happening with her students as a result (personal communication, 2008):

> The prompting questions on the exit ticket allow students the opportunity to self-assess prior to our writing conference. Students come to their conferences with an understanding of how they used the particular part of speech in their writing as well as a personal evaluation

181

Figure 4.22

Writing Exit Ticket	FOR EXAMPLE

Name: A lly _____ Date: 6 - 17

Writing Exit Ticket: Nouns

In your own words, give a definition of a noun.

A noun is

a person, Place, or thing

Choose and list several of the strongest nouns that you used in your writing.

apple, pie, sider, Juice,

Evaluate yourself. How did you do in using nouns in your writing?

I tink I cold of usd more

Source: Used with permission from Laura Grayson, Mehlville School District: St Louis, MO.

of whether it helped make the piece stronger. Students have become aware of nuances in their own writing, such as a strong or weak lead, that in the past I have had to point out to them. Students now make adjustments in their own writing and are eager to share how they have improved it.

High school science teacher Stephanie Harmon (personal communication, 2013) has been able to track the impact of feedback and self-assessment on students that she has had as ninth-graders when they return to her as eleventh-graders. She has established a learning culture with these practices:

From year to year my teaching load changes so some years I have mostly 9th grade students and other years I have mostly 11th grade students.

I am finding that students who return to me in 11th grade excel in the class because they understand what it means to self-assess and to use feedback to direct their effort to achieving the learning targets. This has enabled me to do things I've never had time to do in the past because they come into the classroom as owners of their learning instead of me spending time teaching them how to do this. This year has been particularly powerful as the enthusiasm from returning students rubs off on students who are new to me. I am excited with what they are doing.

Goals and Plans to Achieve Them

Self-assessment forges a commitment to continued learning, and goal setting maps out a path of next steps to sustain the commitment. However, if called on to use assessment results to set goals, without more specific understanding of what learning the assessment represents, students tend to set the most general of goals: "study more," "take my book home," "try harder," "do better." Although noble, these goals don't focus on what students actually need to learn and therefore are of limited use in forming an action plan.

> "A goal is the object or aim of an action, for example, to attain a specific standard of proficiency, usually within a specified time limit."
>
> *Locke & Latham, 2002, p. 705*

Goals that have the greatest impact on performance are what are called *hard goals*: specific rather than vague and challenging rather than easy. Hard goals require students to move beyond their current level of achievement in some significant way (Sadler, 1989). Hattie (2009) summarized the effectiveness of hard goals this way:

> A major reason difficult goals are more effective is that they lead to a clearer notion of success and direct the student's attention to relevant behaviors or outcomes. It is not the specificity of the goals but the difficulty that is crucial to success. There is a direct linear relationship between the degree of difficulty and performance. . . . The performances of students who have the most challenging goals are over 250 percent higher than the performances of the subjects with the easiest goals (Wood & Locke, 1997). (p. 164)

In a summary of 35 years of research on goal-setting theory drawn from the field of organizational psychology, Locke and Latham (2002) found that the specific and challenging goals

> led to higher performance than urging people to do their best. The effect sizes in meta-analyses ranged from .40 to .80 (Locke & Latham, 1990).

"Hard goals work to focus attention, mobilize effort, and increase persistence at a task. By contrast, do-one's-best goals often turn out to be not much more effective than no goals at all."

Sadler, 1989, p. 129

In short when people are asked to do their best, they do not do so. This is because do-your-best goals have no external referent and thus are defined idiosyncratically. This allows for a wide range of acceptable performance levels, which is not the case when a goal level is specified. (p. 706)

According to Locke and Latham (2002, pp. 706–707), specific and challenging goals increase achievement through four mechanisms:

1. They focus attention on activities that will lead to accomplishment of the goal and divert attention from irrelevant activities.

2. They have an "energizing function," triggering greater effort than low-challenge goals.

3. They prolong effort. People with challenging goals demonstrate greater levels of persistence.

4. They cause people to tap into knowledge and strategies they already have and also to look for ways to increase their knowledge and strategy repertoire to accomplish the goal.

Locke and Latham (1990) also explained how feedback can work to support goal attainment. Appropriately difficult goals help students "direct and evaluate their actions and efforts accordingly. Feedback allows them to set reasonable goals and to track their performance in relation to their goals so that adjustments in effort, direction, and even strategy can be made as needed" (p. 23).

Accurate Information

Effective goals rely on accurate gap analysis, so it is important that the information students receive is an accurate representation of their current status relative to the desired learning.

Students won't necessarily engage in goal setting after self-assessment when they have achieved mastery or when no further work will be done on a set of learning targets. But when they have an opportunity to improve after self-assessing, it makes sense to ask them to set goals and create plans for actions they will take. They can base their goals on assessment results, on feedback from you or from peers, on self-assessed areas of need, or on some combination of these sources of information.

Helping Students Create Goals and Plans

The elements of effective goals mirror the three questions that structure the seven strategies of formative assessment: Where am I going? Where am I now?

Figure 4.23

Creating Specific and Challenging Goals

Specific and challenging goals include the following key elements:

- A clear statement of the intended learning: "What do I need to learn?"
- A description of current status: "Where am I now with respect to my goal?"
- An action plan:

  — "What steps will I take?"

  — "When will I do this?"

  — "Where will I work?"

  — "Who can I work with? What materials will I need?"

  — "What will I use as my 'before' and 'after' pictures?"

How can I close the gap? As summarized in Figure 4.23, effective goals identify the intended learning, describe the current status, and outline a plan of action. The plan includes a description of what the student will do, a time frame, a physical location, determination of assistance (if any) and materials needed, and identification of what evidence the student will use to verify accomplishment. The age of your students and the complexity of the learning will guide which of these features you ask students to include in their action plans.

If the time frame for goal accomplishment is lengthy, it can help to build a feedback loop into the plan. A feedback loop is essentially a way for students to know how they are doing in progressing toward their goals. It functions as a course verification or correction, giving students the opportunity to adjust their level of effort or the strategies they are using, if needed. Some students will need external feedback, and others will be able to self-monitor at this stage.

Increasing Persistence in Goal Attainment

The act of specifying *when* and *where* a person will accomplish a goal may be instrumental to follow-through. In one study described by social psychologist Heidi Grant Halvorson (2012), a researcher stopped college students on their way to final exams before winter break and asked if they would be willing to participate in a study of how people spend their holidays. Those who agreed to participate were to write an essay describing in detail how they spent their time on Christmas Day and mail it in by December 27. Half the students were also asked to write down when and where they would write the essay and give the paper to the researcher on the spot. The other half of the students were not asked to make a plan. Of the group that made the *when* and *where* plan, 71% sent back their essays. Of the group without the plan, 32% submitted their essays. The act of determining when and where doubled the chance that these participants would carry through with the intention. Grant Halvorson subsequently tested the impact of intentional planning with a group of 10th-graders who intended to study for the fall PSAT over the summer. All students were given a book of PSAT practice tests in May. Half the students were asked to make a plan for when and where they would work on the practice problems, while the other half were not. As in the previous study, the planners handed their plans to the researcher immediately after writing them. When all students submitted their practice test booklets at the end of the summer, the planners had completed an average of 250 problems, whereas the non-planners completed an average of 100 problems. In this study, the act of determining where and when more than doubled the amount of work participants did.

> ⚠️ **Challenging Goals**
>
> To help students with the "challenging" part of the goal requirement, make sure they are selecting learning targets at the appropriate challenge level—difficult but within reach with effort.

These two studies illustrate what is called *if-then* planning, a strategy that has been repeatedly shown to increase rate of goal attainment in a range of circumstances from wellness goals to achievement goals to personal improvement goals (Gollwitzer & Sheeran, 2006). To apply *if-then* planning to a classroom context, students first identify how, when, and where they will accomplish their goal and then write it or verbalize it in an if-then frame. For example, the student with the goal of doing 10 pushups (Figure 4.24) would say "If it is *6:00 a.m.*, then I will *do pushups in my bedroom.* If it is *7:00 p.m.*, then I will *do pushups in my bedroom.*"

Grant Halvorson (2012) explained the mechanism behind the effectiveness of this frame as follows:

> An amazing thing happens in your brain when you decide when and where you will act on your goal. The act of planning creates a link between the situation or cue (the *if*) and the behavior that should follow (the *when*). Let's say your mother has been giving you a hard time about not keeping in touch, so you set yourself a goal to call mom once a week. After a while, you find that despite your genuine desire to be better about calling, you just keep forgetting to do it. Mom is getting madder by the minute. So you make an *if-then* plan: If it is *Sunday*

Figure 4.24

Status, Target, Plan	FOR EXAMPLE

Status: Right now I can *do 2 pushups*

Target: My goal is to *do 10 pushups* by *2 weeks*

Plan: To reach my goal I will *do 2 pushups morning & night for 2 days. Then 2 sets of 3 pushups morning & night for 2 days. Then 2 sets of 4 pushups morning & night for 2 days. Then 2 sets of 6 pushups morning & night for 2 days. Last 2 sets of 8 push-ups morning & night for 2 days.*

I will get help from *me myself and I*

after dinner, then I will *phone Mom*. Now the situation "Sunday after dinner" is wired in your brain directly to the action "phone Mom." (pp. 178–179)

Research on the impact of specific and challenging goals in the workplace has shown that these types of goals can accomplish changes in behavior, such as reducing absenteeism (Locke & Latham, 2002). In the classroom we can go beyond academic achievement targets and use the same goal and plan process to help students change behaviors interfering with their success, involving attendance, timeliness, appropriate self-control, work habits, and the like.

Carrying out goal intentions requires belief that they are reachable, commitment to attain them, and practical steps to direct effort.

Goal and Plan Frames

For some learning targets, you can use a framework such as "Status, Target, Plan" to guide goal setting. It asks students to begin with *status*—a statement of where they are right now, followed by *target*—a statement of where they're headed, and last, *plan*—a description of how they'll get there. Figure 4.24 illustrates this sequence with a physical education goal. Or you can use a frame that follows the Where am I going?, Where am I now?, and How can I close the gap?

Figure 4.25

High School Health Goal and Plan	**FOR EXAMPLE**

Name: *John Jurjevich*   Date: *Feb. 20*

Learning target: *Explain how the immune system works*
Current level of achievement: *don't understand how a neutrophil works to fight infection* Evidence: *quiz on communicable diseases 2/19*
What I need to learn: *to explain what a neutrophil does at three stages: chemo-taxis, phagocytosis, and apoptosis*
What I will do: *study the pages on pathogens and the immune system in the book and practice drawing the life cycle of a neutrophil, with all stages explained*
When & where: *Mon + Tues night starting at 8 in my room*
Help needed—what and who: *book + me*
Evidence of achieving my goal: *Test 2/26*

Source: Chappuis, J.; Stiggins, R. J.; Chappuis, S.; Arter, J. A., *Classroom Assessment for Student Learning: Doing It Right – Using It Well,* 2nd Ed., ©2012. Reproduced by permission of Pearson Education, Inc.: Upper Saddle River, NJ.

format such as the example in Figure 4.25 for a high school student's goal and plan in health class.

Figure 4.26 shows a variety of frames that illustrate different ways to elicit information about what, how, when, and where from students. In preparation for using a planning frame, you may want to model how to think through each step so students can see how to set goals that relate directly to the learning they are to accomplish and how to create a doable plan that will get them where they want to go. The Chapter 4 DVD file has editable forms of all the self-assessment and goal-setting frames in this chapter.

Helping Students Create a Study Plan

Prior to the end-of-the-unit summative test, middle school mathematics teacher Paula Smith (personal communication, 2013) gives her students a practice test as homework. They correct it in class and then use a study plan

Figure 4.26

Self-Assessment and Goal-Setting Frames

#1

Where Am I Going?	
My goal:	
Where Am I Now?	
What I can already do:	What I need to work on:
How Will I Close the Gap?	
What I will do:	
When I will do it:	
Where I will do it:	
With help from:	
Using these materials:	

#2

Complete this portion at the beginning of an assignment	
Assignment:	Date:
Learning target I am working on:	
Complete this portion after you look at corrections/feedback on your assignment	
Strengths:	
What to improve:	

Figure 4.26 (continued)

#3

Correcting Mistakes	
Learning Target:	
Mistake I made:	Correction:
Mistake I made:	Correction:
Mistake I made:	Correction:

#4

Next Steps
Next steps for my work:
☐ Get feedback from teacher
☐ Get feedback from another student: _____
☐ Self-assess
☐ Revise: _____
☐ Turn in for a grade

⚠ Concrete Targets

Make sure the learning target statements students are setting goals to attain are written as concrete learning targets and not as global or complex content standards.

form shown in Figure 4.27 to determine which learning targets they still need to study and to note the actions they will take to master them prior to the test. She provides them with a list of resources for each learning target—pages in their study guide, online quizzes, and online games—and encourages them to be specific in their plans about the resources they will use. She describes the effect on students as follows:

> Because students help determine their own individualized study plans, they learn valuable lessons on effective ways to study that they can use throughout their careers as students. The task of studying is streamlined to fit their needs so it is not overwhelming or seen as a waste of time. With clear targets in mind, knowledge of their particular weaknesses, and a specific plan, they use their time to study effectively and efficiently. It results in higher levels of understanding and greater achievement.

Figure 4.27

Study Plan	FOR EXAMPLE

Study Plan 3.5–3.7, 5.6 and Inequalities

Name: _____

Parents: Please help your child study and review for the upcoming test by allowing time for the quizzes to be taken at home. Your child will communicate progress, goals, and plans as he/she studies and will benefit from your support and guidance. ☺

Step 1: After reviewing the results of the practice test, you circled the sections below that gave you trouble. Study and practice the circled skills using your pre-assessment, corrected homework, guided notes, and textbook.

3.5   3.6   3.7   5.6

Step 2: Complete the sections in the study guide that correspond to the circled sections. Check your answers using the answer key on the back of this page.

Step 3: Complete the online quizzes. Make and follow a specific study plan if you earn below 80% on a quiz.

Self-Check Quiz	Result %	👍	👎	Next steps . . .	✓
3.5: Solve 2-Step Equations					
3.6: Perimeter and Area					
3.7: Functions and Graphs					
5.6: Multiplicative Inverse					

Step 4: Play some games! Go to Homework Hotline and check out the links to Math Review Games!

Parent signature: _____

Comments:

Source: Reprinted with permission from Paula Smith, Naperville Community Unit School District 203: Naperville, IL. Unpublished classroom materials.

The Goal and Plan Conference

Some students may need individual assistance in completing a frame even after you have modeled the thinking they are to do. For those students, select the frame you want them to use, then meet with them individually or in small groups, using the following protocol to help them think through creating goals and plans. Students can also use the protocol to work with partners to help each other set goals and create plans.

1. Begin by sharing the intended learning in terms they understand. ("Here's what we're working on being able to do.")

2. Next, look together at work they have produced to determine what they already know. Guide them in the formulation of a goal statement regarding what they need to learn.

3. Ask them to describe *how* they might go about accomplishing their goal. Help them identify reasonable actions likely to result in maximum learning, if needed. Have them write down the actions they will take. Also help them identify *when* and *where* they will do the work.

4. Help them determine whether they will need or want assistance from another person and what materials, if any, they will need.

5. Set a time frame for goal attainment, or ask them to identify a completion date. Build a feedback loop into the time frame, if it will help students stay on track for a goal spanning more than a few days. A feedback loop is essentially a check point where you offer feedback regarding progress toward the goal and coach them in adjusting effort or strategies as needed. When students are ready for it, this can be a self-monitored check point, rather than one led by you.

6. Help them identify what artifact(s) they will use as evidence of *meeting* their goal.

Conclusion

Meaningful student self-assessment and goal setting require beginning with clear targets. Beyond that, students need practice with comparing their current status to the targets, justifying their judgments with evidence from their work, and setting specific goals that guide subsequent actions.

When we teach students to self-assess and plan next steps with these conditions in place, they can do it accurately. Indeed, they are often harder on themselves than we would be. If you think back through the activities in this chapter, you'll notice that when students self-assess, they uncover a gold mine of information about what they know and what they need, assessment for learning data that you did not have to create an extra assignment, task, quiz, or test to obtain. Self-assessment and goal-setting activities yield information you can use to group students, to assign partners, to reteach, to dig deeper into understanding, and to enrich their learning. In addition, these activities develop a stronger sense of self-efficacy in students by providing them the information they need to become self-directed learners.

Understanding and Applying the Content of Chapter 4

End-of-chapter activities are intended to help you master the chapter's learning targets and apply concepts to your classroom. They are designed to deepen your understanding of the chapter content, provide discussion topics for collaborative learning, and guide implementation of the content and practices taught in the chapter. Forms and materials for completing each activity appear in editable Microsoft Word format in the Chapter 4 DVD file. Each form needed for an activity is listed after the activity directions and marked with this symbol:

Chapter 4 Learning Targets

1. Understand the impact of self-assessment and goal setting on student motivation and achievement
2. Understand the conditions that maximize the impact of self-assessment and goal setting
3. Know how to teach students to self-assess accurately with a focus on learning targets
4. Know how to prepare students to create specific and challenging goals

Chapter 4 Activities

Discussion Questions (All learning targets)

Activity 4.1 Keeping a Reflective Journal (All learning targets)

Activity 4.2 Determining Readiness to Self-Assess (Learning targets 1 and 2)

Activity 4.3 Selecting a Quick Self-Assessment Activity (Learning targets 2 and 3)

Activity 4.4 Selecting a Self-Assessment Activity for Use with a Selected Response or Written Response Quiz or Test (Learning targets 2 and 3)

Activity 4.5 Preparing a Selected Response Quiz or Practice Test for Use as Self-Assessment (Learning targets 2 and 3)

Activity 4.6 Using Rubrics for Self-Assessment (Learning targets 2 and 3)

Activity 4.7 Selecting and Modifying Goal and Plan Frames (Learning targets 2 and 4)

Activity 4.8 Selecting a Strategy 4 Application (All learning targets)

Activity 4.9 Adding to Your Growth Portfolio (All learning targets)

Chapter 4 Discussion Questions

Discussion questions are also explored in depth in the activities listed in parentheses.

Questions to Discuss Before Reading Chapter 4

1. Self-assessment and goal setting take time. Why might you ask students to do it? (Activities 4.1, 4.8, and 4.9)

2. What do students need to know and be able to do in order to self-assess accurately? (Activity 4.2)

3. What problems do students encounter when setting goals and making plans intended to lead to improvement? (Activity 4.2)

Questions to Discuss After Reading Chapter 4

4. What do you think causes self-assessment to improve achievement? (Activities 4.1, 4.8, and 4.9)

5. Which of the quick self-assessment options might you use? At what points in the unit/ marking period? (Activity 4.3)

6. Which of the self-assessment ideas for use with selected response and written response tasks might you try? At what points in the unit/marking period? (Activities 4.4 and 4.5)

7. Which of the self-assessment ideas for use with rubrics might you try? At what points in the unit/marking period? (Activity 4.6)

8. Which of the goal and plan options might you try? At what points in the unit/marking period? (Activity 4.7)

9. What activities from Chapter 4 did you try in the classroom? How did they work? What successes did you notice? What modifications might you make? (Activity 4.8)

Activity 4.1

Keeping a Reflective Journal

This is intended as an independent activity. If you choose to do it, you may want to discuss the thoughts you record with your learning team.

Keep a record of your thoughts, questions, and any implementation activities you tried while reading Chapter 4.

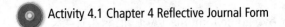 Activity 4.1 Chapter 4 Reflective Journal Form

Activity 4.2

Determining Readiness to Self-Assess

This is intended as an independent activity. If you do it independently, you may want to discuss the results with your learning team. A form for this activity can be found on the DVD.

1. Use this simple yes-no checklist before engaging students in self-assessment to determine whether they are ready to do it.

Self-Assessment Readiness Part 1

☐ Yes ☐ No Does the student have a clear vision of quality (what's expected)?

☐ Yes ☐ No Can the student describe the intended learning?

☐ Yes ☐ No Can the student differentiate between strong and weak examples and/or levels of quality?

☐ Yes ☐ No Has the student practiced using the language of quality to describe attributes of strong and weak examples?

Self-Assessment Readiness Part 2

☐ Yes ☐ No Has the student had experience giving and offering feedback?

☐ Yes ☐ No Has the student received descriptive feedback using the language of quality, with opportunity to act on it?

☐ Yes ☐ No Has the student practiced offering peer feedback using the language of quality?

2. If the answer to one or more of the questions from Part 1 is "no," then you may want to revisit some of the activities described in Chapter 2 before proceeding.

3. If the answer to one or more of the questions from Part 2 is "no," then you may want to revisit some of the activities described in Chapter 3 before proceeding.

4. Once you have asked students to try self-assessing, if some of them have trouble knowing what to write, you can use this checklist as a guide to determine what intervention is most likely to help them.

 Activity 4.2 Determining Readiness to Self-Assess

Activity 4.3

Selecting a Quick Self-Assessment Activity

This is an independent activity, followed by a learning team discussion.

1. Try one of the options explained in the section titled "Ten Quick Self-Assessment Ideas" with a class.

2. As students are engaged in the activity, walk around the room to look and listen for successes and problems they encounter. Record your observations.

3. Meet with your team to share the option you tried, the successes you noticed, and any problems or glitches your students encountered.

4. Discuss ways to solve the problems or remedy the glitches. You may want to refer to the self-assessment readiness checklists in Activity 4.2 for possible next steps if your students experienced difficulty.

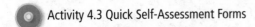 Activity 4.3 Quick Self-Assessment Forms

Activity 4.4

Selecting a Self-Assessment Activity for Use with a Selected Response or Written Response Quiz or Test

This is an independent activity, followed by a learning team discussion.

1. Try one of the options explained in the section "Self-Assessment and Goal Setting with Selected Response and Written Response Tasks" with a class.

2. As students are engaged in self-assessment, walk around the room to look and listen for successes and problems they encounter. Record your observations.

3. Meet with your team to share the option you tried, the successes you noticed, and any problems or glitches your students encountered.

4. Discuss ways to solve the problems or remedy the glitches. You may want to refer to the self-assessment readiness checklists in Activity 4.2 for possible next steps if your students experienced difficulty.

Activity 4.5

Preparing a Selected Response Quiz or Practice Test for Use as Self-Assessment

This is intended as an independent activity. If your learning team teaches the same subjects and grades, you may want to do this activity with a partner or as a team. Three forms for this activity can be found on the DVD.

1. After reading the section titled "Self-Assessment and Goal Setting with Selected Response and Written Response Tasks," find a selected response or short answer written response assignment, quiz, or test that you have used or will use.

2. Identify the learning target that each item on the task addresses. Make a test blueprint like the one below to record your analysis. (Form is on DVD.)

Item #	Learning Target Addressed
1.	
2.	
3.	

3. Determine when you want students to use the results to self-assess and set goals: before the learning, during the learning, or as a review prior to a summative test. Check the items on the task to be sure you have an adequate representative sample for your intended purpose. For more information on ensuring an adequate sample, see Chappuis et al. (2012), pp. 107–112, 126–128, 172–174, and 208–209.

4. Decide whether you want to leave the items on the task in their current order or regroup them according to the learning target each addresses. Discuss with your partner or team the relative advantages and disadvantages of each option.

5. Create a form for students to use to review and analyze their assignment, quiz, or practice test results. Select one of the examples in Chapter 4 to use or modify, or make your own. (Forms are on the DVD.)

6. Have students use the form to interpret the assignment, quiz, or practice test results and set goals for their next steps, following the guidelines in Chapter 4.

7. Bring a few samples of completed forms to your next team meeting to share. If some students were more successful than others with this activity, bring a sample of successful and unsuccessful student attempts. Discuss possible revisions to the process or the form to make it work well for all students. Also consider the questions on the Self-Assessment Readiness Part 1 in Activity 4.2 to determine if more work with Chapter 2 activities might help.

Activity 4.5a Test Blueprint Form   Activity 4.5b Reviewing and Analyzing My Results (Elementary)

Activity 4.5c Reviewing and Analyzing My Results (Secondary)

Activity 4.6

Using Rubrics for Self-Assessment

This is intended as an individual or partner activity, followed by a learning team discussion.

1. After reading the section titled "Self-Assessment with Rubrics," identify a rubric you use that is suited to formative use by students.

2. Select one of the options described, either for formatting rubric text or for using the rubric itself. Prepare the materials needed and have your students engage in self-assessment.

3. Keep track of successes and problems, if any, students had.

4. Bring a sample of the materials students used and their self-assessments to your next learning team meeting. If some students were more successful than others with this activity, bring a sample of successful and unsuccessful student attempts. Discuss possible revisions to the process or the form to make it work well for all students. For self-assessment problems, consider the questions on Self-Assessment Readiness Part 1 in Activity 4.2 to determine if more work with Chapter 2 activities might help.

Activity 4.7

Selecting and Modifying Goal and Plan Frames

This is designed as a partner or learning team activity. A form for this activity can be found on the DVD.

1. After reading the section titled "Goals and Plans to Achieve Them," look over the examples in Figures 4.23 through 4.27. With a partner or your learning team, identify one or more that could be used in your context (grade, subject, learning targets) to help students set learning goals and create workable plans to attain them.

2. Select or modify one of the frames and make a plan to use it by deciding the following:
   - Which unit of study you will use it with
   - What learning target(s) will be the focus of students' goals and plans
   - When students will self-assess and set goals—before or during instruction

3. Have students use the frame. Bring a few samples of completed frames to your next team meeting to share. If some students were more successful than others with this activity, bring a sample of successful and unsuccessful student attempts. Discuss possible revisions to the process or the form to make it work well for all students. For self-assessment problems, consider the questions on Self-Assessment Readiness Part 1 in Activity 4.2 to determine if more work with Chapter 2 activities might help. For goal-setting problems, review the information in Figure 4.23 to determine which part of the process needs more attention.

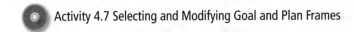 Activity 4.7 Selecting and Modifying Goal and Plan Frames

Activity 4.8

Selecting a Strategy 4 Application

This is intended as an independent activity. If you do it independently, you may want to discuss the results with your learning team.

After reading Chapter 4, choose one activity to use with your students. Then use the form on the DVD to reflect on the activity: what you tried, what you noticed as a result, and what, if any, actions you have taken or will take on the basis of the experience. If you are working with a learning team, consider sharing your reflection with them.

 Activity 4.8 Selecting a Strategy 4 Application

Activity 4.9

Adding to Your Growth Portfolio

This is an independent activity.

Any of the activities from this chapter can be used as entries for your own growth portfolio. Select activities you have completed or artifacts you have created that will illustrate your competence at the Chapter 4 learning targets. If you are keeping a reflective journal, you may want to include Chapter 4's entry in your portfolio. The portfolio entry cover sheet provided on the DVD will prompt you to think about how each item you select reflects your learning with respect to one or more of the chapter's learning targets.

 Activity 4.9 Chapter 4 Portfolio Entry Cover Sheet

How Can I Close the Gap?
Diagnosing Needs for Focused Instruction

Strategy 5
Use evidence of student learning needs to determine next steps in teaching.

> When we teach thoughtfully, we actively seek evidence of what students do not "get." We use assessment processes and instruments with sufficient instructional traction to identify specific learning needs for each student throughout a unit or teaching cycle. And we make sure our diagnostic assessments don't just tell us "Do something." We ensure they help answer the question "Do what?"

*T*he preservice education my teaching colleagues and I received was primarily focused on the act of instructing—different ways to deliver information—and the only response to student work we were prepared to give was a grade. Consequently, I, like many others, began teaching with a repertoire of three steps: plan, instruct, and assess-and-grade. First I planned what I would do and what my students would do. Then, I prepared the materials and resources. Next, I did what I planned, and they did what I planned. Last, I graded what they did. However, learning and teaching turned out to be far messier than I had believed it would be. Somewhere between "I taught it" and "they learned it," the straight shot downstream to mission accomplished diverged into a surprising array of tributaries. Over the course of that first year, I discovered there are a thousand ways for learners to "not get" a lesson.

The belief underpinning my teacher preparation seemed to be that learning trots right along after good instruction, a sort of stimulus-response system, in which instruction alone will create learning. However, if we are teaching along a straight path of "plan, instruct, assess-and-grade" we will miss the true nature of teaching—and the impact of formative assessment. Learning is an unpredictable process, and instructional correctives are part of the normal flow of attaining mastery in any field. Whether learning occurs is directly influenced by the steps we and our students take *after* instruction, so we must plan for reciprocity between *instruct* and *assess*.

Hattie (2009) called this the zone of "what happens next" and described it as a *feedback loop*. The feedback loop begins with a "knowledge-eliciting activity"—what students do in response to instruction. The teacher assesses and then teacher and students take action based on what students' responses reveal they did or did not learn. Subsequent action may or may not include offering feedback to the student. As noted in Chapter 3, feedback isn't always the best teaching tool: identification of the student's learning need determines whether feedback is the appropriate next step or whether further instruction is called for (Wiliam, 2013). Figure 5.1 shows the feedback loop in diagram form.

Figure 5.1

Feedback Loop: The Zone of "What Happens Next"

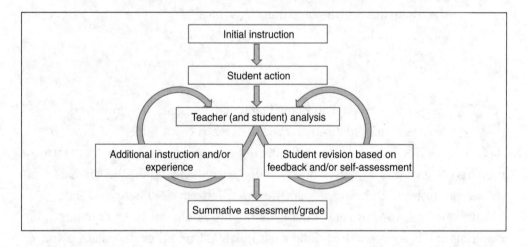

This feedback loop was missing from my beginning teaching. When my students did something in response to instruction, I was not prepared to "loop back" and help them move further along the continuum of learning, either by giving feedback to focus their revisions or by reteaching to the parts not yet learned.

Effective diagnostic assessment tells us where students are in their learning. This is the starting block for the feedback loop. Because it is often *not* a straight shot from instruction to mastery, good teaching includes knowing how to keep learning moving forward to the point of mastery for each student. Hattie's 2009 meta-analysis of research on teaching and student achievement indicated that one of the most powerful influences on teacher effectiveness is the desire to use assessment information to evaluate the effects of their own teaching on student learning. He identified the teacher's willingness to seek *disconfirming evidence*—to actively look for evidence of which parts of the learning need additional focus—as the most crucial factor in doing the best we can to help each student learn. Hattie also found that effective teachers used this disconfirming evidence to

> intervene in calculated and meaningful ways to alter the direction of learning to attain various shared, specific, and challenging goals. In particular, they provide students with multiple opportunities and alternatives for developing learning strategies based on surface and deep levels of learning some content or domain matter, leading to students building conceptual understanding of this learning which the students and teachers use in future learning (p. 22).

In other words, effective teachers build a feedback loop into their instructional sequence by doing three things:

1. They figure out where students are in their learning and what students' learning needs are throughout the instructional sequence for a given learning target.

2. They have a repertoire of teaching strategies from which to choose to develop students' capabilities. And they apply these strategies based on the specific learning needs of their students.

3. They plan time in their instructional sequence to take action on the basis of that information.

Watch Video 5.1 to hear teachers and students describe the impact of using assessment results to shape actions.

Video 5.1: Using Assessment Results to Guide Learning

In this chapter, we look at ways to identify learning gaps—incomplete understandings, misconceptions, partially developed skills, and the like. In Chapter 6 we look at ways to engage students in practice, with feedback, to target the learning gaps identified in Strategy 5. The two strategies work in tandem: Focused diagnostic assessment informs focused instruction and practice.

Types of Learning Needs

You have made the learning target clear to students, and you have engaged them in an initial instructional encounter with that target. The encounter could have been an experience, an activity, a simulation, a demonstration, an explanation, a lecture, a discussion, a passage to read, a video to watch, or a recording to listen to. The students have responded by answering questions, working problems, discussing something, writing something, demonstrating something, designing something, or creating something. You do, they do; now what? At this point, students have mastered the target or they haven't. If the evidence suggests they haven't, your options are (1) grade what they've done and move on, (2) reteach the lesson, or (3) figure out what your students' learning needs are in relation to the target and teach to those needs. Research consistently favors option three.

> When student achievement does not improve over several lessons on the same learning target, it is a good idea to change the teaching method. Offering repeated instances of the same instruction is likely to confirm in students' minds that they will never succeed.

The first step in figuring out students' learning needs is to be able to identify the types of errors they are likely to make. In this book, we will use a three-category classification system: errors due to incomplete understanding, errors due to flaws in reasoning, and errors due to misconceptions (Figure 5.2). Each of these has different precedents, and each calls for a different approach to instruction.

Errors Due to Incomplete Understanding

In the case of errors due to incomplete understanding, students' work demonstrates they know something partially and are ready for further instruction. For example, when primary students are first learning about the use of end

Figure 5.2

Types of Learning Needs

Errors due to incomplete understanding

- Students have partial understanding. They haven't learned it wrong, they just haven't learned it yet.

Errors due to flaws in reasoning

- Students carry out the pattern of reasoning with one or more missteps.

Errors due to misconceptions

- Students have internalized a concept or an explanation of a phenomenon that they believe to be true, but that does not match current best thinking.

---

punctuation, at one stage in development, some children put a period after every word. This shows that they know a period goes at the end of something, but they aren't quite clear about the end of *what*.

Do What?

When students' work exhibits incomplete understanding, next-step instruction takes into account that they haven't necessarily inaccurately learned what's being taught, they just haven't learned it completely yet. This type of learning need is fairly straightforward to address. For example, with the primary students using periods between words, the instructional next step is not to mark the periods as wrong, but rather to move students into stringing words together as units of thought and then guide them to use periods where an idea ends. This approach acknowledges what students know about periods, takes the next step to teach them more about getting ideas into writing, and then circles back to periods. In general, next steps with errors due to incomplete understanding involve further instruction rather than reteaching or simply marking them as incorrect.

Errors Due to Flaws in Reasoning

Patterns of reasoning adhere to rules for their successful application but may also lead to missteps. For example, when students are asked to summarize, they may include details that are not central to the main idea. When they are asked to generalize, they may make a statement that is true for the observed evidence but does not extend to cover a broader array of instances, missing the essence of *generalize* (e.g., "All dogs I have seen have four legs"). Or, they may make a statement that is true for the observed evidence but covers too broad an array of other instances, thus overgeneralizing (e.g., "All dogs have four legs"). When asked to determine cause for an effect, they may offer another effect instead of a cause. These are examples of typical flaws in reasoning.

Do What?

To overcome flaws in reasoning, it is important to help students first identify the flaw. A good way to do this is to use Strategies 1 and 2. Share with students a complete definition of the pattern of reasoning, introduce them to the rubric you will use to assess that pattern of reasoning, and then have them examine some strong and not-so-strong examples and decide, based on the rubric, what the strengths and flaws are in those examples. (The inference scenario at the end of Chapter 2 is an example of this sequence of activities.) Practice with Strategies 1 and 2 helps students recognize a well-executed reasoning process and avoid or correct reasoning flaws they may otherwise demonstrate in their initial attempts at mastery.

Errors Due to Misconceptions

Misconceptions, also known as *alternative* conceptions, involve students' either having learned something inaccurately or having internalized an explanation for a phenomenon that does not fit with current best thinking. For example, when primary students are learning about the solar system, one misconception they may have is that the phenomenon of night and day results from the movement of the sun ("The sun comes up and the sun goes down"). You can teach that it is the earth's rotation that causes our side of the planet to face the sun during the day and then face away from the sun at night. You can demonstrate this using playground balls and a flashlight, papier mache heavenly bodies strung from the ceiling, and simulations ("Partner A, you are the sun. Partner B, you are the earth."), but if you don't also address the misconception, when you ask students to draw the process of how we get night and day, you will still see drawings of the sun coming up and the sun going down. Students have simply put the new concept on top of an existing misconception, and the existing misconception has not gone away. An example of a typical misconception for secondary students is that support for an opinion can be adequately provided by further opinions.

Misconceptions can also present themselves as misapplication of a rule. For example, in language arts a common misapplication of a rule concerns correct use of subject and object pronouns. Students learn that "Him and me went to the store" is not correct, but the rule they tend to internalize is that *me* should be used sparingly. As a result they often use *I* when they should use *me*: "You can give it to him and I." They are operating with rules, just not the correct ones.

Do What?

The challenge with misconceptions is to identify them accurately and then plan lessons to dislodge them. Misconceptions are stubborn. They can't be corrected by papering over them. To illustrate, let's work with a misconception from middle school science. Newton's first law of motion states that a force is not needed to keep an object in motion, yet many students (and adults) will tell you that if an object is in motion, it will require a force to stay in motion, which seems like common sense (and is what Aristotle thought, by the way). Students may memorize the principles of the first law: An object at rest will stay at rest, and an object will continue with constant velocity unless acted on by an unbalanced force. However, memorizing those principles is generally not enough to overcome what our senses tell us about force and motion: If you want a book to keep moving across a table, you have to keep pushing it.

To help students understand why a force is not needed to keep an object in motion, we need to use a teaching strategy specifically designed to dig out misconceptions. One approach derived from research on science misconceptions (Hattie, 2009, p. 148) is to do the following:

- Create an initial awareness of the misconception by generating cognitive dissonance in the students' minds. Provide them with an experience (a demonstration, a reading passage, or some combination of the two) that runs counter to or contradicts the misconception in some way.

- Engage students in discussion to uncover the misconception and to contrast it with the correct interpretation.

- Finish by having students explain why the misconception is incorrect, when they are able to do so.

The teaching challenge is to cause conceptual *change*—to have students *give up* the inaccurate conception they currently hold in favor of an accurate one. Students have to consciously dismantle the old rule or understanding to ensure

Video 5.2: Commit and Toss Activity: Grade 4

that the new takes hold in the long-term memory. Therefore, addressing misconceptions, whether in science, social studies, mathematics, language arts, or any other discipline, requires an intentional approach tailored to the nature of the misunderstanding.

Fourth-grade teacher Crystal Thayer uses an activity called "Commit and Toss" to help students become aware of misconceptions regarding the science topics they are studying. Video 5.2 describes the activity and shows her class in action.

Sources of Information for Identifying Types of Learning Needs

We can uncover evidence of incomplete understanding, flaws in reasoning, and misconceptions informally by noting types of problems in student work, by eliciting explanations, and by asking probing questions. We can use more formal tools, from curriculum documents to quizzes and tests. Discussions with colleagues can also uncover common reasoning errors, instances of incomplete understanding, and outright misconceptions. The operative question for these discussions is "When students go sideways on a given learning target, what are the typical reasons?"

Using Learning Trajectories to Provide Diagnostic Information

Learning progressions, construct maps, developmental continua, and deconstructed standards are all types of learning trajectories. Each provides a way to organize and flesh out instruction. If designed well, each can provide a detailed treatment of how learning a particular concept, procedure, or skill commonly progresses and develops. Learning progressions

> invite a developmental view of learning because they lay out how
> expertise develops over a more or less extended period of time,
> beginning with rudimentary forms of learning and moving through
> progressively more sophisticated states. When teachers' instruction
> and formative assessment practices are undergirded by learning
> progressions, teachers can better use formative assessment to map
> where [an] individual student's learning currently stands and take steps
> to move him or her forward (Heritage, 2013a, p. 37).

Whether learning progressions are developed by experts in the field based on empirical research or by teachers and curriculum content experts based on study and experience, keep these three guidelines in mind (Heritage, 2013b, pp. 188–189):

1. Progressions must be based on the most accurate understanding available of how learning unfolds over time.

2. Teachers must understand them deeply enough to be able to use them effectively.

3. Not all learning is linear, and not all students follow the same trajectory to attain mastery.

With those understandings in place, learning progressions can offer a robust source of information from which to build diagnostic assessments.

Construct maps, developmental continua, and deconstructed standards can also provide information about steps toward developing mastery of a learning target. Several states have published a complete set of deconstructed Common Core State Standards, intended to guide instruction and instructional interventions. Consider this Grade 4 Reading example from Kentucky's document, *4th Grade: Kentucky Core Academic Standards with Targets* (http://education.ky.gov/ curriculum/docs/Documents/Fourth%20Grade%20ELA.pdf): "Refer to details and examples in a text when explaining what the text says explicitly and when drawing inferences from the text." This deconstructed reasoning content standard identifies the following underpinning knowledge targets:

- Explain the difference between explicit and inferred information in a text.

- Identify details and examples when explaining what the text says explicitly.

- Identify details and examples when drawing inferences from a text.

These three learning targets provide guidance not only for instruction, but also for diagnosing specific problems students might have as they attempt to accomplish this standard. Do they know what an inference is? Can they differentiate between explicit and inferred information? Can they find supporting details and examples for an idea explicitly stated? Can they do the same for an idea inferred but not explicitly stated?

With a well-designed learning trajectory, we have a way to determine what comes next in the learning, and we can more easily use our assessments to identify which aspects individual students still need to learn. This in turn enables us to identify appropriate lessons and materials suited to students' specific learning needs.

Using Diagnostic Assessments

An assessment itself can yield solid diagnostic information when its results provide evidence that points to specific learning needs. Such assessments are known as *instructionally tractable* (Andrade, 2013). Not all assessments will work this way, even some assessments purported to be formative in nature. Many assessments yield only a score, which can be used to indicate whether initial instruction was effective or not, and if it was not effective, that further work on the part of the teacher and the student is needed (Wiliam, 2013). However, simply identifying that a particular topic needs attention (e.g., "these students have problems with fractions") does not give an assessment sufficient instructional traction because it does not diagnose the specific learning need.

Selecting or developing assessments with instructional traction requires that we can recognize it when we see it. For example, consider the following item:

Which fraction is largest?

a) $\frac{1}{3}$ b) $\frac{2}{5}$ c) $\frac{7}{9}$

It is likely that many fourth-grade students would be able to correctly choose answer choice *c*, because both the numerator and the denominator are the largest numbers in the set given. This set of answer choices doesn't accurately differentiate between students who understand the concept and students who don't. Students could get it right for the right reason (understanding it is the relationship between the numerator and the denominator that determines size) or for the wrong reason (believing that size is determined by the numerator or by the denominator). The item also doesn't help ferret out misconceptions that may be lurking.

On the other hand, consider the answer choices in this problem:

Which fraction is largest?

a) $\frac{2}{1}$ b) $\frac{3}{8}$ c) $\frac{4}{3}$

Students who understand that it is the relationship between the numerator and the denominator that determines size will choose answer *a*. Students who use the denominator to determine size will likely choose answer *b*. Students who use the numerator to determine size will likely choose answer *c*. With answer choices like these, you not only know who does and doesn't understand magnitude in fractions, you also know what to focus on with students who have selected each wrong answer choice. This diagnostic capability of an assessment is key to its instructional traction.

Assessments of all types—selected response, written response, performance assessment, and personal communication—can be designed to provide results that are instructionally tractable, both as a formal assessment event and as an informal lesson-embedded activity. Some commercially available assessments have been designed specifically for this purpose. For example, the DIAGNOSER Web-based assessment system designed by Minstrell and colleagues is constructed so that each answer choice points to a different science conception (Cowie, 2013). Researchers at Educational Testing Service have developed an item bank known as Diagnostic Items in Mathematics and Science; wrong answer choices to these items reflect research-based misconceptions and incomplete understandings. If we intend to use assessment results formatively, we should require this feature of the assessments provided to us or design them with this feature ourselves.

Instructional Traction with Selected Response Items

Recent research evidence suggests that well-designed multiple-choice items may provide better diagnostic information than open-ended items because the wrong answer choices can give insights into students' understanding, on par with that gained from listening to student "think-alouds" and from interviewing students about their understanding (Andrade, 2013). The wrong answer choices in a multiple-choice problem, known as *distractors*, are crucial to an item's usefulness in diagnosing problems. However, as demonstrated in the previous fraction example, not all distractors are created equal. For an item to function well diagnostically, each distractor must be useful. That means that humorous or throw-away wrong answer choices should not be included. Instead, each distractor should be chosen to represent either incomplete understanding or a "wrong turn." Strong distractors with good diagnostic ability are statements representing incomplete understanding, flaws in reasoning, or misconceptions, the three types of learning needs described previously. To select or create good diagnostic distractors, we must first identify the particular problems students commonly demonstrate when mastering a given learning target.

> **⚠ Distractors**
>
> Multiple-choice distractors should all be plausible choices, each reflecting a misunderstanding or partial understanding of the learning target the item is intended to measure.

Research suggests that providing three possible answers to multiple-choice items is usually adequate (Rodriguez & Haladyna, 2013). The use of more answer choices is often thought to reduce the probability of getting the correct answer through guessing, but researchers have found that, rather than resort to blind guessing, test-takers usually eliminate the least plausible distractors, which reduces the item to two or three options anyway. In their review of research on writing selected response items for classroom assessment, Rodriguez and Haladyna cite agreement among item writers and researchers about the difficulty in coming up with plausible fourth and fifth options. The key in guarding against students' selecting the right answer for the wrong reason lies in the quality, not the number, of the distractors. However, it is fine to include as many functional distractors as needed, as long as each matches a separate typical lack of understanding, or "wrong path" in reasoning or conceptual understanding.

When creating a multiple-choice item addressing a straightforward knowledge target, finding useful distractors is a matter of identifying straightforward, plausible incorrect answers. With continued experience in one content area and one age group, you will notice patterns of incomplete understanding *vis à vis* the knowledge to be mastered, which can be turned into distractors on practice tests. You can develop distractors representing incomplete understanding by framing a multiple-choice question as a fill-in-the-blank question first. Examine students' wrong answers closely to determine typical errors and use the ones that appear most frequently and that are of most use diagnostically.

You can also develop distractors for items measuring reasoning proficiencies by framing a multiple-choice question as a fill-in-the-blank question. Examine students' wrong answers closely to determine typical flaws in reasoning, then describe the characteristics of each typical error. These become your "distractor formulas" for the particular pattern of reasoning. Also, write a description of the characteristics of the correct answer, which should parallel your student-friendly definition of the reasoning target.

For example, if you want to create distractors for the reasoning target "Makes generalizations," you could ask students to read a short text explaining something such as how meat-eating plants function and then pose the following question as an open-ended response item: "What generalization can you make from this passage about how meat-eating plants lure their prey?" Upon examining student responses, you may find the following characteristics:

- Some students answer correctly by providing a statement that is true for the evidence presented and extends the application (generalizes) logically to a broader array of instances.

- Some students offer a statement that is true for the evidence presented, but the application (generalization) includes too broad an array of instances to be supported by evidence (*overgeneralization*).

- Some students offer a statement that is true for the evidence presented, but does not include an extension to other instances (*no generalization present*).

- Some students offer a statement that is not true for the evidence presented and may or may not extend it to a broader array of instances (*incorrect interpretation of evidence*).

By examining the correct and incorrect responses, you can create a list of common errors in reasoning for *generalization*. These right and wrong answer descriptions become an item formula—the blueprint you can use to develop multiple-choice items in any context when you want to assess the learning target "makes generalizations." You will notice in this case that your blueprint allows for four plausible answer choices. However if, for example, none of your students is likely to offer an incorrect interpretation of evidence, you may not want to include a distractor for it.

Figure 5.3 shows item formulas for a sampling of reasoning targets that can be assessed with multiple-choice items. If you can access item formulas for a standardized test, they may work well to help you create diagnostic items with instructional traction, depending on how they were designed.

For further guidance on developing selected response assessment items to measure knowledge and reasoning level targets, see Chappuis et al. (2012), Chapter 5.

Instructional Traction with Written Response Items

An open-ended item requiring a written response may be a better assessment choice than a selected response item when the intended learning target is a complex or multistep pattern of reasoning. Written response items are typically evaluated with a scoring guide in the form of a list or a rubric.

Lists

A scoring guide in list form identifies the possible correct answers and awards points for each. For example, for an item assessing students' knowledge of the Krebs cycle, the list might look like this:

One point for each of the following:

- Cycle describes the sequence of reactions by which cells generate energy

- Cycle takes place in the mitochondria

215

Figure 5.3

| Item Formulas for Reasoning Targets | **FOR EXAMPLE** |

1. Infer

Question: Which idea could you infer from the text? Or which idea does this selection suggest?

Possible Answers:

- The right answer—A guess based on evidence found in the passage
- Distractor—A guess that includes a word or concept from the passage but is not supported by the meaning of the passage
- Distractor—A guess that might seem reasonable but for which there is no evidence in the passage

2. Summarize

Question: Which sentence best summarizes what this passage is about?

Possible Answers:

- The right answer—A statement of the main ideas of the passage
- Distractor—A statement of one main idea not sufficiently broad to represent the whole passage
- Distractor—A statement including an idea not found in the passage
- Distractor—A statement of one fact or detail from the passage

3. Generalize

Question: Which generalization can you support after reading the passage?

Possible Answers:
- The right answer—A statement that is true for the evidence presented and extends the application logically to a broader array of instances
- Distractor—A statement that is true for the evidence presented but the application covers too broad an array of instances to be supported by the evidence
- Distractor—A statement that is true for the evidence presented but does not include an extension to other instances
- Distractor—A statement that is not true for the evidence presented

4. Identify Cause and Effect

Question: Which sentence best explains why _____ (event or action) happened?

Possible Answers:
- The right answer—A plausible statement of causation based on evidence from the text
- Distractor—A statement of causation that is not supported by evidence from the text
- Distractor—A statement that offers another effect rather than a cause

- Cycle consumes oxygen

- Cycle produces carbon dioxide and water as waste products

- Cycle converts ADP to energy-rich ATP (Chappuis et al., 2012, p. 182)

If your list is an accurate description of the requisite knowledge, it is fairly obvious to determine which students need which instruction as a next step while scoring responses.

Task-Specific Rubrics

There are two basic forms of rubrics: *task-specific* and *general*. As you will recall from Chapter 2, task-specific rubrics describe levels of mastery of a learning target with reference to one specific assignment. As such, they are not generalizable across tasks and cannot be handed out in advance to guide student work because they tell students exactly what to do and not do. However, when the learning target calls for conceptual understanding, a task-specific rubric can be quite useful diagnostically. For example, for the learning target "Understand the earth's rotation causes night and day," you can create a task-specific rubric that represents the correct explanation along with the typical incomplete understandings and misconceptions, arranging the problems from slight to severe to make the rubric levels as shown in Figure 5.4. Task-specific rubrics are usually holistic in structure—having only one scoring scale—because the learning targets they are intended to assess are not usually complex enough to require an analytical structure.

Figure 5.4

| **Task-Specific Rubric Used Diagnostically** | **FOR EXAMPLE** |

Level 3:
- The response shows that the earth turns so that one side is facing the sun during the day and away from the sun at night.

Level 2:
- The response shows the sun on one side of the earth and the moon on the other side of the earth. It also shows that the earth turns to face the sun during the day and to face the moon during the night. It does not show the sun moving relative to the earth.

Level 1:
- The response shows that the sun moves relative to the earth.

General Rubrics

As noted in Chapter 2, *general* rubrics describe levels of mastery in terms that can be used to assess any task given for the specific learning target. To understand the diagnostic power of a general rubric designed for use with a written response item, let's use the example of a rubric for a summary (Figure 5.5).

Figure 5.5

Rubric for a Summary	**FOR EXAMPLE**

Level 4:

- The summary states the main ideas and major points of the material to be summarized.
- The summary covers all of the material to be summarized.
- No small details or extraneous information such as personal reflections or opinions are included.
- The summary is written in the writer's own words.

Level 3:

- The summary states most of the main ideas and major points of the material to be summarized.
- The summary covers all of the material to be summarized.
- Very few small details are included. No extraneous information such as personal reflections or opinions is included.
- The summary is written in the writer's own words.

Level 2:

- The summary includes a small portion of main ideas and/or major points of the material to be summarized, or only a portion of the material is represented by the summary.
- Small details and/or extraneous information such as personal reflections or opinions make up a portion of the summary.
- The summary may not be written entirely in the writer's own words; passages may be copied from the text.

Level 1:

- The summary does not represent the main ideas or major points of the material to be summarized.
- The summary consists entirely of small details, unrelated ideas, and/or extraneous information such as personal reflections or opinions.
- The summary may not be written entirely in the writer's own words; passages may be copied from the text.

The rubric helps us understand that students may have problems in one or more of four areas when writing a summary: capturing the main ideas, covering all the material to be summarized, leaving out small details and extraneous information, and writing it in their own words. You can use this rubric diagnostically by identifying the phrases that best describe each student's strengths and problems and then grouping them for further instruction as needed on one or more of the four areas. And as noted previously, well-constructed general rubrics are also useful as feedback and self-assessment tools.

For further guidance on developing written response assessment items, scoring lists, and task-specific rubrics to measure knowledge and reasoning targets, see Chappuis et al. (2012), Chapter 6.

Instructional Traction with Performance Assessment Tasks and Rubrics

When the learning target you are teaching will be assessed through a performance assessment, you will want to use a general rubric. Chapter 2 described three characteristics that make rubrics suited to formative use: they are descriptive of levels of proficiency regarding the intended learning, generalizable across tasks, and analytic in structure if addressing a multidimensional learning target (Figure 2.13). Rubrics used with performance assessments are more likely to be analytic in structure because the learning target is more likely to be multidimensional (e.g., mathematical problem solving, giving an oral presentation, writing an argumentative essay).

It is a good idea to introduce the complete rubric to students at the outset of instruction but to focus on one criterion at a time for diagnostic purposes. Alternatively, you may analyze the students' work for all aspects of quality but then narrow the focus of next steps in teaching and learning by taking into account which criterion needs attention first. For example, when using a mathematics problem-solving rubric (see Figure 2.16), you may decide to work on the trait of *Problem Solving* before moving to the trait of *Mathematical Communication*, because if they don't first learn how to choose an appropriate strategy and follow it through to completion, they won't have much to communicate about.

For further guidance on developing performance assessment tasks and rubrics to measure reasoning, skill, and product targets, see Chappuis et al. (2012), Chapter 7.

Instructional Traction with Questioning and Dialogue

In the context of diagnostic formative assessment, personal communication is one of our most powerful tools. We can ask questions to probe understanding,

and we can listen as students discuss ideas or problems. One crucial prerequisite to eliciting accurate information is that students feel safe in answering and
discussing honestly. When our classroom climate nurtures learning, students
are comfortable answering honestly even though they may not have confidence
in the accuracy of their responses. Assessment, even informally conducted
through questioning in the classroom, has not typically been a comfortable
experience for many students, especially those who are not doing well, who
often dread being called on for a host of reasons. We can turn this around
by establishing a supportive learning environment that allows us to take full
advantage of questions and dialogue. Helpful steps include the following:

- Make sure your instruction and assessment practices all convey
  the message that it is good to uncover what we don't know and
  then go about learning it. That's why we're here.

- Help students understand that a response that hides their true
  understanding gets in the way of their learning. It's a little bit like
  going to the doctor and lying about your symptoms.

- Establish expectations that students will treat each other's
  contributions, mistakes, and misconceptions with respect and
  dignity (Chappuis et al., 2012, p. 271).

As Hattie (2012) noted, the primary purpose of maintaining a classroom environment that is warm, trustworthy, and empathetic is to allow learning to thrive
on error. An essential element of classroom management, then, is to establish
and enforce ground rules that create "a safe harbor for welcoming error and
thence learning" (p. 165).

Once the classroom is conducive to diagnosing student needs through questioning and dialogue, it becomes a matter of formulating the types of questions that
will elicit the best information. Again, we turn to information about incomplete
understanding, flaws in reasoning, and misconceptions to formulate our questions. Strategies that help students think more deeply about their responses
include offering "think time," asking the question before calling on a student,
and making sure that you are calling on students at random. *Think time* is
often referred to as wait time, but in my experience, if you call it that, that's
what you will get—waiting. Students will wait for you to call on someone. Call
it "think time" and explain to students that you will ask questions and then
pause so they have time to think their thoughts before answering. One way to
help them do this is to ask the question and then pause for 7 to 10 seconds. Then
ask students to share what they are thinking with a partner. Give that about a
minute (depending on the question) and then call on someone to answer.

It may seem artificial at first, but students catch on remarkably quickly to this change in routine.

Consider not asking for volunteers to answer, so that all students know they are included in the activity and expected to participate. Money has been made teaching teachers to put students' names on tongue depressors so they can ensure they are offering all students equal opportunity to respond. Whether or not tongue depressors appeal to you, you should develop some systematic way to call on students randomly. When students answer, Heritage (2013b) suggests that teachers not offer a judgment of *correct* or *incorrect* but rather an opportunity to explain the rationale behind the answer. Asking for follow-up explanations is a good idea, especially if you let students know in advance that it is part of the exercise so they will not be surprised when the follow-up question comes at them. You could also work them up to offering the rationale without prompting.

Another source of diagnostic information is walking around the classroom while students are engaged in solving a problem or working on a task and listening to what they are saying. Assuming this is a learning event and not a summative assessment, letting students discuss what they are doing with one another can contribute a great deal to their learning, so let them talk. If they aren't talking, watch what they are doing. Lurk. Teach with your eyes and ears open. Hunter (1993) called this approach "monitor and adjust." It's amazing how many problems you can catch if you're out there among the desks while students are working. There are at least a hundred things that need doing at every moment of a teacher's work day, but the payoff of watching and listening is worth the time it takes, both diagnostically and in terms of creating a caring learning environment. One of the most effective ways we convince our students that their learning is our highest priority is to be physically and mentally present among them while they are at least physically present with us.

Avoiding the Need to Reteach When Possible

When we identify potential problems prior to instruction, either through pretesting or through an understanding of the typical problems and misconceptions students bring to the learning situation, we can often head them off by tailoring the instruction to avoid them.

For example, in the case of misconceptions, we can minimize the need to reteach by helping students to recognize and correct them at the outset of instruction or during the learning—whichever is best suited to the misconception at hand. One simple approach is to list the misconceptions, distribute the list

Figure 5.6

Correcting Misconceptions

Misconception	Date	Correction
1.		
2.		
3.		

to students, and as instruction confronts them, periodically ask students to mark, date, and explain those they can now correct (Figure 5.6). Or, you might make a list of major conceptual understandings you will address in a given unit, mixing in statements reflecting misconceptions students typically have. Ask students to mark "True," "False," or "Unsure" next to each one. Periodically, distribute a fresh copy of the list and have students revisit the statements related to what you have taught to that point, marking the statements as either true or false, accompanied by an explanation: "I think it is true/false because . . ." Figure 5.7 shows a variation of this activity with a seventh-grade mathematics unit.

Figure 5.7

"Buckle Down"—Geometric Measurements	FOR EXAMPLE

Name: _____   Period: _____   Date: _____

Before Reading	Statement	After Reading
True False	Pi ≈ 3.14	True False
True False	Area is the measure of the inside of a two-dimensional figure.	True False
True False	Volume is measured in square units.	True False
True False	The formula to find the area of a triangle is *1/2 bh*.	True False
True False	The area of a composite shape can be found by breaking the shape down into common shapes.	True False
True False	*B* represents a length measurement.	True False
True False	Volume is the amount of space a shape takes up.	True False
True False	The area of a circle is the same as the area of a sector.	True False

Source: Used with permission from Beth Cotsmire, Bucyrus City Schools: Bucyrus, OH.

Using Strategies 1 and 2 can also help students avoid typical problems. When students examine a range of work samples to identify strengths and weaknesses, if you have chosen the work samples to illustrate typical problems they may have, the act of students' identifying and discussing those problems makes it less likely that they will replicate them. Students' initial attempts are often of higher quality as a result, requiring less time spent on instruction in the basics. In Figure 5.8, high school science teacher Ben Arcuri describes an activity he uses to help students recognize and avoid typical mistakes and misconceptions.

Figure 5.8

From the Classroom

Find the Mistake

What I Do

My students use whiteboards for practice activities. The whiteboards are 36 inch $\times$ 24 inch $\times$ ¼ inch thick pieces of white acrylic plastic. They are sturdy and big enough for group work and lengthy written response questions. The students use different colors of dry erase markers to write on the whiteboards in a variety of different activities.

In an activity we call "Find the Mistake," students receive a question and a solution that has a problem or mistake embedded in it. The students work individually or in groups of two to three to find the mistake, correct it, and solve the problem. The left side of the room and the right side of the room complete different questions on a similar topic. I walk around the room and talk to each group or student individually. I can easily see what is going on. If more than one group is having trouble with a specific part of the question, I can address the groups individually or stop the activity, correct the problem with the entire class, then continue the activity. The group members work together to solve the problem. I then ask the students to switch sides of the room. The students go to the other side of the room to a board with the other question, and the group must find the mistake, correct it, and solve the problem. This activity allows the students to see the question and concepts in two completely different ways. Both ways are beneficial.

Impact on Learning

It is incredible to see what happens to students when you give them a marker and a large whiteboard. They become fearless. The students feel confident enough to make mistakes, correct their work, and discuss the problems like politicians. Some days I can sit back and watch the learning take place.

Source: Used with permission from Ben Arcuri, Penticton Secondary School: Penticton, BC.

Conclusion

We know that feedback from the teacher to the student is a powerful formative assessment strategy, but it is preceded by feedback from the student to the teacher. Assessing to find out what our students know, how they are thinking, and how they are progressing, and then building time into the teaching cycle to act on that information creates in students a sense of trust and a belief in themselves as capable learners.

Understanding and Applying the Content of Chapter 5

End-of-chapter activities are intended to help you master the chapter's learning targets and apply concepts to your classroom. They are designed to deepen your understanding of the chapter content, provide discussion topics for collaborative learning, and guide implementation of the content and practices taught in the chapter. Forms and materials for completing each activity appear in editable Microsoft Word format in the Chapter 5 DVD file. Each form needed for an activity is listed after the activity directions and marked with this symbol:

Chapter 5 Learning Targets

1. Understand the importance of the feedback loop to increasing student learning
2. Believe in the necessity of building time for the feedback loop into a teaching cycle
3. Have a repertoire of strategies to diagnose student learning needs

Chapter 5 Activities

Discussion Questions (All learning targets)

Activity 5.1   Keeping a Reflective Journal (All learning targets)

Activity 5.2   Mapping Your Teaching Cycle (Learning targets 1 and 2)

Activity 5.3   Creating Time for the Feedback Loop (Learning targets 1 and 2)

Activity 5.4   Identifying Types of Learning Needs (Learning target 3)

Activity 5.5   Using a Learning Trajectory to Provide Diagnostic Information (Learning target 3)

Activity 5.6   Finding, Modifying, or Creating Diagnostic Assessments (Learning target 3)

Activity 5.7   Avoiding the Need to Reteach When Possible (Learning target 3)

Activity 5.8   Exploring Reactions to Chapter 5 Ideas (All learning targets)

Activity 5.9   Selecting a Strategy 5 Application (Learning target 3)

Activity 5.10   Adding to Your Growth Portfolio (All learning targets)

Chapter 5 Discussion Questions

Discussion questions are also explored in depth in the activities listed in parentheses.

Questions to Discuss Before Reading Chapter 5

1. What do you currently do when students' work demonstrates partial to little mastery of the content standards you are teaching? (Activities 5.2 and 5.3)

2. Consider a unit you are teaching now or will teach this year. What learning difficulties can you predict students will have? What have you done in the past to help students overcome those difficulties? (Activity 5.4)

Questions to Discuss After Reading Chapter 5

3. What actions might you take to identify the types of learning needs students have, prior to offering further instruction? (Activity 5.4)

4. How might you use learning trajectories to help diagnose students' learning needs? (Activity 5.5)

5. How might you use selected response items to help diagnose students' learning needs? (Activity 5.6)

6. How might you use written response items to help diagnose students' learning needs? (Activity 5.6)

7. How might you use performance assessment tasks and rubrics to help diagnose students' learning needs? (Activity 5.6)

8. How might you use questioning and dialogue to help diagnose students' learning needs? (Activity 5.6)

9. Which suggestions for avoiding the need to reteach might you try? (Activity 5.7)

10. Which activities from Chapter 5 did you try in the classroom? How did they work? What successes did you notice? What modifications might you make? (Activities 5.1, 5.2, 5.3, 5.4, 5.5, 5.6, 5.7, 5.9, and 5.10)

Activity 5.1

Keeping a Reflective Journal

This is intended as an independent activity. If you choose to do it, you may want to discuss the thoughts you record with your learning team.

Keep a record of your thoughts, questions, and any implementation activities you tried while reading Chapter 5.

 Activity 5.1 Chapter 5 Reflective Journal Form

Activity 5.2

Mapping Your Teaching Cycle

This activity can be done independently or with a partner or a learning team. If you do it independently, you may want to discuss the results with a colleague. To prepare for this activity, you will need to print the Symbols page on the DVD file and cut out the symbols.

After reading the introductory pages of this chapter describing the feedback loop, select a short unit you have taught or will teach.

1. Identify one learning target for this activity and write it on the teaching cycle map (on the DVD). If you teach two or more learning targets in the same lesson, list them.

2. Briefly describe what form initial instruction for the target(s) will take.

3. Briefly describe what students do in response to initial instruction. Indicate whether it is work intended for practice or work intended to demonstrate level of mastery for a grade.

4. Then using the symbols you have cut out, show what happens between the time that students take action and the summative assessment for the learning target(s).

5. Compare your teaching cycle map to the description of the feedback loop.

6. Note or discuss any changes to your teaching cycle suggested by the comparison.

Variation: If you are currently a student, conduct this activity from your point of view, mapping your instructor's teaching cycle for a given unit or learning target. Discuss the resulting map with your instructor, and together look for any changes that might assist you with your learning.

 Activity 5.2a Teaching Cycle Map   Activity 5.2b Teaching Cycle Symbols

Activity 5.3

Creating Time for the Feedback Loop

This is a partner or learning team activity.

After reading Chapter 5's introductory section, discuss the following questions with a colleague or your learning team.

1. What changes to your instructional and assessment pacing do you believe will help students make more progress in learning?

2. What constraints make these changes difficult?

3. Which changes are within your power to make? What might you do? Who else might need to be involved?

4. Which changes are not within your power to make? Who might need to be involved in the solution? How might you involve them?

Activity 5.4

Identifying Types of Learning Needs

This activity is intended as an independent inquiry, followed by a partner discussion.

After reading the section "Types of Learning Needs," select a unit you have taught in the past and/or will teach shortly.

1. List the learning targets for the unit using the form on the DVD.

2. Think of the difficulties students encountered (or will encounter, based on past experience) with each learning target. List the problems, keying them to their learning targets.

3. Classify the cause of the problem as Incomplete Understanding, Flaw in Reasoning, or Misconception ("IU," "FR," and "M" on the form).

4. For each problem, also estimate its frequency of occurrence and determine importance—how significant a hindrance to learning the problem is—as high, medium, or low.

5. Ask one or more colleagues teaching the same content to do this analysis.

6. Meet with your colleague(s) to compare lists. Add their problems to your list if you think your students also have them. Once you have a complete list, select the incomplete understandings, reasoning flaws, and/or misconceptions you want to address in either whole-class or grouped instruction. Consider frequency and importance in your deliberation. Discuss ways to address those problems for which you won't design whole-class or grouped instruction.

 Activity 5.4 Identifying Types of Learning Needs

Activity 5.5

Using a Learning Trajectory to Provide Diagnostic Information

This is a partner or learning team activity.

After reading the section titled "Using Learning Trajectories to Provide Diagnostic Information," identify what types of learning progression(s) might be available for the subject and grade level you teach. Options include learning progressions, construct maps, developmental continua, and deconstructed content standards. Select one and use it in conjunction with Activity 5.3 to add to your repertoire of what next steps might be most helpful for students with the different types of learning needs you have identified.

Activity 5.6

Finding, Modifying, or Creating Diagnostic Assessments

This is intended as an independent activity. If you do it independently, you may want to discuss the results with your learning team.

The section titled "Using Diagnostic Assessments" describes instructional tractable assessments for each of the four assessment methods: selected response, written response, performance assessment, and personal communication. Practice identifying, modifying, or creating assessment items or tasks so the results function as good diagnostic information by completing the following activity.

1. Begin by selecting a learning target you will be teaching in the near future. Identify the appropriate assessment method to be used to assess it.

2. Find and modify or create one or more assessment items or rubrics by following the guidelines provided in the subsection relating to the method you have chosen. (For more information on creating assessments of all types, refer to Chappuis et al., 2012, Chapters 5 through 8.)

3. Administer the assessment and examine students' results. To what extent do they help in determining next steps in learning? What revisions might you make to increase their instructional traction?

Activity 5.7

Avoiding the Need to Reteach When Possible

This is intended as an independent activity. If you do it independently, you may want to discuss the results with your learning team.

After reading the sections titled "Types of Learning Needs" and "Avoiding the Need to Reteach When Possible," try one of the ideas suggested for correcting misconceptions or for helping students avoid typical problems. Notice what effect the activity has on helping students avoid potential problems. Ask students how or to what extent the activity helped them in their learning. Discuss your observations and your students' comments with a colleague or your learning team.

Activity 5.8

Exploring Reactions to Chapter 5 Ideas

This is intended as an independent activity followed by a learning team discussion.

1. Find a phrase or passage in Chapter 5 that strikes you. Perhaps you agree with it strongly, it goes against your current practice, you disagree with it, or you want to dig deeper into the thoughts it sparks.

2. Write it on a notecard and bring it to your next team meeting.

3. At the meeting, spend 3 to 5 minutes sharing your quote and briefly describing your reaction to it. If appropriate, offer a question to begin the whole-team discussion.

4. Then give 5 to 15 minutes (or longer, if the group decides to continue) for a whole-team discussion.

5. Repeat the process with each team member's quote.

6. Summarize any new conclusions, insights, or questions individually or as a group at the end of the meeting.

Activity 5.9

Selecting a Strategy 5 Application

This is intended as an independent activity. If you do it independently, you may want to discuss the results with your learning team. It is offered as an alternative to the section-by-section activities described previously.

After reading Chapter 5, choose one application to try. After having tried it with students, use the form on the DVD to reflect on the activity: what you tried, what you noticed as a result, and what actions, if any, you have taken or will take on the basis of the experience. If you are working with a learning team, consider sharing your reflection with them.

Activity 5.9 Selecting a Strategy 5 Application

Activity 5.10

Adding to Your Growth Portfolio

This is an independent activity.

Any of the activities from this chapter can be used as entries for your own growth portfolio. Select activities you have completed or artifacts you have created that will illustrate your competence at the Chapter 5 learning targets. If you are keeping a reflective journal, you may want to include Chapter 5's entry in your portfolio. The portfolio entry cover sheet provided on the DVD will prompt you to think about how each item you select reflects your learning with respect to one or more of the chapter's learning targets.

Activity 5.10 Chapter 5 Portfolio Entry Cover Sheet

How Can I Close the Gap?
Focused Practice and Revision

Strategy 6
Design focused instruction, followed by practice with feedback.

> It is in practice that we develop persistence and a commitment to achievement. How we set practice up, what we ask students to do, and what we do in response all have a powerful impact on their behaviors and achievement as learners.

When evidence gained through Strategy 5 tells us that students need more work with a learning target, we move into Strategy 6—focused instruction followed by practice with feedback. Two issues immediately make this difficult in many classroom contexts: finding the time and refraining from grading all student work. Sometimes in order to adhere to a pacing guide, teachers will bypass the feedback loop and move straight to grading. Students who master the learning on the first pass do well, and students who don't, don't. There is no time to act on diagnostic information, so it may not be gathered. If available, it will not be used. Or, there is time to reteach, but not time for students to practice more.

In this chapter, we examine Strategy 6, looking at ways to engage students in practice, with feedback, to target the learning gaps identified in Strategy 5. The two strategies work in tandem: focused diagnostic assessment followed by focused instruction, practice, and revision. Implementing Strategy 6 requires four conditions:

- A belief that further instruction will benefit students

- A desire to devote time to increasing achievement and developing achievement-related attitudes and behaviors

- A repertoire of instructional strategies suited to the learning needs uncovered

- A willingness to leave off grading work that is for practice

Chapter 6 Learning Targets

At the end of Chapter 6, you will know how to do the following:

1. Understand the value of practice in a risk-free zone

2. Have a repertoire of strategies to use as instruction accompanied by

practice and revision before the graded event

Further Learning Opportunities Make a Difference

Some of our students are on a success trajectory—they experience regular success as learners and have confidence that they can achieve with sufficient effort. Many of them have a learning goal orientation toward their work, described in Chapter 1. Other students are on a "no-growth" or failure trajectory. When faced with difficulty, they reduce their aspirations and take fewer risks. University professor Rosabeth Moss Kanter (2004) researched factors that caused winning streaks and losing streaks in business, political, athletic, and education contexts. She also examined how organizations turned losing streaks around. The key factor in each of those contexts was a leader who helped people gain the confidence they needed to invest the effort required to succeed. According to Kanter, failure and success are trajectories, rather than events. Even though each trial seems like a new event, it is influenced by what has happened before unless something intervenes.

Kanter explains the dynamics of a losing streak this way:

> As aspirations diminish, people begin to feel fatalistic—that they can't do anything to help achieve a win. They give up, they retire on the job. They are physically present but mentally absent—a state now labeled as 'presenteeism' to distinguish it from 'absenteeism.' The body is there, but the spirit is gone (p. 109).

The same is true for students on a failure trajectory. Poor performance in the past is a consequence of ineffective actions, and past poor performance leads to diminished motivation to try anything in the present. Because they believe there is nothing they can do about their lack of success, they don't do much of anything.

234

Kanter also examined what leaders did when they were able shift behavior from a losing to a winning mode and found that turnaround leaders

> teach people to see the world differently because they give them new
> opportunities and experiences; it's like handing them a kaleidoscope
> that they can shake to shift the pattern. Then to overcome inertia, they
> move organizational and environmental impediments out of the way.
> Resources must be shifted to support small wins that build confidence
> and then join with others to produce major victories (2004, p. 282).

This is the goal of the feedback loop described within Strategies 5 and 6: to keep students from moving into failure trajectories and to turn around those whose prior experience has convinced them that they are not good at school. The secret to turning students around is to teach them to see themselves differently. This requires that we first have confidence in their ability to learn and our ability to teach them. We inspire their confidence in themselves by setting up conditions that encourage trying and then guiding their efforts into fruitful paths. If, however, we focus on what we believe our students are not capable of, we undermine their confidence in us and in themselves, which reinforces their "losing streak" (Kanter, 2004).

It matters to students whether or not we believe they are capable of succeeding at high levels. Research on *expectancy effects* in the classroom strongly indicates that teacher beliefs about what students are capable of can enhance or inhibit achievement (Hattie, 2009, pp. 123–124). Key findings include the following:

- Students can tell when a teacher expects different achievement levels from different students.

- When teachers treat all students like high achievers and aim to develop all students' learning capabilities, achievement is significantly higher.

- When teachers believe that students' achievement levels are difficult to change (having a "fixed mindset" about achievement), their students achieve at lower levels.

This is not to say that it only takes belief. The *actions that follow the belief* cause the change for students. If we believe we can put all students on the path to achieving at high levels, then we will structure our classroom practices to emphasize that *effort directed at growth*, rather than innate ability, leads to success. We will create instructional experiences that cause students to make progress, and we will stop expecting that prior lack of performance is an

Video 6.1: Creating a
Respectful Learning
Environment

unalterable determinant of future success. We will do whatever it takes to find the time to give students the opportunity to improve. In Video 6.1 fourth-grade teacher Crystal Thayer explains the structures she uses to create a collaborative environment that makes "not knowing" a safe and valued place to begin.

The Role of Practice in Learning

As important as carefully designing next-step instruction is, what we guide students to do during practice determines whether the instruction will take hold.

"What do I need to do today to make this a better learning place for students tomorrow?"

Crystal Thayer, Fourth Grade Teacher

While they are practicing is the point to intervene to help students let go of ineffective strategies and develop new, more productive strategies. We can halt a mistake in the making before they have learned it wrong. When they are ready, we can offer feedback that shows them where they are on track or off track and

that gives guidance for getting back on track. Few would argue that practice isn't important to learning, but assigning practice for practice's sake isn't that powerful. It can be more or less effective depending on how we structure time to practice, the intentionality of the practice, its level of difficulty, and its ability to provide opportunities for incremental improvement (Hattie, 2009). See Figure 6.1.

Video 6.2: Impact of Guided
Practice: Elementary

Watch Videos 6.2 and 6.3 to hear teachers and students explain the impact of guided practice on learning.

Video 6.3: Impact of Guided
Practice: Secondary

Structuring Practice Time

Research studies have shown that *spaced* practice is more effective than *massed* practice (Hattie, 2009). Spaced practice is loosely equivalent to interval training in a sport, while massed practice is basically nonstop. In other words, if given one hour of practice time, it is generally more effective in causing growth to spread it out over several shorter stretches than to stay with one drill or

Figure 6.1

Characteristics of Effective Practice

- Is spaced rather than massed
- Focuses students' attention on and effort toward mastery of the intended learning
- Is at an appropriately challenging level of difficulty
- Is structured to produce incremental growth toward mastery

concept for the whole hour. Studies also indicate the amount of time to plan between intervals depends on the complexity of the intended learning. Simpler targets require shorter rest intervals, and more complex targets require rest intervals of at least a day between practice events. Giving students several shorter practice opportunities rather than one long one has been shown to increase both the amount learned and the length of time students will retain it. In Figure 6.2, middle school mathematics teacher Paula Smith describes how she uses periodic review tasks to space the practice and monitor student learning needs.

Deliberate Practice

A second determinant of effectiveness is whether students are practicing with a learning intention. If students don't know *what* they are practicing, only that they

Figure 6.2

From the Classroom

Station Work

What I Do

In my math classes, throughout a chapter, students do "station work," moving to different areas of the classroom to do different practice activities. The activities look like games to the students, but I use them to check understanding in small groups and one-to-one. At many stations, students have a choice of leveled activities. One of the stations may include a short set of problems that students complete and check over with another student or myself. I already have a good idea of which students I will sit with while they work on the problems and ask them to explain their process as they work. It's a great way to review concepts and get individual time with students while they are engaged in meaningful work. At the end of station time, each student completes an exit slip reflecting on where they are with the concepts they worked with that day and where they still need to go.

Impact on Learning

Students look forward to station work days. They know they will get a choice in how they spend the period, and they have come to realize that it is a safe environment to ask for help from their teacher and peers. They love to collaborate with others, and the result is a classroom where everyone feels they belong, they have something to contribute, and they are successful. There is definitely a feeling of "it takes a village" in the classroom. Students are clear about what they know and don't know, they appreciate the attention they get to help them reach their goals, and they understand what they need to do to get there.

Source: Reprinted with permission from Paula Smith, Naperville CUSD #203: Naperville, IL.

are doing an assignment, they will not be putting forth deliberative effort to master the learning. This reduces the impact of practice on achievement, echoing the findings of goal orientation research: Students who do the work just to get it done or to get the highest grade possible often bypass learning altogether because their attention is not focused on improving. During practice, it is crucial that students understand what learning targets the practice is helping them master.

Video 6.4: Deliberate Practice: Kindergarten to High School

It is also critical that the tasks we give them for practice are directly relevant to the learning they are to master. Both in-class and homework assignments should be chosen to focus directly on the specific next-step learning needs identified by our formal and informal assessments. Watch Video 6.4 to hear teachers and students talk about deliberate practice. In Video 6.5 high school teacher Shannon Braun uses data trackers to identify specific areas to target for further practice.

As described in Chapter 5, sometimes our practice must be designed to uncover and rectify misconceptions. In Figure 6.3, a team of third-grade teachers describes how they help students analyze and correct mistakes that derive from misconceptions during practice. Watch Video 6.6 to see Crystal Thayer guide her fourth-graders in developing understanding and correcting misconceptions about mammals.

Video 6.5: Using Data Trackers to Target Instruction

Level of Difficulty

Practice that moves learning forward requires students to stretch beyond what they already know. While we want to challenge students, we don't want to overwhelm them. We can structure tasks so they present an appropriately challenging level of difficulty by removing some of the complexities so students can pay attention to key concepts, strategies, or skills. This is known as *scaffolding*. For instance, in mathematics, teachers sometimes scaffold the learning by providing the answers to problems so students can concentrate on understanding the process. Thoughtful scaffolding makes learning more manageable, especially for struggling students who may be facing multiple gaps in need of bridging. In Figure 5.8 in Chapter 5, high school science teacher Ben Arcuri describes how he uses scaffolded practice to help students work through problems in understanding. Watch Video 6.7 to see Emily Roberts conduct a scaffolded lesson with her kindergarten students.

Video 6.6: Addressing Partial Understanding and Misconceptions: Grade 4 Science

Video 6.7: Scaffolded Practice: Kindergarten

Opportunities for Incremental Growth

A crucial attribution for students to make is that effort leads to success in mastering learning targets. How we explain the role and importance of practice can

Figure 6.3

From the Classroom

Discovering Misconceptions

What We Do

On practice work, instead of marking the errors with an X, we place a dot next to each error. We then pass the papers back, and students work with a partner to explain why the dots are on their papers—specifically in which part of the process they made the error. Sometimes we also put samples of correct and incorrect answers on the board and have students work individually or with a partner to identify correct and incorrect solutions and to find out in which step of the process the error occurred for the incorrect answers.

Impact on Learning

Students look at their errors differently. They look at their work as steps and then understand their mistakes through their own analysis. They can now draw conclusions about the types of mistakes they are making. Students also are able to analyze other students' work and can more effectively coach them. Essentially, students are discovering their own misconceptions and working with each other to correct them.

What Our Students Say

"I see where I made my mistake," and "I have discovered why I made this mistake."

Source: Reprinted with permission from Kimberly McCabe, Stephanie Arms, Stephanie Selig, Lesley Patrick, and Karla Vinson, third-grade team, Arbor Ridge School: Orlando, FL.

counter misconceptions such as "Kids who are smart don't have to practice" and "If I'm not already good at this, I probably won't be getting better." We can help them establish a mindset that links practice with achievement by giving them opportunities to try, to make penalty-free mistakes, to receive strength and intervention feedback when they are ready for it, to receive further instruction when they are not, and to notice their successive improvements. We can ask them for examples of the connection between practice and becoming an expert, or offer a few of our own such as these described by John Hattie (2012):

- More than 10,000 hours of practice are typically required to develop expertise (Gladwell, 2008).

- People such as Bill Gates and Michael Jordan spent years practicing and learning before they surfaced as experts.

We want students to understand that deliberative practice leads to competence and that mastery requires hard work.

In Figure 6.4, middle school mathematics teacher Paula Smith describes how she ensures that students understand the necessity of practice to achievement and structures their practice to maximize their successes.

Figure 6.4

From the Classroom

Differentiated Units

What I Do

I structure my middle school math classes so students practice what they need to learn. I pretest to determine individual student plans for each two-week unit. Students have specialized agendas for each day that involve individual work, partner work, and small group work. They are grouped according to needs identified by the pretest. During the unit they also have the opportunity to be a peer coach and to apply their understanding to real-life practice tasks. No student time is wasted. Each student is pushed each day and not required to sit through lessons on material they have mastered. Students complete reflective exit slips at the close of each day, and I keep all materials in file folders and check them daily. This system requires work at the planning stage, but the result is an effective, student-run unit.

Impact on Learning

Students are highly engaged and motivated, which maximizes their learning. They love that they have individual plans and the freedom of choice. Each student's strength is highlighted, and each gets a chance to help others, which strengthens fluency of that skill. The feel of the classroom is energized, with students talking about math to each other and showing genuine happiness when another gets a concept. Confidence is high, which has positive effects on learning.

What My Students Say

My students often confess that they have never been good at math before and have never liked it, but because they see their growth, they see proof that they are good at math and that makes them like it. Student reflections often include comments about how their confidence level is higher and how proud they are of themselves. They say that how they learn and how well they understand what is taught are clearer to them. They get how things connect, and they appreciate feedback because it helps them see how holes in learning affect overall understanding. They are not bored because they don't have to do busy work when they understand something. They feel in control of their learning. One of the biggest differences for them is that they are more confident when they take assessments. They are never surprised by material on tests, and they have an accurate impression of how well they will do before they take a test because they are in tune with their level of understanding.

Source: Reprinted with permission from Paula Smith, Naperville CUSD #203: Naperville, IL.

Student-Directed Practice

When we have made the learning clear to students, focused instruction on the intended learning, offered practice opportunities targeted to learning needs, offered feedback on students' learning strengths and needs, and taught them how to self-assess and set goals, we are inches away from students taking initiative to determine what they need practice with and to create their own personalized learning path. Watch Videos 6.8 and 6.9 to hear students and teachers describe how students become self-directed learners.

Video 6.8: Student-Directed Practice: Elementary

Learning from One Another

Each of the strategies we have examined has had a peer interaction component to it. In Strategy 1, students work together to understand the intended learning. In Strategy 2, they collaborate to identify strengths and weaknesses in sample work. In Strategies 3 and 4, they learn to offer feedback to each other and to use it to strengthen their own self-assessment. Even in Strategy 5, students can learn from each other as we diagnose learning needs. Now, in Strategy 6, students can be powerful resources for one another as they engage in the struggle that is natural to moving from "not understanding" to mastery. All of the suggestions that follow include opportunities for students to learn from each other and from you. In Video 6.10 high school students describe the importance of interdependence to their learning.

Video 6.9: Student-Directed Practice: Secondary

Video 6.10: The Value of Learning from Each Other

Strategies to Focus Instruction and Practice

With diagnostic information available and adequate time for practice set aside, the next component to support student learning is focused instruction. There are as many ways to target instruction as there are learning targets in your curriculum. This section offers examples of extending assessment-related activities from Strategies 1 through 4 to offer students additional instruction and practice. The examples in the following sections illustrate uses of short assignments and rubrics to scaffold learning so students are able to practice and experience the small wins that build confidence and create the foundation for major learning victories.

Scaffolding with Knowledge and Reasoning Learning Targets

We can use selected response items and short written-response items diagnostically with knowledge and reasoning learning targets. These items are also useful as teaching tools to move students towards mastery. The following activities show how selected response and short-answer methodology can address problems related to content knowledge and development of reasoning proficiencies.

Instruction and Practice with Multiple-Choice Items

Multiple-choice items whose distractors represent faulty reasoning, misconceptions, or incomplete understanding can act as strong and weak examples. The correct answer is the strong example, and the distractors are the weak examples. As with other activities from Strategy 2, contrasting the two can help students better understand the learning target. When you have distractor descriptions, you can create a variety of practice lessons. The inference example in Figure 6.5 is based on the following item formula:

Question: Which idea does this selection suggest?

Answer choices:

- *The right answer:* A guess based on clues found in the passage
- *A wrong answer:* A guess that includes a word or concept from the passage, but is not supported by the meaning of the passage
- *A wrong answer:* A guess that might seem reasonable, but for which there is no evidence in the passage

In the example in Figure 6.5, two incorrect answers are guesses based on faulty interpretations of different sentences in the reading passage, and one is a guess with no textual trigger. Answer choice (a) is an example of a wrong answer that includes a concept from the passage (ignorance) but is not supported by the meaning of the passage. Answer choice (c) is an example of a wrong answer that might seem reasonable but for which there is no textual evidence. Answer choice (d) is an example of a wrong answer that includes a word from the passage (banjo) but is not supported by the meaning of the passage.

In this activity, students work with each other to identify the correct answer and a wrong answer. They also figure out why the right answer is right and why the wrong answer is wrong. They then can share their choices and explanations with another pair of students. Completing a few of these exercises will go farther in helping students improve their proficiency with making inferences than assigning the traditional multiple-choice practice items. By requiring students to select both a right and a wrong answer, to justify their judgments, and to discuss their reasoning with a partner, such items engage students in thinking more deeply about what makes a strong inference.

Figure 6.5

	FOR
Practice with an Inference Item	**EXAMPLE**

Directions to Students:

The following passage is taken from the book *Down the Great Unknown* by Edward Dolnick, an account of an 1869 exploration of the Colorado River.

Read the paragraph and then read the test question.

> [T]he men were confident about the expedition, the mood a happy mix of can-do optimism and "school's out for summer" boisterousness after the dreary weeks at Green River Station. Ignorance was not quite bliss, but it veered in that direction. Powell, for one, took for granted that outdoor expertise in general would translate into river experience in particular. "The hunters managed the pack train last year, and will largely man the boats this," he wrote matter-of-factly. The tone implied that the switch from horses and mules to boats was trifling, akin perhaps to a switch from guitar to banjo.

Which of the following ideas does this passage suggest about the men of the expedition?

    a. They were not educated.

    b. They did not have experience navigating rivers.

    c. They had just gotten out of school for the summer.

    d. They were going to learn to play the banjo.

Select one of the answers you think is incorrect and explain why you think it is wrong.

Incorrect answer: _____

Why: _____

_____

_____

_____

A simpler approach is to embed the item formula into the practice exercise, as shown in Figure 6.6. In this example, students use the student-friendly definition of an inference to locate the correct answer, then use the distractor descriptions to identify incorrect answers. This removes some of the challenge

Figure 6.6

	FOR EXAMPLE
Why Is This Wrong?	

Which **one** of these answers is a good inference, based on the passage from *Danny the Champion of the World* that you just read? Mark the good inference with a star. The right answer is a good inference because it is a **guess based on clues,** or evidence, from the story.

    a. The BFG could hear extremely well because he could not see very well.

    b. The author loved his father very much.

    c. The father did not finish high school.

    d. The father had a good imagination.

    e. The father wanted people to think he was a serious man.

    f. The father had a well-developed sense of hearing.

    g. The father was a funny person.

Some of these answers are wrong because they are **not inferences at all.** They are just facts that the story tells you outright. Write the letters of those wrong answers here:

_____.

Some of the answers are wrong because, even though they are guesses, **the evidence in the story does not support them.** Write the letters of those wrong answers here:

_____.

Source: Chappuis, J.; Stiggins, R. J.; Chappuis, S.; Arter, J. A., *Classroom Assessment for Student Learning: Doing It Right—Using It Well,* 2nd Ed., ©2012. Reprinted by permission of Pearson Education, Inc., Upper Saddle River, NJ.

present in the example in Figure 6.5, because the explanation of why the answer is right or wrong is provided, which can be helpful for younger or struggling students at the outset.

"I hate those questions where they don't tell you the answers!"

Mary Shannon, 5th-grade student

A third option is to share the item formula and ask students to determine which answer choice matches which formula statement, by treating it as a matching exercise, where the possible answers are listed on the left side, and the item formula statements (the descriptions) are listed on the right side. This approach is shown in Figure 6.7, an example using the item formula for the learning target "Makes generalizations."

Figure 6.7

Matching Answer Choices to an Item Formula

FOR EXAMPLE

(Students read text about a scientific investigation in Death Valley.) *Which statement can you support after reading this selection?* One of these statements is a defensible generalization and the other three are not. Draw a line between each possible answer and the statement that describes it.

Possible Answer	Description
a. Crazy-sounding theories can be ruled out before designing an experiment.	w. Right—True for the evidence presented and extends the application logically to a broader array of instances
b. Sharp and Carey proved to the world that the rocks moved on their own.	x. Wrong—True for the evidence presented, but the statement includes too broad an array of instances to be supported by evidence
c. Death Valley is a place where things happen without explanation.	y. Wrong—True for the evidence presented, but does not include an extension to other instances
d. Questions about the world around us can be answered through scientific investigation.	z. Wrong—Not true for the evidence presented

Each of these practice exercises, summarized in Figure 6.8, helps students realize wrong answer choices are wrong for a reason—it's not actually "mystical choice"—and reinforces why the right answer is right.

Figure 6.8

Practice Options with a Multiple-Choice Item

- Students work in pairs to identify the correct and a wrong answer, explaining why the correct answer is correct and the wrong answer is wrong.
- Students identify a wrong answer, guided by the item formula to help them know what problem to look for.
- Students use the item formula and the answer choices as a matching test.

Instruction and Practice with Graphic Organizers

If you have used activities such as those described in Strategies 1 and 2 to define a reasoning learning target, students can practice applying that definition by using a graphic organizer, which is a visual representation of the elements of quality for that particular pattern of reasoning. Figure 6.9 shows an elementary version of a graphic organizer students can use to practice generalizing, and Figure 6.10 shows a secondary version. If you already use some type of graphic organizer with students to scaffold their thinking, it is also a good idea to include a description of the learning target on the graphic organizer and to refer to the learning they are practicing, or students may have difficulty remembering what they learned when it comes time to complete an assessment item calling for the pattern of reasoning they practiced with the graphic organizer.

Figure 6.9

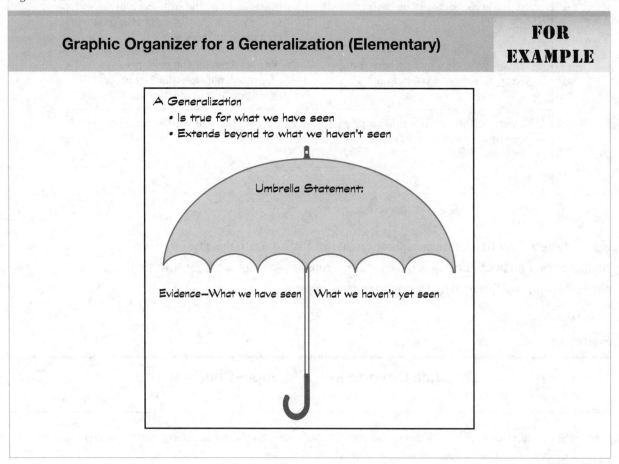

Graphic Organizer for a Generalization (Elementary)

FOR EXAMPLE

A Generalization
- Is true for what we have seen
- Extends beyond to what we haven't seen

Umbrella Statement:

Evidence—What we have seen | What we haven't yet seen

To use a graphic organizer as a teaching tool, find or create several good exercises to practice the pattern of reasoning on which you are focusing. The exercises generally will consist of a question and a short passage of text the question references. Share the learning target, present the question, have

Figure 6.10

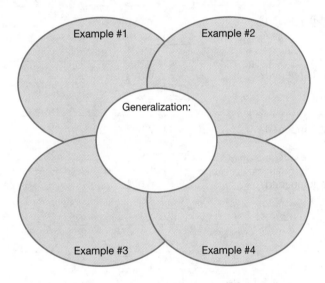

Graphic Organizer for a Generalization (Secondary)   **FOR EXAMPLE**

When we make a generalization, we compare the pieces of evidence at hand to see what they have in common. Then we make a statement that is true for the pieces of evidence at hand and is also true for a broader array of instances. A generalization is an example of inductive inference.

Write the commonalities in the outer circles, then make a statement that would apply to the specific examples and also to others like them.

Example #1 Example #2

Generalization:

Example #3 Example #4

students read the passage, and then work through completing the graphic organizer with them as a large group. Next, ask them to read a different passage and answer the question by completing the graphic organizer with a partner. Let partners share their results in groups of four, then discuss their responses as a large group. Finally, as a self-check and as information for you, have them complete one individually. You might have them follow this with a short reflection on what part was easy to do and what was challenging.

Graphic Organizers for Patterns of Reasoning

For maximum learning, the graphic organizer you choose should be a visual representation of the definition of the learning target you have shared with students.

For example, if you are teaching students to determine cause and effect using the graphic organizer shown in Figure 6.11, locate several short passages that lend themselves to inferring cause and effect. Explain to students that they are

Figure 6.11

Graphic Organizer for Determining Cause and Effect	**FOR EXAMPLE**

Name: _____ Date: _____

When you are figuring out causes and effects, you are looking for a relationship between two or more events or actions. You ask the question, "What happened?" to understand the *effect*. You ask the question, "Why did it happen?" to understand the *cause*.

Effects	Causes
What happened?	Why?
What happened?	Why?
What happened?	Why?
What happened?	Why?

learning to determine cause and effect, remind them of what *cause* and *effect* mean, or introduce those terms if they represent new learning. Have students read the first passage and then demonstrate how to think through completing the first row of the graphic organizer. Have them read the second passage (with a different cause and effect) and work with a partner to fill out the second row. Debrief with another partner group and/or as a whole group so everyone has feedback on how they did, then have them read a third passage and complete the next row with a partner again, if needed. Finally, have them read a passage and complete a row in the graphic organizer independently. As closure, ask students to write a short reflection on the back of the graphic organizer describing what they found easy to do in determining cause and effect and what they found more challenging.

Scaffolding with Performance Assessment Tasks and Rubrics

One barrier to effective diagnostic use that can be present with performance assessment is the length of the task. We need to be able to act on diagnostic information quickly, and yet many tasks students are assigned can take up to several weeks to complete. The problem becomes how, what, and when to diagnose. Consider selecting or designing focused tasks that are *not* longer or more complicated than necessary to elicit the necessary diagnostic information. Or, break the task into sections and check to see that students have sufficient mastery of the learning required by one part before proceeding to another. The rubric you are using to assess the intended learning often will provide guidance on how you might structure the task so you can diagnose problems during the learning, rather than at the end, along with the grade.

For example, if you are teaching students to give an effective oral presentation, the content standard may include characteristics of the content of the presentation, the organization of the presentation, and the delivery of the content. Therefore, your rubric will also describe each of these categories, most likely on separate scoring scales. You might work first with students to develop content that does the following:

- Adheres to a clear main topic

- Includes details that support the topic and are important to understanding the topic

- Includes facts, anecdotes, and/or examples as appropriate to make the topic come alive for the audience

Then review their drafts to see who needs more work on focus or support before moving on to fine-tuning the organization or practicing the delivery.

If your ultimate learning target calls for completion of a complex task (such as solving a multistep mathematics problem, writing a research paper, conducting a science investigation, or writing an analysis of primary source documents), you can design practice around aspects of the task that you know will be difficult for some or all students. The following examples illustrate focused use of tasks in mathematics, writing, and science. The examples illustrate a process useful in any discipline: identify one part of a complex task and teach to it specifically, engaging students in practice and discussion, before having them take on the full-blown assignment.

Elementary Mathematics Scaffolded Task Examples

In elementary mathematics, one challenge is to help students learn to select an appropriate strategy for solving a problem and then to know how to work it through to completion. Offering focused instruction and practice begins with selecting a series of three to four relatively short problems. Share one problem with them and demonstrate one problem-solving strategy (e.g., drawing a picture) that is suited to solving it. Next, give students a different problem to solve using the strategy you demonstrated. They can work with partners or alone for this activity. Ask them to share their work with a small group and together come up with an answer to the question, "How does drawing a picture help us solve the problem?" Discuss answers as a class. Give them a third problem to solve independently using the "draw a picture" strategy and debrief with students showing different ways they represented the important information in the problem to arrive at the correct answer, or not.

The next day, demonstrate a second problem-solving strategy (e.g., make a tree diagram) with a different problem and repeat the process, described in the previous paragraph. Finally, give them a new problem (one that could be solved with one or both of the strategies they have practiced) and ask them to choose which of the two strategies to use. You can have them work in pairs to make the decision and write an explanation of why they chose that strategy, then compare their thinking with another pair, before conducting a large-group discussion of what each strategy is best suited for and when you might use it. Figure 6.12 shows a list of problem-solving strategies from which you could select to support your mathematics problem-solving content standards.

Another way to scaffold the learning in mathematics is to provide the answers to problems so students can concentrate on understanding the process. Teachers

Figure 6.12

Mathematics Problem-Solving Strategies	**FOR EXAMPLE**

- Draw a picture or diagram
- Use objects or manipulatives
- Look for a pattern
- Make a table
- Make a list
- Substitute simpler numbers

- Work backwards from the solution
- Generalize from special cases
- Write an equation
- Use logical reasoning
- Use trial and error

who use this practice often have students work with a partner to reason "backwards."

Elementary mathematics specialist Janna Smith advocates using smaller numbers when helping students learn a process. For example, when teaching bar model drawing to third graders, we can begin with two-digit numbers rather than with numbers in the thousands, which they have been learning to add and subtract. Because visually representing number relationships with bar models is a new process, we reduce the cognitive load by allowing them to practice initially with numbers they can more easily manipulate (personal communication, 2013).

English/Language Arts Scaffolded Task Example

In writing, students often have difficulty narrowing a topic so that their writing has one distinct focus. To help them, you can prepare a list of topics, some of which are narrow enough to be addressed fully in the given time and some of which are not. Have students work in pairs or small groups to discuss which topics fit each category and why. Next, you can select one of the broad topics and model how to narrow it. Finally, students can select a topic and rework it so that it is narrow enough to address in the given time.

Science Scaffolded Task Example

In science, if students need work with preparing accurate and understandable data displays, you can first model options to use with different data sets. For each given data set, explain the thought process you would use to select the type of display most suited to the type of data, and then demonstrate how you would construct the display so that it is complete, accurate, well-organized, and easy to interpret (or whatever characteristics for display of data your rubric specifies). Next, give them a new data set and have them work in pairs to create a display that is suited to the data and is complete, accurate, well-organized, and easy to interpret.

Practice Guided by a Rubric

When you are planning to evaluate students' final products or performances with a scoring rubric, first introduce the language and concepts of the rubric using Strategy 1 activities. Then give them practice using the rubric to differentiate between strong and weak samples following the suggestions given in Strategy 2. You may want to look at a sample of student work to determine which aspect of the rubric to focus on (identifying their learning needs as described in Strategy 5). Then you can use one or more of these options, which function as both instruction and practice:

1. Students work with a partner to revise a previously scored weak sample. They focus on one criterion from the scoring rubric and use its phrases to guide their revision. They can compare their new draft to that of another pair, then revise again, if needed. Or, they can decide which is the better revision and describe why. They can also use the rubric to score their final revision.

2. Share a sample of work from published sources (e.g., newspapers, magazines, pamphlets, government documents, videotaped footage) that falls in the mid to low range on one criterion of your scoring rubric. Have students evaluate the sample using the rubric, discuss its problems, and then revise it based on their observations about what it needs.

3. Students work with a partner to create a revision plan describing what the author of a previously evaluated anonymous sample can do to make it strong for the specified criterion or criteria. Or they write a letter to the author of the sample ("Dear Anonymous, . . ."), explaining what steps to take to improve it for one or more selected aspects of quality.

4. Students work individually or in pairs to revise their own work, using the scoring rubric to point the way to an exemplary product or performance.

5. Students write an explanation of what they can do to make their product or performance exemplary for the specific criterion. Or, they write themselves a revision letter ("Dear Me, . . .") detailing the steps they can take to improve their work. In an assessment *for* learning context, students do not necessarily need to execute their plans. The plans can function as evidence of whether they have as yet grasped the central concepts of quality, leading you either to continue focused teaching or to move on to the revision stage.

6. Another way to give students practice with selected criteria is to take a shot at developing the product or performance in front of your class. Don't be afraid to model the messy underside. Students can benefit when you model using concepts from the scoring rubric to help you think your way through the problems you encounter. Let students use the scoring rubric concepts to give

you suggestions along the way. This activity can also function as preparation for students to give peer feedback.

7. Let students share their process and reasoning by modeling them for the class.

Grading Too Soon

If we grade their practice work and use that information in figuring their final grade, students who have a steeper learning curve will receive a lower grade than those who had less to learn. There are a number of arguments for why we should not grade practice work, but I believe the strongest arguments are that (1) it harms learning and (2) it misrepresents the final level of achievement. If the assignment is the last one students will do to show level of mastery on the learning target, then by all means grade it. If it isn't, then consider using the information formatively, tracking it if needed and acting on it.

A grade on an assignment often signifies "you're done." If they aren't "done" with the learning, it is a mixed message. Grading practice work and attempts at mastery during a unit or teaching cycle can put a high grade out of reach for students who need the practice to improve. We cannot underestimate the negative impact this has on student motivation. Our assessment practices must reinforce the message that if students work hard and do the learning, the grade will follow. This is not to say that students should be working solely for the grade. Research on goal orientations (see Chapter 1) shows the negative impact of believing the grade is the only reason to do the work. Nor is it to say that grades should be awarded for effort. However, if we want students to understand that we learn from mistakes and to regard mistakes and wrong turns as learning opportunities, we have to build time for instructional correctives and penalty-free practice into the pacing of our teaching. We also have to pay attention to when students are working hard but not making progress and help them adopt more profitable approaches.

In Figure 6.13, high school science teacher Jeanette Kenney shares an excerpt from her grading policy statement as an example of how the feedback loop can be woven into the teaching, learning, and assessing cycle in a high school mathematics class. In Figure 6.14, high school science teacher Ben Arcuri explains how he balances formative and summative assessment and the benefits to learning of doing so. And in Figure 6.15, high school science teacher Stephanie Harmon explains what she grades, what she doesn't grade, and how that differentiation affects student motivation and achievement. Watch Video 6.11 to hear teachers and students discuss how they approach grading in a classroom centered on learning.

Video 6.11: Grading Revisited

Figure 6.13

Excerpt from a High School Mathematics Grading Policy	FOR EXAMPLE

Assessment for Learning

In this course, our main focus is for each student to understand the concepts of Pre-Calculus and be able to apply them to solve problems. In order to best promote and support students' learning, we are going to shift our assessment practices so students will have a clear understanding of what they are expected to know and be able to do. Students will be given many opportunities to practice these skills and work to master the content through classroom activities, homework, and penalty-free quizzes before showing what they know on our summative tests. Students will frequently be asked to self-assess their understanding, and to work in pairs, small groups, or as a class to improve each others' comprehension.

Homework

Students will be given homework assignments to practice their skills individually on a regular basis. These assignments are crucial for students to expand their understanding, and will give both the students and me an opportunity to check their comprehension of small chunks of material before moving on. It is very important that the students attempt and give serious thought to all problems, as our difficult content is best learned through this individual practice and sometimes struggle. Homework assignments will be discussed and checked the next day in class, giving students the opportunity to ask questions of each other and me to further increase their understanding.

Formative Quizzes

We will have short, penalty-free quizzes about once a week throughout the year. The sole purpose of these quizzes is for students to gauge their current understanding and correct misconceptions. These quizzes will not count as a part of a student's grade, but will be used to determine which concepts each student needs to work with more to master. I will record scores to keep track of students' progress with the material as we move through a unit, and may use quiz scores to determine homework or to group students for appropriate class work to help each student improve understanding.

Summative Tests

At the end of each unit of material, we will have a test where students will be asked to show that they have learned the material, can perform necessary skills, and can apply concepts to solve problems. These tests will be the great majority of students' grades each quarter. Students can expect about three summative tests each quarter, and they will be able to retake any test to show later mastery.

Figure 6.13 (continued)

Projects/Class Assignments

There may be a few projects or other classroom assignments where students will be asked to apply previous knowledge to real-life tasks or in-depth problems. These assignments may be graded and count toward students' quarter grades.

Test Retake Policy

Each student has the option to retake each unit test once and will receive the higher score. If you want to retake a unit test you must meet these conditions:

—Have all homework from the unit complete.

—Complete test corrections from the original test.

—Turn in these corrections and your original test to me.

—Schedule a time to retake the test.

Source: Reprinted with permission from Jeanette Kenney, Olentangy Local School District: Lewis Center, OH. Unpublished classroom materials.

Figure 6.14

From the Classroom

Balancing Formative and Summative Assessment

What I Do

In my senior chemistry classes there is a balance between formative and summative assessment. The summative assessment is only used for grading. The formative assessment is strictly used as a guide for each individual student.

Quizzes are specifically designed for practice. Students complete the quiz individually, then I mark it and return it the next day. The feedback is immediate and effective and is used to improve learning. The quiz results directly guide my teaching practice. I address common problems in a variety of ways, sometimes reteaching a concept to the whole class. The quiz results show students which concepts they know and don't know. They use checklists to organize their study and complete specific questions from the textbook and worksheets on the concepts they don't yet know. The students complete the practice they feel is most

Figure 6.14 (continued)

beneficial to them individually. I record the practice that students are completing in my grade book, but it is not calculated in the grade. The answer keys to every worksheet can be found on my website. Students come to me with questions, and we discuss them individually or as a class. Following practice, students have an opportunity to complete an optional re-quiz. The re-quiz is made up of different questions on the same concepts. I mark the re-quiz and return it to the student. The hope is that the students' level of understanding has increased. A higher score on the re-quiz is a powerful way to increase the level of motivation, confidence, and overall disposition of the students.

Students complete many quizzes and re-quizzes throughout the chapter to prepare for the important chapter test. The chapter test is worth 70% of the grade. Laboratory work makes up the other 30%. Doing well on the test is completely determined by the work completed to prepare for the quizzes because the test questions mirror the quiz questions. I don't like surprises on tests. If the students complete the quizzes, review or relearn specific concepts, and re-quiz on the concepts to check their new level of understanding, they will be successful on the tests.

Impact on Learning

This system has been shown to create a positive, motivating, and confidence-building environment. The fact that the quiz score is not used in calculating the grade allows students to answer the questions without the fear of failing and also reduces test anxiety. Students understand that the system is in place to help them through the course and that they are in full control of their learning.

I no longer assign the entire class worksheets and assignments. I no longer spend hours marking questions and corrections. I no longer have to deal with late work slowing down classroom progress. There are no longer deadlines, late marks, or any other factors that can skew the students' grade. The grade at the end of the semester represents the students' level of understanding.

I can say with confidence that teachers have the ability to increase the overall motivational and confidence level of their students by incorporating characteristics of formative assessment into their classroom, resulting in more students striving to maximize their success in the class.

I have documented positive changes in my classroom and students in the following areas:

- More questions asked in class and outside of class

- Increased participation in classroom discussions

Figure 6.14 (continued)

- Better preparation for quizzes and tests

- A reduction in test anxiety

- More practice and review completed

- More confidence in ability to achieve higher grades and maintain higher grades

- Less competition

- An increase in intrinsic motivation

What My Students Say

One of the best comments I have ever received from a student is "This class makes me feel better about myself."

Source: Reprinted with permission from Ben Arcuri, Penticton Secondary School: Penticton, BC.

Figure 6.15

From the Classroom

What I Grade . . . What I Don't

What I Do

I am frequently asked questions about how I get students to do practice work if it isn't graded. The answer is: I am honest with my students as to why I am making an assignment, and I explain how the assignment relates to the learning target. If I am not satisfied with my reason for the practice work, I need to rethink why I am assigning it.

At the beginning of each course I talk to my classes about the difference between formative and summative assessments. I want them to understand and use this language as we work together in their learning experience. On our progress reports, I use "FA" and "SA" as part of the assignment descriptions so that students can track what they have completed. I track progress on formative assessments with a nonnumerical coding system:

* = On time and complete

P = On time and partially complete

L = Late and complete

PL = Partially complete and late

0 = No attempt

Figure 6.15 (continued)

This helps me with students who are absent or who develop a pattern of not completing practice work. In my class there is no penalty for not completing practice work. If students don't do it, then I'll ask why. If the student can demonstrate mastery without doing it, that's great! If it is due to not understanding the assignment, then I need to know that. I try to create a classroom environment where I can have these conversations with my students and deal with whatever the situation may be.

I assign numeric grades for summative items and give feedback on formative items. The intention is that the feedback helps the student improve before taking the summative assessment. For some practice assignments, students self-assess and then come to me with questions. Several times each week, I set up a question desk where students can receive individual assistance. They can also bring items for clarification on what the feedback means.

I also teach students to self-assess, both within the unit after students have practiced and in a more formal way after completing a summative assessment. Self-assessing as a checkpoint within the learning helps students focus on the feedback they have received and determine how they are going to use it to improve. Students set goals for what needs to be done to show mastery before the summative assessment. After the summative assessment, students self-assess by comparing their performance on each learning target to what is necessary to show mastery of the learning target. They identify which targets were mastered or not mastered and develop a plan for practice and retesting.

Impact on Learning

Once students realize the direct connections among the learning targets, the practice, and the summative assessments, completing the practice is no longer an issue because they see it as an opportunity to truly practice, receive feedback, and improve before the summative assessment.

Clear, specific feedback is so important to this process. I have found that I spend less time marking papers when I am focused on providing descriptive feedback than years ago when I tried to fairly assign points to all work. When I focus on helping students understand and build quality into their work, it makes the learning process more productive for all of us.

It takes time to teach students how to self-assess with confidence, but it is time well spent. In the beginning, I model the process, focusing on how the learning target and the work are related. It also takes time for students to trust feedback and not expect a grade on everything. They begin to realize that learning is an ongoing process, and if they are willing to put forth the effort, they can understand the content. The quality of their work improves because they have a deeper understanding of the content.

Figure 6.15 (continued)

What My Students Say

"I used to focus on the grade I made and move on because I couldn't do anything about it. Now I know that I can do something about it—I can do practice, ask questions, study, and retest. I remember and apply things we learn and I'm constantly learning and applying new things in this class."

Amethyst C., 11th grader, Rockcastle County High School

Source: Reprinted with permission from Stephanie Harmon, Rockcastle County High School: Mt. Vernon, KY.

Conclusion

With Strategy 5, we assess formally or informally to become aware of each student's learning gaps. Within Strategy 6, we incorporate the first four strategies to build a bridge our students traverse over to achieve the desired learning. Together, Strategies 5 and 6 answer the question fourth-grade teacher Crystal Thayer asks herself: "What do I need to do today to make this a better learning place for students tomorrow?" In seeking answers to the question, we demonstrate that we care for the learning of each student, engendering their trust and willingness to learn from us, with us, and from and with each other.

Understanding and Applying the Content of Chapter 6

End-of-chapter activities are intended to help you master the chapter's learning targets and apply concepts to your classroom. They are designed to deepen your understanding of the chapter content, provide discussion topics for collaborative learning, and guide implementation of the content and practices taught in the chapter. Forms and materials for completing each activity appear in editable Microsoft Word format in the Chapter 6 DVD file. Each form needed for an activity is listed after the activity directions and marked with this symbol:

Chapter 6 Learning Targets

1. Understand the value of practice in a risk-free zone
2. Have a repertoire of strategies to use as instruction accompanied by practice and revision before the graded event

---

Chapter 6 Activities

Discussion Questions (Both learning targets)

Activity 6.1   Keeping a Reflective Journal (Both learning targets)

Activity 6.2   Rethinking Practice Opportunities (Learning target 1)

Activity 6.3   Developing Lessons Around Multiple-Choice Items (Learning target 2)

Activity 6.4   Selecting and Modifying Graphic Organizers (Learning target 2)

Activity 6.5   Creating Focused Tasks (Learning target 2)

Activity 6.6   Using Rubrics as Teaching Tools (Learning target 2)

Activity 6.7   Creating Time for the Feedback Loop (Both learning targets)

Activity 6.8   Exploring Reactions to Chapter 6 Ideas (Both learning targets)

Activity 6.9   Selecting a Strategy 6 Application (Both learning targets)

Activity 6.10 Adding to Your Growth Portfolio (Both learning targets)

Chapter 6 Discussion Questions

Discussion questions are also explored in depth in the activities listed in parentheses.

Questions to Discuss Before Reading Chapter 6

1. What do you do currently when student work indicates the need to reteach? (Activities 6.2, 6.3, 6.4, 6.5, 6.6, and 6.7)

Questions to Discuss After Reading Chapter 6

2. Which suggestions for offering instruction and practice with multiple-choice items might you try? (Activity 6.3)

3. Which suggestions for offering instruction and practice with graphic organizers might you try? (Activity 6.4)

4. Which suggestions for offering instruction and practice with scaffolded tasks might you try? (Activity 6.5)

5. Which suggestions for offering instruction and practice with rubrics might you try? (Activity 6.6)

6. What might you do to alter your grading practices to avoid grading too soon in the learning? (Activities 6.7 and 6.8)

7. Which activities from Chapter 6 did you try in the classroom? How did they work? What successes did you notice? What modifications might you make? (Activities 6.1, 6.2, 6.3, 6.4, 6.5, 6.6, 6.7, 6.9, and 6.10)

Activity 6.1

Keeping a Reflective Journal

This is intended as an independent activity. If you choose to do it, you may want to discuss the thoughts you record with your learning team.

Keep a record of your thoughts, questions, and any implementation activities you tried while reading Chapter 6.

Activity 6.1 Chapter 6 Reflective Journal Form

Activity 6.2

Rethinking Practice Opportunities

This is intended as an independent activity. If you do it independently, you may want to discuss the results with your learning team.

After reading the section titled "The Role of Practice in Learning," select a short unit you have taught or will teach and identify one learning target as the focus of this activity.

1. Using the form on the DVD, briefly describe each practice activity students engage in prior to the summative assessment.

2. Audit the practice activities against the four characteristics for effective practice listed in Figure 6.1. To what extent is each characteristic fulfilled?

3. Note or discuss any changes in the pacing of instruction, practice, and assessment you might make.

Activity 6.2 Rethinking Practice Opportunities

Activity 6.3

Developing Lessons Around Multiple-Choice Items

This activity can be done independently or with a partner or a learning team. If you do it independently, you may want to discuss the results with a colleague.

After reading the section titled "Instruction and Practice with Multiple-Choice Items," select a concept or pattern of reasoning that your students need more work with.

1. Following the suggestions in the section, write or revise a multiple-choice item (stem plus possible answer choices) that addresses the concept or pattern of reasoning. You may want to do this with a partner or with your team.

2. Select one of the practice lesson options described in the section and summarized in Figure 6.8.

3. Format your multiple-choice item to match the practice lesson option you have selected. Refer to the examples in Figures 6.5, 6.6, and 6.7 for suggestions.

4. Conduct the practice lesson with students. Look for impact on their learning.

5. Share a few samples of student responses with a colleague or your learning team meeting and discuss the impact of the lesson on their understanding. You may want to create additional items using the same or a different lesson option if students would benefit from continued practice.

Activity 6.4

Selecting and Modifying Graphic Organizers

This is intended as an independent activity. If you do it independently, you may want to discuss the results with a colleague or your learning team.

After reading the section titled "Instruction and Practice with Graphic Organizers," select a pattern of reasoning your students need practice with.

1. Review the graphic organizers in the section and those on the DVD to see if one might be useful. Also look through your teaching materials to see if you can find one to use or modify.

2. If you decide to use one that has already been created, check to see that it includes a description of the pattern of reasoning (basically the student-friendly definition) and that it matches the one you have given students. If you need to insert a definition or revise it, you may also need to revise the graphic organizer. It will be important that the definition and the graphic organizer match conceptually.

3. If you have no graphic organizer for the pattern of reasoning your students need practice with, work with a partner or your team to create one that helps students understand the elements of quality. Begin by developing a clear statement that defines quality, and then create a diagram that guides students to include all relevant components. Refer to examples on the DVD for guidance.

4. Let students use the graphic organizer when they are practicing answering questions calling for the targeted pattern of reasoning.

5. Bring samples of student work to share with your learning team. If some students were more successful than others, bring samples of successful and unsuccessful student attempts. Discuss with your team possible solutions: modifications to the graphic organizer, refinement of the definition of quality, or further use of strong and weak examples, as described in Chapter 2.

 Activity 6.4 Examples of Graphic Organizers

Activity 6.5

Creating Focused Tasks

This is intended as an independent activity, but you may find it useful to engage in steps 1 and 2 with a partner or team of colleagues teaching the same unit/subject.

After reading the section titled "Scaffolding with Performance Assessment Tasks and Rubrics," select a learning target that calls for completion of a complex task. Identify one or a small number of aspects of quality (as represented on your rubric) that you want students to practice with.

1. Design or select a task so that students will be able to focus on just the aspect(s) of quality you want them to practice.

2. Teach strategies they can use to accomplish the task, if needed, then give students the practice task.

3. Offer feedback on the aspect(s) of quality students are practicing, if student work demonstrates readiness for feedback. Allow them time to act on the feedback and/or provide further instruction, as needed.

4. Repeat the process with one or more additional tasks.

5. Ask students their opinion of the impact this kind of practice has on their learning.

6. Bring a few samples of student work to share with your learning team. Explain what you tried, what you noticed happening with student motivation and achievement as a result, and what students said. Discuss possible revisions or extensions to the practice activities.

Activity 6.6

Using Rubrics as Teaching Tools

This is intended as an independent activity. If you do it independently, you may want to discuss the results with your learning team.

After reading the section titled "Practice Guided by a Rubric," select one or more of the seven options described to try with your students.

1. Conduct the activity; notice the impact on student motivation and learning.

2. Ask students for their thoughts on the impact of the activity.

3. Discuss with a colleague or your learning team what you tried, what you noticed, what your students said, and what, if any, modifications you might make were you to use it again.

Activity 6.7

Creating Time for the Feedback Loop

This is a partner or learning team activity.

After reading Chapter 5's introductory section and the Chapter 6 sections titled "Further Learning Opportunities Make a Difference" and "Grading Too Soon," discuss the following questions with a colleague or your learning team.

1. What changes to your instructional and assessment pacing do you believe will help students make more progress in learning?

2. What constraints make these changes difficult?

3. Which changes are within your power to make? What might you do? Who else might need to be involved?

4. Which changes are not within your power to make? Who might need to be involved in the solution? How might you involve them?

Activity 6.8

Exploring Reactions to Chapter 6 Ideas

This is intended as an independent activity followed by a learning team discussion.

1. Find a phrase or passage in Chapter 6 that strikes you. Perhaps you agree with it strongly, it goes against your current practice, you disagree with it, or you want to dig deeper into the thoughts it sparks.

2. Write it on a notecard and bring it to your next team meeting.

3. At the meeting, spend 3 to 5 minutes sharing your quote and briefly describing your reaction to it. If appropriate, offer a question to begin the whole-team discussion.

4. Then give 5 to 15 minutes (or longer, if the group decides to continue) for a whole-team discussion.

5. Repeat the process with each team member's quote.

6. Summarize any new conclusions, insights, or questions individually or as a group at the end of the meeting.

Activity 6.9

Selecting a Strategy 6 Application

This is intended as an independent activity. If you do it independently, you may want to discuss the results with your learning team. It is offered as an alternative to the section-by-section activities described earlier.

After reading the section of Chapter 6 dealing with Strategy 6, choose one application to try. After having tried it with students, use the form on the DVD to reflect on the activity: what you tried, what you noticed as a result, and what, if any, actions you have taken or will take on the basis of the experience. If you are working with a learning team, consider sharing your reflection with them.

Activity 6.9 Selecting a Strategy 6 Application

Activity 6.10

Adding to Your Growth Portfolio

This is an independent activity.

Any of the activities from this chapter can be used as entries for your own growth portfolio. Select activities you have completed or artifacts you have created that will illustrate your competence at the Chapter 6 learning targets. If you are keeping a reflective journal, you may want to include Chapter 6's entry in your portfolio. The portfolio entry cover sheet provided on the DVD will prompt you to think about how each item you select reflects your learning with respect to one or more of the chapter's learning targets.

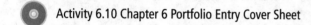

Activity 6.10 Chapter 6 Portfolio Entry Cover Sheet

How Can I Close the Gap?
Tracking, Reflecting on, and Sharing Learning

Strategy 7
Provide students opportunities to track, reflect on, and share their learning progress.

> [We] help our students become increasingly efficacious when we . . . help them learn how to improve the quality of their work one key attribute at a time, when we help them learn to see and keep track of changes in their own capabilities, and when we help them reflect on the relationships between those improvements and their own actions.
>
> *—Stiggins, 2007, p. 75*

With Strategy 7, students look back over time to notice their successes and progress, to reflect on them, and to share them. Knowing you have made progress toward a goal reinforces the value of effort. Incremental success leads to incremental growth in students' confidence in their capabilities as learners, which promotes greater effort, which in turn leads to higher achievement.

When students keep track of their progress and regularly reflect on it, they are paying attention to their learning. This is a form of *metacognition*, or thinking about thinking. Research supports the inclusion of metacognition into a teaching and learning cycle to increase achievement. In one study, for example, students in grades 4, 5, and 6 were given personal analyses of their reading comprehension strengths and weaknesses based on the Woodcock-Johnson III test (Allen & Hancock, 2008). Students used their profiles regularly during the study to reflect in writing about their strengths as readers. The researchers found that this group attained greater learning gains than did a control group (no reflection) or another group of students experiencing a different intervention (Andrade, 2013).

Researcher Paul Black (2013) reminds us that learning takes place on two levels—developing mastery of the content standard and also of self-regulation processes—and that we help students create the inner dialogue of self-regulation by giving them opportunities to pay attention to their learning and to talk about it. To engage in these self-monitoring activities successfully, students need a clear vision of where they are headed and where they are now, and they need to have made some gains along the way. Strategies 1 through 6 prepare students with the information and the progress required to answer the questions implicit in Strategy 7: "What have I learned?" and "How far have I come?" In this chapter, we'll examine ways to help students track their learning, reflect on it, and share it with others.

> The process of learning includes the ability to monitor progress and adjust strategies with the aim of attaining mastery.

Chapter 7 Learning Targets

At the end of Chapter 7, you will know how to do the following:

1. Have a repertoire of strategies for keeping students in touch with their learning progress

2. Have a repertoire of strategies for engaging students in metacognitive reflection on their learning and on themselves as learners

3. Have a repertoire of opportunities for students to share their learning progress with others

4. Be able to track, reflect on, and share your own learning progress throughout your study and application of the Seven Strategies of Assessment for Learning

Students Keeping Track of Their Learning

One of the main purposes of having students track their learning is to help them celebrate having moved in a positive direction. Computer games are built on the premise of incremental gain: People play them again and again to get a little farther, and each time they get farther, players are willing to put in more time to continue the trajectory. As long as there is hope of progress, they will stay at it. When they encounter a setback, players keep playing until they repeatedly don't make progress, at which point they look for another game to play that will allow them to get better incrementally and will give them regular evidence of their improvement.

We can build this motivational cycle into learning by establishing one or more ways for students to track their progress and watch themselves grow. Simply noticing progress is a powerful tool in helping students believe in the connection between their effort and their success. We in turn must keep an eye on their progress, intervening with guidance or reteaching when they encounter setbacks, to keep the hope of eventual success alive.

Students can track achievement progress by recording information from assignments and assessments, by keeping learning journals, and by collecting evidence in a portfolio.

Tracking learning helps students link effort with improvement. Without that link, motivation dries up.

Figure 7.1 summarizes the three tracking options discussed in this section. Later in the chapter, we'll look at ways for students to reflect on their learning and themselves as learners based on these records and the evidence they collect.

Figure 7.1

Tracking Options

- Recording information from assignments and assessments
- Keeping learning journals
- Collecting evidence in a portfolio

Recording Assignment and Assessment Information

Any time students track their progress, the record should link each entry to a learning target. Because Strategy 7 includes looking back over time to reflect on growth, tracking forms should also include a place for students to record and date their results on multiple trials, as illustrated in Figures 7.2 through 7.5.

Some assignment and assessment results lend themselves to tracking progress by assignment. The form in Figure 7.2 is organized this way and includes the following:

- The name of the assignment (e.g., page number, title, project name)

- The date turned in and identifying information for learning target(s) addressed (e.g., numbers transferred from a list of learning targets given to students for the unit or marking period)

Figure 7.2

Tracking Progress by Assignment

Assignment	Date	Target	Score	F/S	★ ⌐_⌐

- The mark or score the assignment received (e.g., points earned/ points possible)

- Classification of the assignment as formative (for practice) or summative (for a mark or grade)

- Space for students to record strengths, which they mark with a star symbol, and area(s) for improvement or next steps, which they mark with the stair-step symbol

Figure 7.3 shows an example with mathematics targets using the "Stars and Stairs" format, where students color in the star and record the date as they achieve the target on each step. You can use a form like this with any developmentally sequenced set of learning targets written in student-friendly language.

Figure 7.4 shows an example of students graphing their results on practice assignments and tests for a collection of reading learning targets. Two of the targets, "I can identify synonyms and antonyms" and "I can tell the meaning of prefixes and suffixes," are knowledge targets practiced and assessed with one-right-answer selected response questions—multiple-choice and fill-in items. The third target, "I can read aloud with fluency," is a skill target evaluated with a five-point scoring rubric. This example demonstrates that students can graph their results with any combination of learning targets to help them see their progress assignment by assignment, or task by task.

Figure 7.3

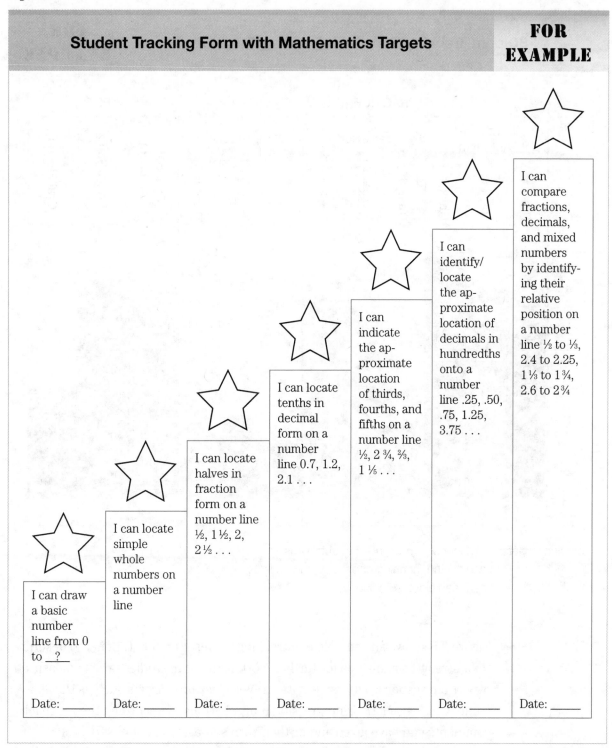

Student Tracking Form with Mathematics Targets **FOR EXAMPLE**

I can compare fractions, decimals, and mixed numbers by identifying their relative position on a number line ½ to ⅓, 2.4 to 2.25, 1⅓ to 1¾, 2.6 to 2¾

I can identify/locate the approximate location of decimals in hundredths onto a number line .25, .50, .75, 1.25, 3.75 . . .

I can indicate the approximate location of thirds, fourths, and fifths on a number line ½, 2¾, ⅔, 1⅕ . . .

I can locate tenths in decimal form on a number line 0.7, 1.2, 2.1 . . .

I can locate halves in fraction form on a number line ½, 1½, 2, 2½ . . .

I can locate simple whole numbers on a number line

I can draw a basic number line from 0 to _?_

Date: _____   Date: _____   Date: _____   Date: _____   Date: _____   Date: _____   Date: _____

Source: Reprinted by permission from Rick Croom, San Juan Unified School District: Carmichael, CA. Unpublished classroom materials.

Figure 7.4

Student Tracking Form with Reading Targets	FOR EXAMPLE

	PRACTICE									TEST		
	Synonym/Antonym			Prefix/Suffix			Oral Fluency			Synonym/Antonym	Prefix/Suffix	Oral Fluency
	(Task #)	(Task #)	(Task #)	(Task #)	(Task #)	(Task #)	(Task #)	(Task #)	(Task #)			
10												
9			■									
8						■				■	■	
7		■			■							
6	■											
5				■								
4												■
3								■				
2							■					
1												
Date												

Learning targets: I can identify synonyms and antonyms.
I can tell the meaning of prefixes and suffixes.
I can read aloud with fluency.

Figure 7.5 shows an example of a tracking form set up for students to describe their strengths and areas for further work with social studies targets measured by written response assessment items. With learning targets such as these, students can track their progress on multiple trials by recording the feedback comments you have given and/or their own self-assessment observations.

Keeping Learning Journals

Learning journals are in essence a collection of thoughts about any aspect of learning—questions, insights, observations about things that are important,

Figure 7.5

Student Tracking Form with Social Studies Learning Targets			FOR EXAMPLE
Learning Target	Date	What I did well	What I need to work on
1. I can explain the constitutional structure of our government.			
2. I can describe the processes that have been used to create, amend, and repeal laws.			

likes and dislikes, progress, strengths, areas for improvement, and so forth. They can be purposefully comprehensive or idiosyncratic, elaborate in style or made from whatever is at hand. They can be kept electronically, video-recorded, or handwritten. Students can create their own journal books, or they can use spiral-bound notebooks. Even a manila folder will do. The purpose for keeping a journal determines its contents. In this section, we'll look at two options for structuring learning journals for the purpose of tracking learning: dialogue journals and learning logs (Figure 7.6).

Figure 7.6

Learning Journal Options

Dialogue Journals

Students convey thoughts and ideas about what they are learning. Teachers respond, within the journal or through further instruction.

Learning Logs

Students keep ongoing records to document learning, progress made, and processes and resources used.

Source: Chappuis, J., Stiggins, R. J., Chappuis, S., & Arter, J. A. *Classroom Assessment for Student Learning: Doing It Right—Using It Well,* 2nd Ed. © 2012 Reprinted by permission of Pearson Education, Inc., Upper Saddle River, NJ.

Dialogue Journals

Dialogue journals are conversations about learning between students and teachers. Over the course of a unit of instruction, students record their interpretation of the learning to be accomplished (what they think they are supposed to be learning), self-appraisals of their progress, points of confusion, and new understandings (Chappuis et al., 2012). Dialogue journals offer teachers insights into how the learning is going and what might be needed in the way of course correction. For example, fourth-grade students at Mark Twain Elementary School in Houston, Texas, make subject-specific journals out of lined paper with construction paper covers. They record facts and concepts they are learning, describe experiments, pose questions, express opinions, and note insights. Teacher Kathleen Blakeslee (personal communication, 2013) explains how the journals help the teachers and students:

> The journals provide the students and teachers with regular descriptive feedback, which guides instruction for the next day. The teachers love reading these journals because they can see what's in students' heads and thereby see the misconceptions and what needs reteaching. As the teachers read the students' journals, they take notes to modify their instruction. The teachers believe that the purpose and success of the journal is its accessibility. It gives everyone a voice, validates every student's thinking because not everyone speaks up in class. It engages students in self-reflection and lets them keep track of and share their learning.

Learning Logs

A learning log is another option for students to keep an ongoing record to document actions they have taken, the processes they have used, and the learning progress they have made. It is similar to a dialogue journal, in that both the teacher and the student use the information, but with a learning log, students are keeping a record of everything they do primarily as an aid to focus their study efforts. Teachers regularly check learning logs to make sure students are on track and to offer additional guidance or correctives as needed. In Figure 7.7, high school teacher Andy Hamilton explains how learning logs function in his classroom.

Collecting Evidence in a Portfolio

Another way for students to track their progress is to keep a portfolio, either in hard copy or electronically (known as *e-portfolios*). A portfolio is simply an *intentional* collection of artifacts that tells a predetermined story. Common types of portfolios, their purposes, and kinds of artifacts to collect for each are shown in Figure 7.8.

Figure 7.7

From the Classroom

Learning Logs

What I Do

My primary mode of in-class assessment these days is a variation of the learning log. Students include all of their practice work and notes, and it helps them keep track of which things we do to provide evidence for specific targets. They self-evaluate throughout, and if they run into difficulty, they can easily find the notes and practice that match the target they are struggling with. Practice quizzes are correlated to specific learning targets so they can evaluate their evaluations from time to time. The entire learning log is assembled throughout a unit and collected at the end of a grading cycle. Labs are about the only thing excluded from the logs. These are graded with quality in mind. For this reason, they are collected as we go, a few days after the lab is completed in class.

Impact on Learning

I have noticed that my students are more independent as learners with a learning log in hand. They spend time using the learning log to figure out problems and rely less on outside help at first. They know where to go to find information and are generally more willing to do the assignments when they see exactly what targets they relate to. When the evaluations are honest, they are able to spend time studying what they need most. It also provides a way for me to track their learning without constantly collecting or checking homework. I can see with a glance how they have been doing on practice quizzes and what their self-evaluations say. I can easily determine which students are struggling or which concepts are causing widespread confusion. The time I save processing homework daily allows me to do more formative assessment.

What My Students Say

Some of my students say they used to spend hours studying but now get better results with less time because they know exactly what they need to study.

Source: Used with permission from Andy Hamilton, West Ottawa Public Schools: Holland, MI. Unpublished classroom materials.

When carefully thought out, portfolios can keep students organized, strengthen their sense of responsibility for their own learning, and function as evidence for self-reflection, demonstrating the link between their effort and their improvement.

All types of portfolios can be used for tracking and self-reflection, but it is important to be clear at the outset what kind of story the evidence is to tell, because

Figure 7.8

Types of Portfolios

Type of Portfolio	Purpose	Artifacts to Collect
Growth	To show progress toward one or more learning goals	Artifacts from before, during, and after learning
Project	To document the trajectory of a project	All drafts of work during the creation of the product or performance
Achievement	To demonstrate current level of achievement over a collection of learning targets	Artifacts comprising a representative sample of achievement
Competence	To provide evidence of having attained competence in one or more areas	Artifacts representing highest level of achievement
Celebration	To showcase best work or what the student is most proud of	Student choice based on quality of work or preference

Source: Based on Stiggins, R., Arter, J., Chappuis, J., & Chappuis, S. (2008). *Classroom Assessment for Student Learning: Doing It Right—Using It Well.* Pearson Assessment Training Institute: Portland, OR.

"Becoming reflective learners, developing an internal feedback loop, learning to set goals, and noticing new competencies and new challenges are all habits of thought we can cultivate in students through the use of portfolios."

Chappuis, Stiggins, Chappuis, & Arter, 2012, p. 364

that will determine the artifacts to include. In any type of portfolio, entries collected should be dated, and students should know what learning target(s) each entry relates to. Entries accompanied solely by a grade or a mark often do not provide enough information for in-depth self-reflecting or explaining achievement to others. The examples in this section will refer to portfolios documenting growth, completion of a project, and achievement.

Collecting Evidence for a Growth Portfolio

Growth portfolios show progress toward mastery on one or more learning targets, documenting increasing levels of competence, so they include evidence of levels of achievement at different times during the unit or teaching cycle to show growth over time. To assemble a growth portfolio, students can keep all of their artifacts (e.g., assignments, quizzes, feedback, self-assessments) in a working folder and select portfolio contents from the working folder to illustrate their beginning level of achievement, their developing level of achievement, and their final level of achievement on one or more learning targets.

Each selection can document either best work or typical work at the time represented. To be of maximum use, each sample should show what students have learned or done well and what, if anything, they have yet to learn or need to improve. For selections illustrating learning targets they have mastered, students can write the learning target as an "I can" statement and attach it to the work. Or, they can complete a sentence such as one of these:

- My _____ meets these criteria: _____ because _____.
- My strengths in this _____ are _____.

With complex learning targets, you may want to use a cover sheet such as one of those shown in Figure 7.9 to capture a more complete description of the learning the artifact demonstrates.

Figure 7.9

Portfolio Entry Cover Sheets

Form A

Date:_____   Title of Entry: _____

Learning target(s) this entry demonstrates:

What this entry shows about my learning:

Why I chose this entry:

Form B

Date: _____   Title of Entry: _____

What this shows I am good at/have mastered/know how to do:

What this shows I need to keep working on:

Many teachers have students collect evidence of their growth in a notebook, sometimes called a *data notebook*. One type of data notebook includes a place for students to record their scores on pretests, organized by learning target; a place for them to set goals and make plans for improvement on specific learning targets; a place for them to record their posttest scores, again organized by learning target; and finally a place for them to reflect on their learning and progress.

Video 7.1: Students Keeping Track of Their Learning

High school mathematics teacher Jennifer McDaniel has each student compile a three-ring binder that includes their target tables (Figure 2.11), completed practice work and assessments, and test reflections and corrections (Figures 4.16 and 4.17). Students use binders to keep themselves organized during the learning, as well as to reflect on their progress at the close of a unit. In Video 7.1, a third-grader describes how he uses his data notebook, and Ms. McDaniel and one of her students explain how the three-ring binders are used in her class.

Collecting Evidence for a Project Portfolio

Project portfolios document the steps taken to complete a project—the execution of a performance or the creation of a product, or a combination of the two. Their purpose is to allow students to look back over the life of the project and reflect on what they learned by doing the project. Each piece of evidence selected for a project portfolio is accompanied by an explanation of the learning it is intended to document (e.g., some version of "This entry shows _____.").

Selections can be chosen to illustrate successful attainment of intermediate learning targets necessary for mastering the ultimate learning targets represented by the performance or product. For example, for a research project artifacts might include the work a student did to develop the initial research question and then work done at each major step through to the completion of the final paper.

They can also be chosen to document evidence of mastery of processes attained by working through a project. For example, students might keep all drafts of a paper for the purpose of documenting their use of the writing process and reflecting on what they had learned about the writing process by doing the project. Or, they might keep all artifacts related to a scientific investigation and reflect on what they learned about scientific processes by conducting the investigation.

Collecting Evidence for an Achievement Portfolio

Achievement portfolios comprise the best, most recent evidence of level of achievement attained on one or more learning targets at the end of a unit or teaching cycle. They are in essence a collection of artifacts to support a summative assessment claim regarding ultimate level of mastery. When selecting evidence for an achievement portfolio, it is important to attend to the sampling question of how much evidence is sufficient to support the claim being made. As with other portfolio types, each entry should be accompanied by a clear connection to the learning target.

A Word About Comparisons

Setting up a tracking system and having students compare their progress against the progress of others is not recommended (Hattie, 2009, p. 214). Introducing an element of competitiveness in hopes of increasing motivation creates artificial winners and losers,

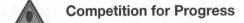

> **⚠ Competition for Progress**
>
> Tracking progress should not be set up so students compete against each other.

which is the antithesis of the intent of tracking as a way to enhance effort. To be fair to all students, comparisons, when made, should be in reference *only* to their own previous status.

Comparison issues also arise with portfolios. There are sometimes efforts to standardize the portfolio so comparisons can be made regarding student learning across groups of students. However, in the classroom, the power of the portfolio lies in its responsiveness to the vibrancy of the learning happening now and the needs of the teacher and the student, which standardization removes. Portfolios are a collaboration between student and teacher. Teachers give guidance about what goes into the portfolio and teach students how to self-reflect, but it is ultimately a collection of each student's learning, best used by them individually to learn about *how to learn* and about *how they learn*. Standardization does not meet any student needs and it takes the process and the ownership away from students. It puts the portfolio in the category of things that must be done to satisfy someone else. Imposing an externally driven summative purpose for the sake of accountability sacrifices learning. Maximize the time you spend developing the learner, minimize the time you spend on requirements that get in the way, and actively work to protect your classroom and students from those practices that harm their learning.

Students Reflecting on Their Learning

As important as it is, a record of progress of a collection of work does not guarantee reflection will occur. After students have recorded or assembled the evidence, it's time to have a second look at it. When students engage in self-reflection, they revisit progress made over time, thinking metacognitively about their learning. The difference between self-assessment in Strategy 4 and self-reflection in Strategy 7 is that *self-assessment* centers on reviewing individual pieces of evidence to identify specific strengths and areas for further work, whereas *self-reflection* refers to a more global process of looking back over a collection of evidence. It involves students in drawing conclusions about what they have learned, how they have learned it, what worked and didn't work, what they would do differently, or how far they have come. In this section, we will look at structuring self-reflection to focus on growth, on learning from a project, and on achievement.

Reflecting on Growth

When students reflect on growth, they compare what they used to know or do and what they now know or can do, a process that is more successful when you have made the learning targets clear along the way. It is also helpful if students have evidence (or a record of evidence as described in the previous section) at hand to inform their thinking. The reflection generally includes two parts. The first part makes an assertion of growth and the second part describes the evidence: "I have become better at _____. I used to _____, but now I _____."

Students can state how they have changed in specific or general terms. They can be specific in their assertion by stating one or more learning targets, such as a key understanding, skill, or proficiency: "I have developed a better understanding of major structures of government"; "I have become better at shooting layups"; or "I have become better at explaining similarities and differences." Or, they can make a general statement: "I have become better at volleyball"; "I have become better at drawing"; or "I have become better at math."

A general assertion of change is fine as long as the comparison of previous and current status offers details that support it. Figure 7.10 illustrates what specific supporting evidence could look like with the volleyball example.

You may want to modify the call for evidence to suit your content and students. With younger students, instead of "I used to . . . /Now I . . . " you may ask them to describe (or draw) their "before" picture and their "after" picture as illustrated

Figure 7.10

Reflecting on Growth: Volleyball	FOR EXAMPLE

I have become better at *volleyball*

I used to *I didn't use to be able to keep my serves inbound, I wasn't good at serve receive, I didn't like to block.*

Now I *can aim my serve. I get low and absorb the force of a serve so I can pass it more accurately. I'm better at jumping to block hits if I'm ever in the front row.*

Figure 7.11

"Before" and "After"	FOR EXAMPLE

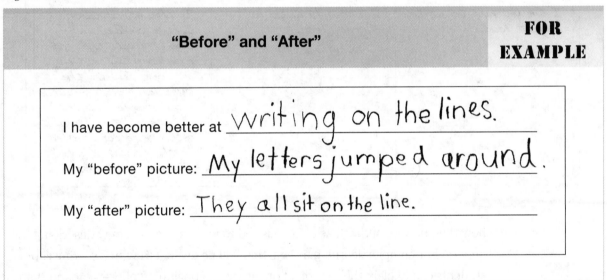

I have become better at writing on the lines.

My "before" picture: My letters jumped around.

My "after" picture: They all sit on the line.

in Figure 7.11 and attach samples of their work that match their "before" and "after" descriptions. Figure 7.12 shows examples of "before" and "after" statements accompanied by short descriptions of the evidence of current status.

Older students can write a paper reflecting on their growth. One way to do this is to have them write a short essay describing what they know about the topic they will be studying at the beginning of the unit or marking period. Keep this essay. At the conclusion of the unit or marking period, ask students to reread it, to consider

Figure 7.12

"Before" and After" with Evidence		FOR EXAMPLE

This is my "before" picture	This is my "after" picture	This is my evidence
I am learning to convert fractions to decimals.	I know how to convert fractions to decimals.	This paper shows that I can convert regular fractions like √8, improper fractions like 5/4, and mixed numbers like 2 2/3 to decimals.
Inferences: I am learning to make guesses based on clues in what I read.	I can make good inferences. I can make guesses based on clues in what I read.	This is an example of a good inference. I made a guess about why Laurie lied by using clues from the story.
I am learning to write a great lead.	I know how to write a great lead.	In this introduction I have asked a question that gets the reader wondering and sets up my topic. I think the question works because most people wouldn't have thought of it and it gets the reader directed to the focus of what I am going to say.

how their understanding has changed, and to write a second essay describing their growth. For complex learning targets that will be evaluated with a scoring rubric, students can explain their vision of quality at the beginning of the year and then again at the end of the year and compare the two to see how it has changed.

The following is an example of an assignment calling for a reflection on growth from a course, "Educational Technology in My Classroom," offered in a teacher preparation graduate program:

Reflect on the essay you composed the first class session related to the concept of integrating technology into your classroom. Based on our reading of the text, the assignments, in-class activities, and any additional resources you have encountered over the past several weeks, compare and contrast your current views on how you plan to integrate technology into your classroom. Cite specific tools, websites, and practices that you intend to employ in order to enhance your course content (Osborne, 2008).

The instructor, John Thomas, described the assignment's effects on his students this way (personal communication, 2008):

> Without exception, the students had arrived at the end of the course very tired, a little frustrated with the volume of work, and the constant, unrelenting pace of the work resulted in most of the students grumbling. The second assessment of their beliefs and ideas about how they would use technology in their classrooms focused their attention on what they had learned and helped them realize the amount of new information and new knowledge they had acquired. Each student had the same epiphany. For me as the instructor, it was a very powerful assurance of the learning that had taken place during the course.

Figure 7.13 includes excerpts from one student's response. Her remarks reveal the deeper learning that arises from reflecting on how far she has come.

Figure 7.13

Excerpt from a Reflection on Growth in a College Course	FOR EXAMPLE

After reviewing my essay from the first class I realize how much I have actually learned in class over the past seven weeks. It has not always been evident that I was truly encountering experiences that definitely have to be used in the classroom of today. Today's classroom is so vastly different from the classroom of my childhood and it is different today in comparison to ten years ago. I have seen my view evolve just as the technology has evolved. My first essay was so rudimentary in its content and my understanding of what technology in the classroom is has changed with each and every lesson and assignment. Some of the lessons were overwhelmingly challenging, but once completed showed a wonderful tool that can be used to enhance the lessons to be learned by the students. . . .

[In my initial essay] I mentioned using a microscope and viewing movies as examples of integrating technology into the classroom. The two examples do not even scratch the surface of what is available. As mentioned in Lever-Duffy & McDonald (2008), there are digital technologies . . .

In conclusion I can honestly say that comparing and contrasting my views from eight weeks ago to now has been eye opening. I see it more as a time of growth with technology than as a contrast in viewpoints. . . . I look forward to putting my knowledge to use in the classroom, and now I can appreciate the past eight weeks of anxiety and learning.

Source: Reprinted with permission from Mishell Mueller, Mount Vernon Nazarene University Adult and Graduate Studies: Mount Vernon, OH. Unpublished classroom materials.

Reflecting on a Project

Challenging projects also offer opportunities for deepened self-awareness and metacognition. Students can document the steps they took and reflect on the effectiveness of their process—what worked and what didn't and what they would do differently. They can reflect on what they learned about themselves as learners by completing the project. Or, they can reflect on what the project caused them to think or feel about the topic or subject. The following list offers examples of questions to trigger insights generated by the experience of completing a project:

- What steps did you go through to complete this project? Did your process work throughout completion? Did you encounter difficulties? If so, what were they? How did you solve them? What would you do differently next time?

- What did you learn about yourself as a learner by doing this project?

- What skills did you develop as a result of doing this project? What skills would you like to develop or refine as a result of doing this project?

- How did your thinking about _____ change as a result of doing this project?

- What impact has doing this project had on your interests regarding _____?

- What did you like most about doing this project? Why? What did you like least? Why?

- What did doing this project teach you about _____?

You can select one for a short reflection or put together a combination and ask students to write a *process paper* that answers those questions. Or, you could let students choose which question or combination of questions to answer in a shorter essay.

Reflecting on Achievement

When students reflect on achievement, they look back over a record (e.g., a completed tracking form) or a collection of their work to identify what they have mastered and what, if anything, they still need to focus on. It is important that the record or collection of work provide clear evidence of what their strengths and needs are. You can use questions such as the following to trigger this kind of self-reflection:

- What did I learn?

- What learning targets have I mastered?

- What are my strengths in this subject?

- What do I still need to work on?

- What learning targets have I not yet mastered?

Reflecting on a record of achievement or a collection of work can also elicit thoughts about the process that led to the achievement. Sometimes this can be even more productive than focusing on the achievement itself or achievement alone. The following are examples of questions you can use to prompt reflection on process:

- What did I learn?

- How did I learn it?

- What would I change about what I did?

- What should I remember to do again?

- What did I learn about myself as a learner?

Students can reflect more generally on their learning over time by responding to a series of prompts: what was interesting, what I have learned, what I am proudest of, and so forth. After you have read the reflections, students can keep them in a learning journal and look back on them to summarize or comment on their learning in preparation for conferences with parents. Figure 7.14 shows an example of a periodic reflection from a middle school social studies class; Figure 7.15 is a weekly reflection from a middle school language arts class. Again, it is helpful if students have access to data or artifacts when completing these forms.

You can have students reflect in groups or as a class as well as individually. Using one or more self-reflection prompts, students can discuss their learning for the week, for a unit, for the month, or for the marking period and create a display such as a poster to sum up what they have learned. In Figure 7.16, teacher Laura Grayson explains how this works with her fourth-graders.

Figure 7.14

Reflecting on My Social Studies Achievement	FOR EXAMPLE

Name: _____

Please complete the following stems with thoughtful responses and complete sentences. You may use your social studies binder to help you review your work so far this year.

So far, this year, I have learned . . .

I still have questions about . . .

I can find answers to these questions by . . .

I need more practice on . . .

My goal for the end of the grading period is . . .

Source: Reprinted with permission from Brenda Doyle, Olentangy Local Schools: Lewis Center, OH. Unpublished classroom materials.

Figure 7.15

Weekly Reflection	FOR EXAMPLE

Week of _____

Three interesting things that I learned this week are:

1.

2.

3.

One thing that I am proudest of in my student notebook this week is:

One thing that I want to improve on next week is:

Next week I want my teacher to do the following:

Source: Reprinted with permission from Jessica Hendershot, Olentangy Local School District: Lewis Center, OH. Unpublished classroom materials.

Figure 7.16

From the Classroom

Gifts of Learning

What I Do

One thing that I have tried new this year is a yearlong reflection of learning in my classroom. I have hung nine canvases on my wall (one for each month of the school year) and titled it as "Gifts of Learning." At the end of the month, in a class meeting format my students reflect on their personal learning for that month, and we decide how we might represent that learning for that month.

Impact on Learning

This has been a powerful piece for the students in my classroom in terms of reflecting on their own learning, working collaboratively with classmates, and finding ways to represent the learning. It has also allowed us to reflect back on previous learning. We have these on our wall the whole year to include in our discussion.

What My Students Say

I have heard students say, "Oh remember in November when we studied the states and capitals. That fits with what we are learning now."

Source: Used with permission from Laura Grayson, Kirkwood School District: Kirkwood, MO. Unpublished classroom materials.

Reflecting on Self as a Learner

Reviewing a record of progress, a series of reflections in a learning journal, a collection of evidence, or a project's artifacts all offer students an opportunity to learn more about themselves. This form of metacognitive thinking involves answering questions such as the following:

- What helps me as a learner?

- What gets in my way as a learner?

- What things are difficult for me as a learner?

- What used to be difficult that is easier now?

- How did that happen?

- What did I do to make it happen?

Our students can also profit from self-assessing and reflecting on behavior, work completion, and study habits. Figure 7.17 gives an example of what

Figure 7.17

Reflecting on the First Nine Weeks	FOR EXAMPLE

NAME: _____   **DATE:** _____

Overall

This grade/class is _____. (harder, easier or about what I expected)

Socialization

The first nine weeks, I socialized:	Too much	Enough	Not enough
The first nine weeks, my parents think I socialized:	Too much	Enough	Not enough

Homework

I complete homework on time in ALL classes.	Yes	No
I check my agenda book AT HOME EVERY night.	Yes	No
I have a comfortable, well-lit place for doing homework.	Yes	No
I have a regular homework time.	Yes	No
I complete my homework before picking up the phone or turning on the TV etc . . .	Yes	No

Study Habits

The first nine weeks, I studied:	Too much	Enough	Not enough
The first nine weeks, my parents think I studied:	Too much	Enough	Not enough
I typically wait until the night before a test to study.	Yes	No	

Class

I ask questions in class.	Too much	Enough	Not enough
I feel comfortable asking teachers for help.	Yes	No	
I participate in classroom discussions.	Yes	No	

Figure 7.17 (continued)

Report Card Reflection

I think I did my best work during the first grading period.	Yes	No
My parents will think I did my best during the first nine weeks.	Yes	No
My teachers think I did my best during the first nine weeks.	Yes	No
My grades represent what I have learned in class.	Yes	No

I learned best when I was able to _____

_____

_____

If I had the quarter to do over again, I would _____

_____

_____

For the second nine weeks, I have decided to _____

_____ so that I'll be more satisfied with my report card.

After reviewing my first nine weeks reflection I have decided that . . .

My challenge is:

My goal is:

Source: Reprinted with permission from Jessica Hendershot, Olentangy Local School District: Lewis Center, OH. Unpublished classroom materials.

sixth-grade language arts teacher Jessica Hendershot asks her students to do. Here is how she describes the benefits of taking the time to have students complete this reflection:

> By talking with students about their learning and not just about particular projects, I felt that I had a clearer picture of my students' learning habits and expectations they set for themselves. The reflections were also useful in helping students set goals for their future learning.

Students Sharing Their Learning

Students have kept a record of their learning journey, and they have reflected on it. The final step is to share their reflections with an audience. That audience can be parents, other significant adults in students' lives, other students, or teachers.

One immense benefit of students talking with their parents about their learning progress is that these conversations contribute to parents developing higher learning expectations for their children. In analyzing research on home-related factors and their influence on achievement, Hattie (2009) found that parents' hopes and expectations for children's levels of achievement were the strongest contributing factor to high achievement *across all home variables*. In the meta-analyses he reviewed, the beliefs and expectations of the adults in the home contributed significantly more to level of achievement than other factors such as family structure, amount of supervision, or homework or study rules. Students' discussions with parents about their learning when they have made progress strengthen their parents' beliefs about their capabilities.

Video 7.2: Students Sharing Their Learning Progress: Elementary

We can develop students' confidence in their learning capabilities through assessment for learning practices. Their confidence, coupled with the evidence they share, helps parents believe in their children's ability to succeed in school, which in turn influences students' expectations for themselves. In addition, when students describe what they are learning, where they have succeeded, and where they are struggling, parents are better equipped to support learning at home. Watch Video 7.2 to hear teachers and a student talk about the impact of students sharing their learning progress with parents.

There are many ways for students to discuss their progress and achievement. In this section, we will look at providing opportunities to share through writing and conferencing.

Sharing by Writing to Others

Students can write a note, a letter, a journal entry, or an email message to their parents or another adult in the home, describing what they have mastered or learned or worked on during the week, unit, or marking period. Second-grade teacher Amy Meyer creates a list of the learning targets her class has worked on for the week and uses them in communication with parents (Figure 7.18):

> Every Friday students in my class check off which targets they have met, then I check off the ones they have met. For example, the last

Figure 7.18

Learning Targets in a Family Message Journal	FOR EXAMPLE

_____ I can use correct friendly letter format that includes a date, greeting, indentation, body, closing, and signature.

_____ I can write two paragraphs about two topics with supporting details.

_____ I can write sentences that sound right or make sense.

_____ I can use correct punctuation and capitalization.

_____ I can write using my best handwriting.

_____ I can stretch out my words so they look right (spelling).

Source: Reprinted with permission from Amy Meyer, Worthington City Schools: Worthington, OH. Unpublished classroom materials.

couple of weeks the targets have focused on writing a paragraph with a topic sentence and supporting details. Then my students write a letter to someone at home who will write back to them in their family message journal. These back-and-forth written conversations are all kept in a notebook, and then parents and child can look at them when they read the letters.

Primary students can complete a daily calendar of accomplishments and take it home at the end of the week along with their work so they and their parents can talk about their successes at school. Figure 7.19 is an example of a daily calendar designed for students who are not yet writing full sentences.

Figure 7.19

Look What I Accomplished This Week					**FOR EXAMPLE**
	Monday	Tuesday	Wednesday	Thursday	Friday
📖	I read:	I read:	I read:	I read:	I read:
✏️	I wrote:	I wrote:	I wrote:	I wrote:	I wrote:
+ & −	I added and subtracted:	I added and subtracted:	I added and subtracted:	I added and subtracted:	I added and subtracted:

Source: Used with permission from Donna Snodgrass, Cleveland State University, Cleveland, OH. Unpublished classroom materials.

Participating in Conferences

Students can lead conferences either at home with parents or other significant adults or at school with peers, teachers, parents, or other adults. They can discuss their improvement on one learning target, improvement in a unit or subject over all learning targets, their current level of achievement, or their progress toward goal attainment. Figure 7.20 summarizes the discussion options and evidence needed for each. Which one or ones you select will be determined by the kind of information your students are prepared

Figure 7.20

Student-Led Conferences

Discussion Topic	Evidence	Participants	Location
Improvement on one learning target	• Tracking form • Two or more dated work samples showing progress over time or project portfolio • Student reflection on growth	• Student and parent • Student and other adult • Two or more students • Student and teacher	• Home • School
Improvement in a subject overall	• Tracking forms • Dialogue journal • Learning log • Growth portfolio • Project portfolio	• Student and parent • Student and other adult • Two or more students • Student and teacher	• Home • School
Current level of achievement in a subject	• Tracking forms and samples of work • Achievement portfolio	• Student and parent • Student and other adult • Student and teacher	• Home • School
Attainment of goals	• Short- or long-term goals and evidence of progress or goal attainment	• Student and parent • Student and other adult • Two or more students • Student and teacher	• Home • School

to share and context considerations such as students' ages and the logistics involved.

Conferences at Home

Any artifact—a quiz accompanied by feedback or self-evaluation, a record of progress the student has kept, a learning journal, or a portfolio—can be the focus of a conference at home with a parent or significant adult, especially if the artifact shows growth. We don't need to wait until the end of the marking period for parents to hear from their own children about how they are doing. Yet as students get older, they are less likely to volunteer this information spontaneously. You can make it a homework assignment for students to share their growth, current level of achievement, or progress toward goal attainment with adults at home one or more times during the quarter and ask that the adults and students write a brief reflection or summary regarding what was discussed. The reflection or summary can become part of the student's portfolio and can be useful to refer to during parent conferences at the end of the marking period.

Conferences at School

Students can discuss their growth or progress toward goal attainment at school with peers, teachers, parents, or other significant adults. It is a good idea to save the discussions about current level of achievement for conversations between the student and adults to avoid the negative consequences that can occur when students compare their learning status to that of peers.

You can set up student-parent conferences to run simultaneously in the classroom throughout the course of a morning or afternoon or over several days. You can run a handful of student-parent conferences simultaneously in rotating shifts in the classroom during the day, stopping by to check in with each one. You can schedule student-parent-teacher conferences during the marking period or at its conclusion.

Preparing for a Student-Led Conference

Participating in activities drawn from Strategies 1 through 6 will have prepared your students to talk knowledgeably about their growth, achievement, strengths, goals, and needs as learners. You choose the focus, give students opportunity to reflect on the pertinent artifacts, help them set an agenda for the kind of conference they will be leading, and plan for time for practicing with a peer.

Inviting Parents to School

When inviting parents to a conference or presentation during the day, it is helpful to give them some time options and ask them to commit to one. Figure 7.21 is an invitation preschool teacher Beth Fujikawa created to encourage parents to attend their children's project presentations. She reports that both she and another teacher using this form had all students' parents attend, whereas in previous years, using a shorter invitation without the choice of time slots, only one in three students had a parent who came to watch the presentations.

Many teachers report that when each student writes an invitation to his or her parents, attendance increases. It is helpful if parents receive information that lets them know what to expect and offers suggestions for their participation. You can also let parents know how to schedule a separate conference at a different time without their child present, if they wish to discuss a concern.

Figure 7.21

| Preschool Parent Invitation | FOR EXAMPLE |

Dear Parents,

Your child has been working on an end of the year project and would like to make a personal presentation—just for you! It should only take 15 minutes or so. Please complete this survey and return it to school tomorrow.

❑ I would prefer to come during the school day on Monday, June 2 (between 8:30 and 10:30).

❑ I would prefer to come with my child after school (between 1:30 and 2:00) this week.

Please circle which day you prefer: Thursday or Friday.

❑ I am unable to come to the school. Please send my child's project home at the end of the year.

Thank you for supporting your child's education!

—Mrs. Fujikawa

Source: Reprinted with permission from Beth Fujikawa, Central Oahu School District: Mililani, HI. Unpublished classroom materials.

Conducting a Student-Led Conference

During a student-led conference, typically the student opens by making introductions, if needed, and sharing the agenda. Then the student shares the learning targets or goals that are the focus of the conference and presents and discusses the artifacts selected to illustrate the topic (e.g., growth, achievement, successful completion of a project, or attainment of goals). Parents may ask clarifying questions and discuss the work or the learning. Students should think in advance about the kinds of questions their parents may have and be prepared to answer them. The conference closes with the student thanking the parents for coming.

Figure 7.22

Grade 7 Self- and Teacher Evaluation			**FOR EXAMPLE**	

		Reading	Trimester 1		Trimester 2		Trimester 3	
			Student	Teacher	Student	Teacher	Student	Teacher
K E Y		5 = Exceeds standards 4 = Meets, and sometimes exceeds, standards 3 = Consistently meets standards 2 = Meets some standards 1 = Does not meet standards						
7-1	Word Analysis & Vocabulary	I can use the meaning of parts of a word (prefix, suffix, and root words) to understand the word in text.						
7-2	Comprehension Strategies	I can make connections to what I am reading and I can tell if the connections I am making are helping me to better understand the text.						
7-3		I can figure out the main idea/theme of the text.						
7-4		I can consider information from a variety of texts and judge the value of those ideas.						
7-5		I can make text-to-world and text-to-self connections that increase understanding of the text.						
7-6	Reading Skills	I can summarize or make a short statement of the main points of the text.						
7-7		I can tell the main idea and details in a text.						
7-8		I can develop an accurate summary that includes important ideas from the text as well as my conclusions.						
7-9		I can explain how text features (headings, charts, diagrams, chapter summaries, specialized print, captions, etc.) show the meaning of the text.						
7-10		I can figure out the point of view through the author's language and word choice.						
7-11		I can compare different authors' ideas and opinions about the same event, experience, or topic (point of view).						

Source: Reprinted with permission from Jill Meciej, Community Consolidated School District 93: Bloomingdale, IL.

Depending on the type of conference you have selected, you may want to send work samples home in advance for parents to review. Or you and the student may complete a joint report of progress and send that home in advance of a parent conference. Figure 7.22 is an example of a report card completed by both teacher and student, which can form the basis of a student-parent or student-parent-teacher conference. Students can also share with parents the records they have kept, in preparation for or instead of a conference at school.

Debriefing the Experience

After the conferences, debrief with the class. You can do this formally with a conference evaluation form (Figure 7.23) or informally, using the questions on the conference evaluation form as a discussion guide. You can also ask parents to give you feedback on their experiences using this form.

Figure 7.23

Conference Evaluation Form

Name: _____   Date: _____

What I learned from this conference	
What I liked about it	
What I would change about the conference	
Other comments	

Source: Chappuis, J., Stiggins, R. J., Chappuis, S., & Arter, J. A. *Classroom Assessment for Student Learning: Doing It Right—Using It Well,* 2nd Ed. © 2012 Reprinted by permission of Pearson Education, Inc., Upper Saddle River, NJ.

Conclusion

Strategy 7 brings assessment for learning full circle. Assessment processes and results develop in students an intrinsic motivation to learn when we give them structured opportunities to notice their learning, to reflect on it, and to share it with others who are important to them. Engaging in the metacognitive processes of Strategy 7 deepens both students' achievement and their insights into themselves as learners.

Closing Thoughts

A secondary foreign language department created an audiotape of each first-year student's initial attempts to speak the language they were studying. At intervals throughout the year students added three-minute segments to their tapes, and at the end of the year they were able to hear the progress they had made. The tapes followed them through their years of foreign language study as they periodically recorded three-minute segments of conversation. The tapes became a portfolio of sorts, a record of growth that students could tune into at any time. And at graduation, the teachers giftwrapped each cassette and presented them to their students.

Assessment *for* learning is a gift we give our students. It is a mirror we hold up to show them how far they have come. It is a promise that we will use assessment, not to punish or reward, but to guide them along the path of their learning journey.

Understanding and Applying the Content of Chapter 7

End-of-chapter activities are intended to help you master the chapter's learning targets and apply concepts to your classroom. They are designed to deepen your understanding of the chapter content, provide discussion topics for collaborative learning, and guide implementation of the content and practices taught in the chapter. Forms and materials for completing each activity appear in editable Microsoft Word format in the Chapter 7 DVD file. Each form needed for an activity is listed after the activity directions and marked with this symbol:

Chapter 7 Learning Targets

1. Have a repertoire of strategies for keeping students in touch with their learning progress
2. Have a repertoire of strategies for engaging students in metacognitive reflection on their learning and on themselves as learners
3. Have a repertoire of strategies for offering opportunities for students to share their learning progress with others
4. Be able to track, reflect on, and share your own learning progress throughout your study and application of the Seven Strategies of Assessment for Learning

Chapter 7 Activities

Discussion Questions (All learning targets)

Activity 7.1 Keeping a Reflective Journal (All learning targets)

Activity 7.2 Tracking Learning (Learning targets 1 and 4)

Activity 7.3 Reflecting on Learning (Learning targets 2 and 4)

Activity 7.4 Sharing Learning (Learning targets 3 and 4)

Activity 7.5 Selecting a Strategy 7 Application (All learning targets)

Activity 7.6 Adding to Your Growth Portfolio (All learning targets)

Activity 7.7 Tracking Your Own Learning (All learning targets)

Activity 7.8 Reflecting on Your Own Learning (All learning targets)

Activity 7.9 Sharing Your Own Learning (All learning targets)

Chapter 7 Discussion Questions

Discussion questions are also explored in depth in the activities listed in parentheses.

Questions to Discuss Before Reading Chapter 7

1. How do the processes of tracking, reflecting on, and sharing learning work to "close the gap"? (Activity 7.1)

2. What activities do your students currently engage in that you would classify under the umbrella of Strategy 7? (Activity 7.1)

Questions to Consider During or After Reading

3. Which of the tracking options is best suited to your context (grade level, subject, learning targets)? (Activity 7.2)

4. How would you differentiate between the self-assessment activities described in Strategy 4 and the self-reflection activities described in Strategy 7? (Activity 7.1)

5. Which of the self-reflection options is best suited to your context (grade level, subject, learning targets)? (Activity 7.3)

6. Which of the sharing options is best suited to your context (grade level, subject, learning targets)? (Activity 7.4)

Closure Questions

7. What activities from Chapter 7 did you try in the classroom? How did they work? What successes did you notice? What modifications might you make? (Activities 7.5 and 7.6)

Activity 7.1

Keeping a Reflective Journal

This is intended as an independent activity. If you choose to do it, you may want to discuss the thoughts you record with your learning team.

Keep a record of your thoughts, questions, and any implementation activities you tried while reading Chapter 7.

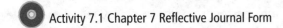 Activity 7.1 Chapter 7 Reflective Journal Form

Activity 7.2

Tracking Learning

This is intended as an independent activity, but you may find it useful to engage in steps 1–4 with a partner or team of colleagues teaching the same unit/subject.

1. After reading the section titled "Students Keeping Track of Their Learning," make a list of the learning targets you will teach for a given unit or grading/marking period.

2. Decide for each learning target which tracking option will work best. You may use one option for all targets or a combination of options, depending on the kinds of learning targets on your list. Tracking options include recording progress by learning target or by assignment, keeping learning journals, or collecting and annotating evidence in a portfolio.

3. Determine how often students will keep track of their learning and how long it will take them each time to complete the tracking activity. Build that time into your teaching plans.

4. Create the form(s) students will use. (Forms in this chapter can be found on the DVD.)

5. Let students keep track of their learning for the duration of the unit or grading/marking period. Consider asking them to share what they think this activity did for them. Keep track of students' comments about the activity, about their learning, or about themselves as learners while they are recording their progress.

6. At the end of the unit or grading/marking period, share samples of students' completed forms or journals with your learning team. Discuss students' comments and reactions to the activity and any changes you noticed in their motivation and achievement.

7. Note any revisions you want to make to the process or the forms for later use.

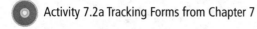 Activity 7.2a Tracking Forms from Chapter 7    Activity 7.2b Portfolio Entry Cover Sheets

Activity 7.3

Reflecting on Learning

Successful completion of this activity requires completion of Activity 7.2. This is also intended as an independent activity, but you may find it useful to engage in steps 1 and 2 with a partner or team of colleagues teaching the same unit/subject.

1. After reading the section titled "Students Reflecting on Their Learning," identify the reflection option that best suits the learning targets you will teach, the tracking option(s) you have selected, the evidence students will have at hand (which is determined by the learning targets you are focusing on), and the age of your students. Options include reflecting on growth, reflecting on a project, reflecting on achievement, and reflecting on themselves as learners.

2. Determine what evidence students will need to refer to and how you will elicit their reflection: through a form, a writing prompt, or a series of questions. (Blank versions of the reflection forms described in Chapter 7 are found on the DVD.)

3. Have students use the reflection form, prompt, or questions. Consider asking them to share what they think this activity did for them. Keep track of your impressions regarding the activity's impact on students' understanding of themselves as learners, motivation to continue learning, and achievement.

4. Bring a few samples of students' reflections to share with your learning team. Discuss students' reaction to the activity and your impressions about its impact.

5. Note any revisions you might like to make to the process or to the form, prompt, or questions for future use.

 Activity 7.3 Self-Reflection Forms from Chapter 7

Activity 7.4

Sharing Learning

Successful completion of this activity requires prior completion of Activities 7.2 and 7.3. Again, this is intended as an independent activity, but you may find it useful to engage in steps 1 and 2 with a partner or team of colleagues teaching the same unit/subject.

1. After reading the section titled "Students Sharing Their Learning," decide which sharing option best suits the learning targets you will teach, the tracking and reflecting students will do, your students' age, and the time available. Options include written communication, discussions at home, and conferences at school.

2. Prepare the form and/or the protocol you will use. Determine what artifacts students will need to have on hand to share or refer to.

3. Explain the process and its purpose to students and to parents.

4. Let students engage in the sharing option you have selected.

5. If students have been involved in a conference, debrief the experience with all participants following the suggestions in Chapter 7. (A full-page version of the Conference Evaluation Form in Figure 7.23 is found on the DVD.) Keep track of your own impressions regarding this activity's impact on students' understanding of themselves as learners, their motivation to continue learning, and their achievement.

6. Share a few samples of either students' written communication or their debrief comments regarding the oral sharing experience with your learning team. Discuss your observations about its impact on students and parents.

7. Note any revisions you might like to make to the form(s) or the protocol for future use.

Activity 7.4a Sharing Learning Planning Form   Activity 7.4b Conference Evaluation Form from Chapter 7

Activity 7.5

Selecting a Strategy 7 Application

This is intended as an independent activity. If you do it independently, you may want to discuss the results with your learning team. It is offered as an alternative to the section-by-section activities described earlier.

After reading Chapter 7, choose one application to try. After having tried it with students, use the form on the DVD to reflect on the activity: what you tried, what you noticed as a result, and what, if any, actions you have taken or will take on the basis of the experience. If you are working with a learning team, consider sharing your reflection with them.

◉ Activity 7.5 Selecting a Strategy 7 Application

Activity 7.6

Adding to Your Growth Portfolio

This is intended as an independent activity.

Any of the activities from this chapter can be used as entries for your own growth portfolio. Select activities you have completed or artifacts you have created that will illustrate your competence at the Chapter 7 learning targets. If you are keeping a reflective journal, you may want to include Chapter 7's entry in your portfolio. The portfolio entry cover sheet provided on the DVD will prompt you to think about how each item you select reflects your learning with respect to one or more of the chapter's learning targets.

◉ Activity 7.6 Chapter 7 Portfolio Entry Cover Sheet

Activity 7.7

Tracking Your Own Learning

Activities 7.7, 7.8, and 7.9 are set up so that you can share with others selections from your own learning through study, discussion, and application of the concepts in this book. This activity is intended as an independent activity.

Part A

1. Make an inventory of practices you now use for each of the seven strategies.

2. Compare your current practices to the practices you listed in the Chapter 1 Activity 1.6, "Inventorying Formative Assessment Practices."

3. Write a description of how your classroom assessment practices have changed as a result of your study.

Part B

Review the learning targets for each of the seven chapters of the book. Select one or more artifacts from your growth portfolio that represent aspects of your own learning that you would like to share with others.

Activity 7.7 Tracking Your Own Learning

Activity 7.8

Reflecting on Your Own Learning

Once you have a collection of artifacts representing your learning, you can select one or more of the following reflection options. You can use each chapter's learning targets for purposes of self-reflection.

1. Use or adapt one of the student suggestions from the section "Reflecting on Growth" to reflect on your own learning as demonstrated by your collection of artifacts. You may wish to use one of the portfolio entry cover sheets shown in the chapter (and found on the DVD in Activity 7.2).

2. Use or adapt one of the student suggestions to reflect on changes you have seen in your students' motivation and achievement that you believe have been influenced by implementing one or more of the strategies described in this book.

3. Use or adapt one of the suggestions for reflecting on a project to reflect on your own learning with *Seven Strategies of Assessment for Learning*.

4. Create and complete your own reflection prompt or form to (a) capture your learning and the conclusions you have drawn and (b) demonstrate your mastery of the self-reflection portion of Strategy 7.

Activity 7.9

Sharing Your Own Learning

Your learning team can plan a "share fair" to let others know what you have been doing in your classrooms and team meetings with assessment for learning. The success of this activity depends on having completed Activity 7.7 and Activity 7.8. Your audience can be other learning teams or colleagues who are not participating in this study. Both options are explained in the following sections.

Option 1: Sharing with Other Learning Teams

1. Each learning team meets separately to plan what they will share. Learning team members bring the work they have done with Activity 7.7 and Activity 7.8 to a meeting, and each spends a few minutes explaining his or her artifacts and what they illustrate.

2. Each learning team selects the artifacts they would like to share with others and prepares a display that includes the key idea or ideas illustrated by each artifact, any brief explanatory information needed, the artifact(s), a reflection from Activity 7.8, and the name(s) and contact information of person(s) submitting the artifact(s). Often teams spend one meeting sharing and selecting artifacts and another preparing them for display.

3. Find a good place to stage your "Share Fair." Have each team set up around the room.

4. Assign one person to stay with the team's display to give a short explanation and/or to answer questions. The rest of the team circulates to other displays. You can rotate the responsibility of staying with the display so all have a chance to see what others have done.

Option 2: Sharing with Colleagues Who Are Not Part of a Learning Team

1. Learning team members bring the work they have done with Activities 7.7 and 7.8 to a team meeting, and each spends a few minutes explaining his or her artifacts and what they illustrate. Each person on the team then selects his or her own artifacts to share with others.

2. The team decides how and when to conduct the sharing. Here are some options:

   - In a large group setting, such as a faculty meeting, you each can give a short description of the key idea your artifact illustrates and a brief explanation of how you used it and what you noticed happening with students as a result. You can involve the audience in a brief activity that simulates a part of what you had your students do, if appropriate.

   - You can follow the same procedure in a smaller group format, such as a department meeting.

   - You can each create a display similar to the one described above, and set the displays up in a room such as the cafeteria or library. You can each give a short presentation to small groups as they rotate through your team members' displays.

3. In each of the sharing options, be sure to include a reference to the learning target illustrated by each artifact and a reflection on its impact on motivation and/or achievement.

Appendix
Index to DVD Files

Chapter 5

5.0   Chapter 5 Discussion Questions
5.1   Chapter 5 Reflective Journal Form
5.2a Teaching Cycle Map
5.2b Teaching Cycle Symbols
5.4   Identifying Types of Learning Needs
5.9   Selecting a Strategy 5 Application
5.10 Chapter 5 Portfolio Entry Cover Sheet

Chapter 6

6.0   Chapter 6 Discussion Questions
6.1   Chapter 6 Reflective Journal Form
6.2   Rethinking Practice Opportunities
6.4   Examples of Graphic Organizers

6.9   Selecting a Strategy 6 Application
6.10 Chapter 6 Portfolio Entry Cover Sheet

Chapter 7

7.0   Chapter 7 Discussion Questions
7.1   Chapter 7 Reflective Journal Form
7.2a Tracking Forms from Chapter 7
7.2b Portfolio Entry Cover Sheets
7.3   Self-Reflection Forms from Chapter 7
7.4a Sharing Learning Planning Form
7.4b Conference Evaluation Form from Chapter 7
7.5   Selecting a Strategy 7 Application
7.6   Chapter 7 Portfolio Entry Cover Sheet
7.7   Tracking Your Own Learning

VIDEO CLIPS

Chapter 1

1.1   Impact of the Seven Strategies in Elementary Classrooms
1.2   Impact of the Seven Strategies in Secondary Classrooms
1.3   Developing a Learning Culture in the Classroom
1.4   Formative Assessment Practices and Grading Issues
1.5   Implementation Advice: Elementary Teachers
1.6   Implementation Advice: Secondary Teachers
1.7   Implementation Advice: Administrators

Chapter 2

2.1   Making Targets Clear to Students: Kindergarten
2.2   Making Learning Targets Clear to Students: Grade 4
2.3   Dissecting Learning Targets with Students
2.4   Making Targets Clear to Students: AP Calculus
2.5   Co-Creating Criteria with Students
2.6   Revisiting the Learning at the End of the Lesson: Kindergarten
2.7   Revisiting the Learning at the End of the Lesson: Grade 1
2.8   Revisiting the Learning at the End of the Lesson: Grade 3
2.9   Using Strong and Weak Models: Kindergarten
2.10 Using Strong and Weak Models: Grade 1
2.11 Using Strong and Weak Models: Middle School Science
2.12 Using Strong and Weak Models: High School Science
2.13 Using Strong and Weak Models: AP Calculus
2.14 Using Classwork as Strong and Weak Models: AP Calculus

Chapter 3

3.1   Effective Feedback Focused on the Learning: Middle School Students
3.2   Offering Effective Feedback: Kindergarten
3.3   Offering Effective Feedback: Grade 3
3.4   Peer Feedback: Kindergarten to High School

Chapter 4

4.1   Self-Assessment and Goal Setting with Target Tables
4.2   Self-Assessment and Goal Setting with Test Corrections
4.3   Peer Feedback and Self-Assessment: Grade 1

Chapter 5

5.1   Using Assessment Results to Guide Learning
5.2   Commit and Toss Activity: Grade 4

Chapter 6

6.1   Creating a Respectful Learning Environment
6.2   Impact of Guided Practice: Elementary
6.3   Impact of Guided Practice: Secondary
6.4   Deliberate Practice: Kindergarten to High School
6.5   Using Data Trackers to Target Instruction
6.6   Addressing Partial Understanding and Misconceptions: Grade 4 Science
6.7   Scaffolded Practice: Kindergarten
6.8   Student-Directed Practice: Elementary
6.9   Student-Directed Practice: Secondary
6.10 The Value of Learning from Each Other
6.11 Grading Revisited

Chapter 7

7.1   Students Keeping Track of Their Learning
7.2   Students Sharing Their Learning Progress: Elementary

Bibliography

Allen, K., & Hancock, T. (2008). Reading comprehension improvement with individualized cognitive profile and metacognition. *Literacy Research and Instruction, 47*, 124–139.

Ames, C. (1992). Classrooms: Goals, structures, and student motivation. *Journal of Educational Psychology, 84*(3), 261–271.

Andrade, H. (2010). Students as the definitive source of formative assessment: Academic self-assessment and the self-regulation of learning. In H. Andrade & G. Cizek (Eds.), *Handbook of formative assessment* (pp. 90–105). New York, NY: Routledge.

Andrade, H. (2013). Classroom assessment in the context of learning theory and research. In J. McMillan (Ed.), *The SAGE handbook of research on classroom assessment* (pp. 17–34). Los Angeles, CA: SAGE Publications, Inc.

Arter, J., & Chappuis, J. (2006). *Creating & recognizing quality rubrics.* Portland, OR: Pearson Assessment Training Institute.

Bennett, R. E. (2011). Formative assessment: A critical review. *Assessment in Education: Principles, Policy and Practice, 18*, 5–25.

Black, P. (2013). Formative and summative aspects of assessment: Theoretical and research foundations in the context of pedagogy. In J. McMillan (Ed.), *The SAGE handbook of research on classroom assessment* (pp. 167–178). Los Angeles, CA: Sage.

Black, P., Harrison, C., Lee, C., Marshall, B., & Wiliam, D. (2002). *Working inside the black box: Assessment for learning in the classroom.* London, England: King's College Press.

Black, P., & Wiliam, D. (1998a). Assessment and classroom learning. *Assessment in Education, 5*(1), 7–74.

Black, P., & Wiliam, D. (1998b). Inside the black box: Raising standards through classroom assessment. *Phi Delta Kappan, 80*(2), 139–148.

Blackwell, L., Trzesniewski, K., & Dweck, C. (2007). Implicit theories of intelligence predict achievement across an adolescent transition: A longitudinal study and an intervention. *Child Development, 78*(1), 246–263.

Brown, G., & Harris, L. (2013). Student self-assessment. In J. McMillan (Ed.), *The SAGE handbook of research on classroom assessment* (pp. 367–393). Los Angeles, CA: SAGE Publications, Inc.

Butler, R. (1988). Enhancing and undermining intrinsic motivation: The effects of task-involving and ego-involving evaluation on interest and performance. *British Journal of Educational Psychology, 58*, 1–14.

Chappuis, J., Stiggins, R., Chappuis, S., & Arter, J. (2012). *Classroom assessment for student learning: Doing it right—Using it well* (2nd ed.). Portland, OR: Pearson Assessment Training Institute.

Chappuis, S., Stiggins, R., Arter, J., & Chappuis, J. (2010). *Assessment* for *learning: An action guide for school leaders*. Portland, OR: Pearson Assessment Training Institute.

Cizek, G.J. (2010). An introduction to formative assessment: History, characteristics, and challenges. In H. Andrade & G. Cizek (Eds.), *Handbook of formative assessment* (pp. 3–17). Routledge, NY.

Common Core State Standards Initiative. (2010a). *Common core state standards for English language arts & literacy in history/social studies, science, and technical subjects.* Washington, DC: Council of Chief State School Officers & National Governors Association. Retrieved January 2011 from http://www .corestandards.org/assets/CCSSI_ELA%20Standards.pdf

Common Core State Standards Initiative. (2010b). *Common core state standards for mathematics.* Washington, DC: Council of Chief State School Officers & National Governors Association. Retrieved January 2011 from http://www.corestandards.org/ assets/CCSSI_Math%20Standards.pdf

Cowie, B. (2013). Assessment in the science classroom: Priorities, practices, and prospects. In J. McMillan (Ed.), *The SAGE handbook of research on classroom assessment* (pp. 473–488). Los Angeles, CA: Sage.

Crooks, T. (2007, April 9). Key factors in the effectiveness of assessment for learning. Paper presented at the 2007 Annual Meeting of the American Educational Research Association, Chicago, IL.

Dweck, C. S. (2007). The secret to raising smart kids. *Scientific American Mind,* November 28, 2007. Retrieved November 12, 2008, from http://www.sciam.com/ article.cfm?id=the-secret-to-raising-smart-kids&print=true

Gladwell, M. (2008). *Outliers: The story of success.* New York, NY: Little, Brown.

Gollwitzer, P. M., & Sheeran, P. (2006). Implementation intentions and goal achievement: A meta-analysis of effects and processes. *Advances in Experimental Social Psychology, 38*, 66–119.

Gregory, K., Cameron, C., & Davies, A. (2000). *Knowing what counts: Self-assessment and goal-setting.* Merville, BC: Connections.

Halvorson, H. G. (2012). *Succeed: How we can reach our goals.* New York, NY: Penguin.

Harlen, W. (2007). Formative classroom assessment in science and mathematics. In J. H. McMillan (Ed.), *Formative classroom assessment: Theory into practice* (pp. 116–135). New York, NY: Teachers College Press.

Harlen, W., & James, M. (1997). Assessment and learning: Differences and relationships between formative and summative assessment. *Assessment in Education: Principles, Policy, & Practice, 4*(3), 365–379.

Hattie, J., & Timperley, H. (2007). The power of feedback. *Review of Educational Research*. Retrieved October 9, 2007 from http://rer.sagepub.com

Hattie, J. (2009). *Visible learning: A synthesis of over 800 meta-analyses relating to achievement*. New York, NY: Routledge.

Hattie, J. (2012). *Visible learning for teachers: Maximizing impact on learning*. New York, NY: Routledge.

Heritage, M. (2013a). *Formative assessment in practice*. Cambridge, MA: Harvard Education Press.

Heritage, M. (2013b). Gathering evidence of student understanding. In J. McMillan (Ed.), *The SAGE handbook of research on classroom assessment* (pp. 179–196). Los Angeles, CA: SAGE Publications, Inc.

Hunter, M. (1982). *Mastery teaching: Increasing instructional effectiveness in elementary, secondary schools, colleges and universities*. El Segundo, CA: TIP.

Hunter, M. (1993). *Enhancing teaching*. Upper Saddle River, NJ: Pearson Education.

Kanter, R. M. (2004). *Confidence: How winning streaks and losing streaks begin and end*. New York, NY: Three Rivers Press.

Kluger, A.N., & DeNisi, A. (1996). The effects of feedback interventions on performance: A historical review, a meta analysis, and a preliminary feedback intervention theory. *Psychological Bulletin, 119*(2), 254–284.

Locke, E. A., & Latham, G. P. (1990). *A theory of goal setting & task performance*. Englewood Cliffs, NJ: Prentice Hall.

Locke, E. A., & Latham, G. P. (2002). Building a practically useful theory of goal setting and task motivation. *American Psychologist, 55*(9), 705–717.

Rodriguez, M. C., & Haladyna, T. M. (2013). Writing selected-response items for classroom assessment. In J. McMillan (Ed.), *The SAGE handbook of research on classroom assessment* (pp. 293–313). Los Angeles, CA: SAGE Publications, Inc.

Sadler, D. R. (1989). Formative assessment and the design of instructional systems. *Instructional Science, 18,* 119–144.

Sadler, D. R. (1998). Formative assessment: Revisiting the territory. *Assessment in Education, 5*(1), 77–84.

Schunk, D. (1996). Goal and self-evaluative influences during children's cognitive skill learning. *American Educational Research Journal, 33*(2), 359–382.

Shepard, L. A. (2008). Formative assessment: Caveat emptor. In C. Dwyer (Ed.), *The future of assessment: Shaping teaching and learning* (pp. 279–303). New York, NY: Lawrence Erlbaum.

Shepard, L. A. (2008/2009). The role of assessment in a learning culture. *Educational Researcher, 29*(7), 4–14.

Spandel, V. (2009). *Creating writers through 6-trait writing assessment and instruction.* Boston, MA: Pearson.

Stiggins, R. (2007). Assessment for learning: An essential foundation of productive instruction. In Douglas Reeves (Ed.), *Ahead of the curve* (pp. 59–76). Bloomington, IN: Solution Tree Press.

Stiggins, R., Arter, J., Chappuis, J., & Chappuis, S. (2004). *Classroom assessment for student learning: Doing it right—Using it well.* Portland, OR: Pearson Assessment Training Institute.

White, B. Y., & Frederiksen, J. R. (1998). Inquiry, modeling, and metacognition: Making science accessible to all students. *Cognition and Instruction, 16*(1), 3–118.

Wiliam, D., & Lee, C. (2001, September). Teachers developing assessment for learning: Impact on student achievement. Paper presented at the 27th annual conference of the British Educational Research Association, University of Leeds, England.

Wiliam, D. (2013). Feedback and instructional correctives. In J. H. McMillan (Ed.), *SAGE handbook of research on classroom assessment* (pp. 197–214). Thousand Oaks, CA: SAGE Publications, Inc.

Index

Credits

Text Credits

Page 18: Reprinted by permission from "Align, Assess, Achieve" produced by Westerville City Schools District, Westerville, OH. DVD copies Available for purchase by calling 614-797-5934. Copyright © by Westerville City Schools District.

Lessons 1, 2 (pp. 62 and 63): Reprinted by permission from Jill Meciej & Jerry O'Shea, personal communication.

Lesson 3 (p. 64): Reprinted by permission from Jill Meciej, Core Service Director for Student Effectiveness, Community Consolidated School District.

Page 80, Page 115: Reprinted by permission from Amy Meyer, personal communication. Olentangy Local School District.

Pages 182–183: Reprinted by permission from Stephanie Harmon Rockcastle, County High School, Mt Vernon, KY.

Page 188: Reprinted by permission from Paula Smith, personal communication. Naperville Community Unit School District.

Page 276: Reprinted with permission from Kathleen Blakeslee.

Pages 284–285: Reprinted with permission from Damon Osborne, Mount Vernon Nazarene University, Mount Vernon, OH.

Page 285: Reprinted by permission from John Thomas, personal communication.

Page 292: Reprinted by permission from Jessica Hendershot. Copyright © Olentangy Local School District.

DVD Credits

Activities 1.1, 1.8–1.11, 2.12, 3.1–3.9, 4.9, 5.10, 6.10, 7.6: Chappuis, Jan; Stiggins, Rick J.; Chappuis, Steve; Arter, Judith A., Classroom Assessment For Student Learning: Doing It Right—Using It Well, 2nd Ed., © 2012. Reprinted and Electronically reproduced by permission of Pearson Education, Inc., Upper Saddle River, NJ.

Activity 4.3: Adapted with permission from Donna Snodgrass, unpublished classroom materials, Cleveland State University: Cleveland, OH.

Activity 7.2: Adapted with permission from Rick Croom, unpublished classroom materials, San Juan Unified School District: Carmichael, CA.

Activity 7.3: Adapted with permission from Jessica Hendershot, unpublished classroom materials, Olentangy Local School District: Lewis Center, OH.